Sea Changes

Sea Changes
Historicizing the Ocean

Edited by
Bernhard Klein
and **Gesa Mackenthun**

ROUTLEDGE

NEW YORK AND LONDON

Published in 2004 by
Routledge
29 West 35th Street
New York, NY 10001
www.routledge-ny.com

Published in Great Britain by
Routledge
11 New Fetter Lane
London EC4P 4EE
www.routledge.co.uk

Copyright © 2004 by Taylor and Francis Books, Inc.

Routledge is an imprint of the Taylor and Francis Group.
Printed in the United States of America on acid-free paper.

10 9 8 7 6 5 4 3 2 1

Library of Congress Cataloging-in-Publication Data
    Sea changes : historicizing the ocean / edited by Bernhard Klein and Gesa Mackenthun.
       p. cm.
    ISBN 0-415-94650-6 (hardback : alk. paper) — ISBN 0-415-94651-4 (pbk.: alk. paper)
1. Ocean and civilization. 2. Ocean—History. 3. Ocean travel. I. Klein, Bernhard, 1963–
II. Mackenthun, Gesa, 1959–
    CB465.S44 2003
    910.4'5—dc21

                                   2003009693

CONTENTS

List of Illustrations   vii

Acknowledgments   ix

Introduction   1
The Sea Is History
BERNHARD KLEIN AND GESA MACKENTHUN

1 Deep Times, Deep Spaces   13
Civilizing the Sea
GREG DENING

2 Costume Changes   37
Passing at Sea and on the Beach
VANESSA SMITH

3 The Global Economy and the Sulu Zone   55
Connections, Commodities, and Culture
JAMES FRANCIS WARREN

4 Ahab's Boat   75
*Non-European Seamen in Western Ships
of Exploration and Commerce*
DAVID A. CHAPPELL

5 Staying Afloat   91
Literary Shipboard Encounters from Columbus to Equiano
BERNHARD KLEIN

6 The Red Atlantic; or, "a terrible blast swept over
the heaving sea"   111
MARCUS REDIKER

7 Chartless Voyages and Protean Geographies   131
Nineteenth-Century American Fictions of the Black Atlantic
GESA MACKENTHUN

8 "At Sea—Coloured Passenger"   149
ALASDAIR PETTINGER

9 Slavery, Insurance, and Sacrifice in the Black Atlantic   167
TIM ARMSTRONG

10 Cast Away   187
The Uttermost Parts of the Earth
PETER HULME

Select Bibliography   203

Contributors   209

Index   213

Illustrations

Figure 1.1   *Endeavour* at Port Philipp (1998). Photograph by Greg Dening.

Figure 1.2   *Hokule'a* at Kaneohe (1975). Photograph by Greg Dening.

Figure 1.3   Philippe Jacques de Loutherbourg, *The Apotheosis of Captain Cook* (1785). By permission of the British Museum.

Figure 1.4   John Webber, *Portrait of Captain James Cook RN* (1782). Oil on canvas. Collection: National Portrait Gallery, Canberra. Purchased 2000 by the Commonwealth Government with the generous assistance of Robert Oatley and John Schaeffer. Photograph by David Reid.

Figure 1.5   Fort Venus. By permission of the Hakluyt Society.

Figure 1.6   Fort Venus Plan. By permission of the Hakluyt Society.

Figure 1.7   Transit of Venus (photographed in 1874). By permission of The Royal Observatory, Greenwich.

Figure 1.8   *Endeavour* launching. Photograph by John Lancaster. By kind permission of HM Bark Endeavour Foundation.

Figure 1.9   *Hokule'a* arriving. Photograph by Nicholas DeVore.

Figure 1.10   *Hokule'a* at sea. Photograph by Frank Wandell.

Figure 1.11   *Hokule'a* voyaging. Photograph by Frank Wandell.

Figure 1.12   Nainoa. By permission of The University of Hawaii Press.

Figure 1.13   Stars Rising. By permission of The University of Hawaii Press.

Figure 1.14   Compass. By permission of The University of Hawaii Press.

Figure 1.15   Calibration. By permission of The University of Hawaii Press.

Figure 1.16   Polaris–Southern Cross. By permission of The University of Hawaii Press.

Figure 1.17   Voyage of *Hokule'a*. By permission of The University of Hawaii Press.

Figure 1.18   *Hokule'a* arriving. Photograph by Frank Wandell.

Figure 3.1   Map of Sulu and Celebes Seas.

Figure 3.2   Map of Iranun Maritime Raiding and and the Malay Archipelago in the first half of the nineteenth century.

Figure 6.1   William Blake, "Orc," from *America, a Prophecy* (1793).

Figure 6.2   William Blake, "A Negro hung alive by the Ribs to a Gallows," from John Gabriel Stedman's *Narrative of a Five Years Expedition against the Revolted Negroes of Surinam* (1790).

Figure 6.3   William Blake, "The Execution of Breaking on the Rack," from John Gabriel Stedman's *Narrative of a Five Years Expedition against the Revolted Negroes of Surinam* (1790).

Figure 10.1   The beach at Zahara de los Atunes, Spain. Photograph by Javier Bauluz. By permission of White Star.

Acknowledgments

We are grateful to our editor at Routledge, Karen Wolny, and her assistant, Jaclyn Bergeron, whose enthusiastic support of this project has made the task of editing much less of a burden. Numerous colleagues and friends have helped us at various stages of the project; we would like to thank especially Jürgen Kramer, Hartmut Lutz, and all the speakers and delegates at the Sea Changes symposium in Greifswald, July 2000, where most of the essays in this collection started life as humble conference papers. Marcus Rediker must be singled out for special praise (though he won't like it) since without his generosity, unconditional support, and expert advice we might never have brought this ship safely to port. Thanks to Greg Dening for the warmth and wisdom of his scholarship and for his help in securing permissions; and to Peter Hulme and Susan Forsyth for tracking down evasive copyright holders. For their financial support, of the initial conference, thanks are due to the Thyssen-Stiftung, the Deutsche Forschungsgemeinschaft, and the Dekanat der Philosophischen Fakultät, Universität Greifswald. Finally, we owe a debt of gratitude to our fine crew of contributors, who have responded with patience and good humor to our numerous queries. It was an honor to have you as our shipmates.

Introduction
The Sea Is History

BERNHARD KLEIN AND GESA MACKENTHUN

Few texts could serve as a better introduction to the present volume than Derek Walcott's 1979 poem "The Sea Is History." In its programmatic opening, the sea encompassing the poet's Caribbean island home of St. Lucia is served up as the imaginative principle of an alternative or counter-history "which has far more relevance to the lived experience of Caribbean peoples than the linear records of colonial society":[1]

> Where are your monuments, your battles, martyrs?
> Where is your tribal memory? Sirs,
> in that grey vault. The sea. The sea
> has locked them up. The sea is history.[2]

In these lines, the sea is imagined both as the guardian of a history that has gone unrecorded by traditional Western forms of preserving the past—narrative, museum, monument—and as a release from the oppressive regime of "tribal memories" and embittered ancestral ghosts. It is seen as opening up a discursive space beyond the repetitive schisms of colonial history, a space—"all subtle and submarine"[3]—of new perspectives, fresh colors, and imaginative liberation, reaching far beyond the crippling binaries characteristic of much retrospective processing of colonial encounters. And while in the last few centuries, the cultural signification of the sea has traveled all the way from a demonic and anti-human principle to an atemporal figure of forgetting and oblivion,[4] Walcott here suggests a different perspective entirely. His poetic metaphor works to restore the sea to the dynamics of the historical process, energizing it for the project of re-imagining, re-writing, and re-membering the past as a complex and polysemic dialogue, a meeting place of different cultures rather than solely the battleground of antagonistic forces.

Taking its cue from this poetic foray into an imaginative maritime historiography, the present volume is motivated by the same urge to venture beyond outworn patterns of historical causality and explanation, and to recover in the history of the sea a paradigm that may accommodate various revisionary accounts—revisionary in the sense of seeing things in new ways, of seeing them differently—of the modern historical experience of transnational contact zones. Such contact zones, according to a recent definition, are "social spaces where disparate cultures meet, clash, and grapple with each other, often in highly asymmetrical relations of domination and subordination—like colonialism, slavery, or their aftermaths as they are lived out across the globe today."[5] Many of these lopsided cultural encounters, the speaker in Walcott's poem knows, took place not beyond but literally in or on the seas, making the ocean itself a prime example of such contact zones, and investing it with both historical meaning and cultural agency.

In exploring the diverse and complex histories of maritime contact zones, *Sea Changes* starts on the premise that the ocean itself needs to be analyzed as a deeply historical location whose transformative power is not merely psychological or metaphorical—as its frequent use as a literary motif might suggest—but material and very real. The essays in this volume all take issue with the cultural myth that the ocean is outside and beyond history, that the interminable, repetitive cycle of the sea obliterates memory and temporality, and that a fully historicized land somehow stands diametrically opposed to an atemporal, "ahistorical" sea. Such a mythical view of the sea—as a symbol of madness, irrational femininity, unruly or romantic anti-civilization—arguably serves only to consolidate the dualistic structure of Western modernity whose definition of knowledge and reason has a remarkably *landed* quality, as Foucault suggested long ago in *Madness and Civilization*.[6] In fact, the impact of the ocean on the course of modern history has been as enormous as its roles have been contradictory: the sea has served as an agent of colonial oppression but also of indigenous resistance and native empowerment, it has been a site of loss, dispersal, and enforced migration but also of new forms of solidarity and affective kinship, a paradigm of modern capitalism but also of its creative reinterpretation, a figure of death but also of life. Whether as the Mediterranean *omphalos*, the Arcadian Pacific, or more recently the Black Atlantic, the sea has occasioned radical changes in human lives and national histories, and it continues to be encompassed—in myth and symbol, in lyric and song, in culture and thought—within the full expressive range of human desire.

Redirecting the historical gaze in this fashion requires some additional conceptual adjustments. Walcott's poem reminds us that with such an agenda, we need to register first of all that the "grey vault" of his ocean, that in-between space of transformation and change where nothing is ever fixed but everything always in flux, will not yield to just any kind of history making. Instead of discovering the martial components of linear history's very public, frontal imagery—"monuments, battles, martyrs"—the poet unexpectedly hears a chorus of quiet, unassuming, hardly audible voices: "[T]here was the sound / like a rumour without any echo // of History, really beginning."[7] Those voices, like the roaring inside a shell, will put our listening skills to the test:

> [T]hat child who puts the shell's howl to his ear,
> hears nothing, hears everything
> that the historian cannot hear, the howls
> of all the races that crossed the water . . .[8]

As the present volume sets out to trace some of the hidden human histories in the vast oceanic archives of which Walcott speaks, readers are invited to discover in the pages that follow the often elusive traces of the many voyagers who "crossed the water"—whether out of their own accord or against their will—as well as the shifting semantic contours of the maritime spaces through which they moved.

This project of unearthing alternative maritime histories takes some inspiration from the practitioners of history from below. Eric Wolf's analysis of the Western colonial system's transactions with non-European cultures and his plea for a transnational historical practice is of particular importance here,[9] and even more pertinent to new forms of maritime history have been Marcus Rediker's efforts—especially in his pioneering study *Between the Devil and the Deep Blue Sea*[10]—to retrieve the physical and often dangerous reality of the lives of seafarers from the widespread romanticization of seafaring in the popular imagination, as well as in earlier historical work. "The romantic perspective," Rediker asserts, "has . . . misrepresented or omitted vital segments of the seaman's experience," concentrating on the universal theme of the struggle between "man" and "nature" instead of considering the historically more specific struggle of "man against man."[11] The most important effect of bringing the critical categories of working-class history to bear on the analysis of seafaring is that the history of modern maritime capitalism can now be viewed from the bottom up—in keeping with the precept that "the history of seafaring people can and must be more than a chronicle of admirals, captains, and military battles at sea: It must be made to speak to larger historical problems and processes."[12] In Rediker's own and in other contributions to this volume, the limited ground of national historiography is transcended to enable a conception of seafarers as "workers of the world," and special attention is placed throughout on the mental and material forms of resistance devised by seamen against the often oppressive social regimes that defined their lives.[13]

In recent years, this line of research has sparked a new interest in the living conditions and cultural experiences of men and women who go to sea; and a number of studies in this field have already stressed the necessity of looking across national and ethnic boundaries in order to get a proper historical sense of the social dynamics that characterized shipboard life in the Age of Exploration and beyond.[14] A number of works have also begun to revise the predictably simplistic understanding of gender relations in a field that has until recently been regarded as a classic resort of masculinity. To see the ocean and the social space of the ship as exclusively male spheres of action is to ignore both the many women who traveled on board ship in various capacities, and the ways in which the life of seafaring men interacted with that of women on shore. As Margaret Creighton and Lisa Norling observe in the introduction to their groundbreaking collection *Iron Men, Wooden Women*, "gender is a fundamental component of seafaring,"[15] and its inclusion in studies of oceans and voyagers changes our view of the history and culture of seafaring as a whole. For to focus on gender means not only to speculate on the number of women who might have engaged in cross-dressing in order to remain undetected on board. Far more complex cultural negotiations are at stake here. For example, as Vanessa Smith shows in her contribution, the understanding of gender codes is central to the analysis of the cross-cultural encounter in the Pacific, where the perception of Polynesian cultures by Western seafarers is crucially disrupted by male anxieties about the role of women in the largely masculine maritime projects of exploration and empire.

The collection by Creighton and Norling on gender and seafaring, from which we have just quoted, is perhaps more than simply a related work that shares many of our critical concerns. Given the focus throughout our volume on transnationality and the multi-cultural maritime encounter, *Sea Changes* could be considered an immediate response to Creighton and Norling's call for future studies that would "acknowledge seafaring as the site of multiracial and multicultural interactions."[16] The need to critically reevaluate Western-dominated thought patterns and Eurocentric historical assumptions has been accepted in many disciplines now, and *Sea Changes* aims to take seriously the critical challenge to not only be interdisciplinary in approach but also remain open to the culturally and historically diverse experiences of modernity. In studies of both the Atlantic and Pacific Ocean, the "multi-cultural" and "postcolonial" turn in the human sciences is becoming especially visible. In Pacific studies, the work of Greg Dening—who is also a contributor to this volume—can be seen to have initiated forms of anthropological research that acknowledge the "performative" response to the cultural encounter as it was acted out on both sides of the beach. In *Mr Bligh's Bad Language*, for instance, Dening writes an ethnographic history of the mutiny on the *Bounty* by applying the theoretical categories of Victor Turner and others to the situation on board, showing that the ritualistic enactment of social hierarchies is just as much part of Western shipboard culture as it is of indigenous cultures of the South Seas.[17]

In these and other studies, the sea has begun to emerge as a truly interdisciplinary field of inquiry. One of the aims of the present volume is to expand on current research by taking its cue from several fields, most importantly—as we have pointed out—critical maritime history and historical anthropology, but also, and no less decisively, postcolonial theory and historiography. In this expanding field, Paul Gilroy's *The Black Atlantic* has been a particularly important intervention, to which several of the essays in this volume are indebted. Gilroy reconceptualizes the Atlantic Ocean in terms of what he calls a "counterculture of modernity," providing cultural historians with a "single, complex unit of analysis" that would enable "an explicitly transnational and intercultural perspective" on the history of modernity.[18] The ship—a "living, micro-cultural, micro-political system in motion"—serves Gilroy as an image for the "rhizomorphic, fractal structure of the transcultural, international formation" of the Black Atlantic as a whole.[19] Like Rediker in his essay on the "Red Atlantic," Gilroy stresses the incompatibility of the Atlantic as a cultural unit with the academic logic of viewing history in nationalist terms. While offering a viable alternative to the nationalist paradigm in the study of Atlantic cultures, the concept of the Black Atlantic can also be seen as a "cultural" response to the predominantly culture-blind, statistical studies of the transatlantic slave trade and their exclusion of the humanistic aspect of the Atlantic experience.[20]

In the light of much of this innovative research, oceans and ships can now be newly assessed as spaces and sites of cultural conflict (as well as, crucially, though less obviously visible, of cooperation). While Dening suggests that the complex social theater enacted on board the *Bounty*, which culminated in open mutiny, is directly related to the ship's spatial organization, Gilroy's concept of the Black Atlantic shifts our attention away from continents as defining geographical entities to the ocean itself as a hybrid cultural space. In this volume, David Chappell shows how the triumphalist tale of European modernity's "discovery of the sea" largely ignores the contribution of indigenous seafarers around the globe, who often responded to the European exploration of their shores with a counter-exploration of Western ships and living conditions. On a more abstract level, such studies can be seen as analogous to Martin Lewis and Kären Wigen's critique of traditional ways of subdividing continents—above all, the Cold War division of the globe into First, Second, and Third World—and their attempt to replace this concept with a culturally less hierarchical scheme of different geopolitical regions.[21] Oceans can be conceptualized in similar ways. Notwithstanding seemingly monolithic terms such as *Black Atlantic,* the essays collected in this volume strongly suggest that there is no single "Atlantic" culture or "Pacific" experience but that both oceans are subdivided into discrete but related and inherently polymorphous sociopolitical contact zones.

These new departures in the historicizing of the sea have an important bearing on the *literary* study of the sea as well. Just as conventional historical approaches to the sea have been limited to specific nations and social groups, the critical engagement with sea fiction, too, has frequently suffered from being conducted within conceptual frameworks far too narrow to match the global scale of their topic (structured, as they frequently are, around limiting themes such as genre, character, or region).[22] Literature remains a dominant point of reference in this volume, too, but the attempt here is to widen the historical and generic contexts within which its maritime variety is studied, and to move beyond the Romantic paradigm that is still too often taken as its defining characteristic. Several essays presented here follow the lead of scholars who approach maritime fictions from an explicitly postcolonial perspective,[23] for it is here that the sea is read not as a catalyst for modern forms of metaphysical and/or psychological brooding but as one of the principal engines of historical change. One recent author of sea fiction, Fred D'Aguiar, for instance, opens his novel about the notorious case of the slaver *Zong*—discussed in this book by Tim Armstrong—with an imaginative, historicized response to Walcott's poem: "The sea is slavery."[24] In the present volume, sea fiction is made to speak for the cultural energies that have been invested in the maritime encounter, and the result, we believe, is a far more resonant and dynamic conception of how the literary representation of the sea interacts with the historical contexts it openly or silently reflects.

We have decided to group the essays in geographical rather than chronological sequence—starting with the Pacific and moving on to the Atlantic—and we will briefly present them here in this order. All respond in different ways to the many sea changes—both real and symbolic—in our historical understanding of ships, oceans, and voyagers, placing special emphasis either on the specific cultural forms that the various oceanic spaces have generated, or on the voyagers who have moved through them—out of free will or by force, driven by economic need, curiosity, or by the desire for change. Perhaps the project of studying the sea as a cultural and historical space takes its inspiration not so much from critical historiography as from maritime archaeology, where the "question of cultural diffusion by contact from the sea"[25] has long been considered one of the most important areas of current research. In our interdisciplinary age, such questions of influence have thankfully become less important, and while each essay included in this book explores the idea of the transnational maritime contact zone from a different methodological angle, each makes the sea the focal point of a critical inquiry into the historical force fields from which our modern notions of self and other have emerged. Despite these common concerns, interdisciplinarity is to be taken literally as a defining principle of this book, in which historians, anthropologists, as well as cultural and literary critics all offer their different stories of the ocean, and in which theoretical and disciplinary perspectives vary accordingly from essay to essay.

Greg Dening opens the section on the South Seas with a suggestive analysis of two "theaters" of reenactment that produce cultural identity in the double encompassment of Oceania, native and stranger: the building of the replica of Cook's *Endeavour* and a journey from Tahiti to Hawaii in the Polynesian voyaging canoe *Hokule'a*. Drawing on a wide frame of theoretical and historical reference, Dening richly contextualizes both these projects, moving back and forth among their practical realization, their implications for the study of cultural identity, and their multiple and complex forms of historical address. Both vessels represent alternative traditions of navigation, both make different cultural claims on the ocean they encompass in their voyages, and both are ultimately, as Dening shows, different expressions of a theatrical language that demands from us an understanding of the deep times and deep spaces of Pacific history. Directing our attention away from the *longue durée* of the historical process and toward the human details of eighteenth-century linguistic and textual transactions that occurred in the context of voyages of exploration, Vanessa Smith then focuses on two individual stories from the first French maritime expedition to the Pacific: the exposure by native Tahitians of the cross-dressing of Jeanne Baré, a French sailor on board one of Bougainville's ships, and the metropolitan experience of Aotourou, the Tahitian traveler who eventually returns to Paris with the expedition. As Europeans and Polynesians gaze at each other from both sides of the beach, Smith argues, cultural fixities threaten initially to disintegrate, exploding the myth of European superiority. But even as native Tahitians are shown in both stories to expose European pretensions of "civility" in Rousseauesque fashion, they are ultimately reinstated in their speaking positions as wild and oversexed "savages," representatives of an essential cultural difference.

While these two opening essays both locate their encounter histories in the Pacific, a different kind of contact between European and indigenous cultures is explored by James Warren in his analysis of the maritime raiding practiced in the Sulu-Mindanao region in Southeast Asia in the eighteenth and nineteenth centuries. As a regionally specific contact zone, this area grew in strategic importance alongside the emergence of a global network of commerce—structured principally around that new hot commodity, "tea"—that connected Britain, China, the Sulu Sultanate, and a variety of smaller places within an expanding trading circuit. Focusing on the impact of these economic changes on local culture, Warren sketches an ethnohistorical framework to show how the Iranun and Balangingi, a maritime people that engaged in what Western sources identified as "piracy," developed their ethnic identity in response to these processes of economic transformation and enormous growth. In the next essay, David Chappell also focuses on what could be called the "local" effects of early globalization by examining the history of seafarers indigenous to the regions explored by Europeans in the Age of Sail and beyond. Chappell reminds us that the newly "discovered" oceanic spaces were no empty "plates" prior to the arrival of the Europeans but had been charted and traversed for thousands of years by the oceangoing ships and canoes of indigenous cultures. The success of European shipping in foreign waters often depended on this local knowledge and expertise, and Chappell spells out the hidden history of this two-way process of cultural exchange in his survey of four groups of non-European seamen: Asian lascars, Oceanian kanakas, African Kru, and the hybrid shipboard category of (mainly East Asian) "Manila-men."

In participating in Western projects of exploration and trade, these indigenous seafarers often displayed a significant—and perhaps unexpected—degree of personal agency. In his analysis of the "literary shipboard encounter," Bernhard Klein explores how this reversal of traditional accounts of native victimization can already be extracted, even if only at a subtextual level, from the writings of various early modern and eighteenth-century "maritime" authors—ranging from Columbus, Brant, and Shakespeare to Behn, Defoe, and Equiano. Taking on board Foucault's reading of the ship as a "heterotopic" social space, Klein shows how textual constructions of the ship and the ocean crossing can function as reflectors of a narrative that reverses the more conventional readings of European colonization: even as Western seafarers master and conquer the Atlantic, their culture has an increasingly incomplete control over the definition of ethnic and national boundaries that their projects were meant to sustain. Marcus Rediker, in the next essay, widens the scope of this analysis by focusing on what he calls the "Red Atlantic": a vibrant maritime space of revolutionary dynamics, incipient capitalism, and transgressive politics that spanned the four corners of the eighteenth-century Atlantic world: northwestern Europe, West Africa, the Caribbean, and North America. Using William Blake's *America, a Prophecy* (1793), a profound meditation on the Age of Revolution in the Atlantic world, as a lead into contemporary perspectives on this turbulent maritime space, Rediker examines two sides of this Atlantic scenario—the violence from above and the resistance from below—to show how the color of blood was mixed in with the color of revolution: expropriation, the Middle Passage, exploitation, and repression were the fourfold forms of violence that constituted the hallmark of maritime capitalism in the Atlantic.

Gesa Mackenthun continues the focus on the Atlantic Ocean in her analysis of the shifting conceptualizations of U.S. national identity in the antebellum period. Focusing principally on literature, Mackenthun traces various instances of discursive translation—that is, the transfer of thought patterns between one historical arena and another—from the Mediterranean of antiquity, to the Atlantic sea of slavery, and from there to the imperial future to be enacted in the Pacific, showing how the fictional ships and protean maritime spaces of American literary discourse often resonate with echoes of the Black Atlantic past. As Mackenthun shows, the ideological certainties and the idealist rhetoric of colonial discourse cannot be sustained when historicized in the light of the hybrid geographies and shape-shifting ships of American sea fiction. Mackenthun discusses these issues with regard to novels by Edgar Allan Poe, Maxwell Philip, and Herman Melville, but considers other writers as well, including, for instance, Olaudah Equiano and Frederick Douglass. The latter is also an important point of reference for the next essay in the volume, in which Alasdair Pettinger considers cases of open discrimination (including one involving Douglass) on Cunard Line steamers crossing the Atlantic in the nineteenth century. As Pettinger shows, the (unofficial) practice of racial segregation on board—itself more widely linked to contemporary U.S. legislation on maintaining order in public spaces—helped to define races as much as keep them apart, and is a much more complex issue than is usually thought when viewed in terms of its experimental and improvisatory character. This examination of the special "contact zone" of the transatlantic steamer strongly suggests that cases of racial discrimination have to be assessed within wider considerations of the social dynamics peculiar to the passenger ship.

Tim Armstrong then turns to the famous case of the slave ship *Zong*, whose captain in 1781 ordered 134 slaves to be thrown overboard in order to have the loss covered by insurance. Armstrong contextualizes this horrific case within the history of life insurance and the maritime practice of casting lots after shipwreck to determine which of the survivors is to die so that the others can survive. As Armstrong argues, life insurance began at sea, and is in its modern conception a product of the confluence of economic expansion and African slavery that is the Black Atlantic. In particular, the debate over the status of the insured slave as either person or property, and over the question of how the value of a life can be quantified, proved influential in the development of life insurance. Instances of maritime cannibalism, another secularized form of "sacrifice at sea," where the victim is chosen by the supposedly random (but actually rarely transparent) operation of lots, relate to this history in ways that reveal the continuing centrality of the transatlantic slave trade to our contemporary culture of catastrophe and compensation. In the final essay of the volume, Peter Hulme develops the trope of the castaway into a critique of many of the cultural assumptions that still determine global politics today, drawing together several thematic strands of the book. Hulme reconstructs an imaginative geography of the world that began to take shape in the sixteenth century, but that was not fully developed until much later, when first Patagonia and then Tasmania came to be scripted as the "uttermost parts of the earth," places whose distance from the scientific center of Europe was measured not only in space but also in time, culture, and civilization. The round shape of the earth is thus overlaid with covert ideological and hierarchical divisions that allow us to be blind to the thousands of drowned, "cast away" African bodies that today wash ashore at Gibraltar—which is no longer the ancient *limit* of knowledge but the frontier between First and Third Worlds.

In this elegiac coda, Hulme draws widely on texts that span the historical period covered in this book, roughly the early sixteenth to the late nineteenth century. As Shakespeare's *Tempest* is read alongside *Robinson Crusoe*, Baudelaire's "Le Cygne" and other texts that use the trope of the castaway in various forms, including Marx's description of the urban raggle-taggle of Paris in "The Eighteenth Brumaire," Hulme exemplifies in his essay what we have attempted to achieve with this book: to explore from as many angles as possible the global scale of the maritime imaginary.

Notes

1. John Thieme, *Derek Walcott* (Manchester and New York: Manchester University Press, 1999), 160.
2. Derek Walcott, "The Sea Is History," *Collected Poems, 1948–1984* (London: Faber, 1984), 364.
3. *Ibid.*, 365.
4. For an excellent account, see Alain Corbin, *The Lure of the Sea: The Discovery of the Seaside in the Western World, 1750–1840* [French original 1988], trans. Jocelyn Phelps (Cambridge: Polity Press, 1994).
5. Mary Louise Pratt, *Imperial Eyes: Travel Writing and Transculturation* (London and New York: Routledge, 1992), 4.
6. Michel Foucault, *Madness and Civilization: A History of Insanity in the Age of Reason*, trans. Richard Howard (New York: Random House, 1965), chapter 1.

7. Walcott, "The Sea Is History," 367.
8. Walcott, *Another Life*, chapter 22, *Collected Poems*, 285. For some thoughts on Walcott's use of the ocean as a figure of history, see Tobias Döring and Bernhard Klein, "Of Bogs and Oceans: Alternative Histories in the Poetry of Seamus Heaney and Derek Walcott," Bernhard Klein and Jürgen Kramer (eds.), *Common Ground? Crossovers between Cultural Studies and Postcolonial Studies* (Trier: Wissenschaftlicher Verlag, 2001), 113–36.
9. Eric Wolf, *Europe and the People without History* (Berkeley: University of California Press, 1982).
10. Marcus Rediker, *Between the Devil and the Deep Blue Sea: Merchant Seamen, Pirates, and the Anglo-American Maritime World, 1700–1750* (Cambridge: Cambridge University Press, 1987). See also his more recent book, cowritten with Peter Linebaugh, *The Many-Headed Hydra: Sailors, Slaves, Commoners, and the Hidden History of the Revolutionary Atlantic* (Boston: Beacon Press, 2000).
11. Rediker, *Between the Devil*, 5.
12. *Ibid.*, 7.
13. For other studies along these lines, see, for example, Eric W. Sager, *Seafaring Labour: The Merchant Marine of Atlantic Canada, 1820–1914* (Kingston: McGill-Queen's University Press, 1989); and Colin Howell and Richard Twomey (eds.), *Jack Tar in History: Essays in the History of Maritime Life and Labour* (Fredricton, New Brunswick: Acadiensis Press, 1991).
14. See, for instance, David Chappell, *Double Ghosts: Oceanian Voyagers on Euroamerican Ships* (New York: M. E. Sharpe, 1997); and Jeffrey Bolster's *Black Jacks: African American Seamen in the Age of Sail* (Cambridge, MA: Harvard University Press, 1997), based on the groundbreaking but unpublished research of Julius Sherrad Scott III: "The Common Wind: Currents of Afro-American Communication in the Era of the Haitian Revolution" (unpublished Ph.D. thesis, Duke University, 1986).
15. Margaret Creighton and Lisa Norling (eds.), *Iron Men, Wooden Women: Gender and Seafaring in the Atlantic World, 1700–1920* (Baltimore: Johns Hopkins University Press, 1996), vii. Studies on seafaring women include Linda Grant de Pauw, *Seafaring Women* (Boston: Houghton Mifflin, 1982); Daniel A. Cohen (ed.), *The Female Marine and Related Works: Narratives of Cross-Dressing and Urban Vice in America's Early Republic* (Amherst: University of Massachusetts Press, 1997); and Suzanne Stark, *Female Tars: Women Aboard Ship in the Age of Sail* (London: Pimlico, 1998). On gender and the sea, see also a number of important essays by Valerie Burton, especially "'Whoring, Drinking Sailors': Reflections on Masculinity from the Labour History of Nineteenth-Century British Shipping," Margaret Walsh (ed.), *Working Out Gender* (Aldershot et al.: Ashgate, 1999), 84–101; and "'As I wuz a-rolling down the Highway one morn': Fictions of the 19th-Century English Sailortown," Bernhard Klein (ed.), *Fictions of the Sea: Critical Perspectives on the Ocean in British Literature and Culture* (Aldershot et al.: Ashgate, 2002), 141–56.
16. Creighton and Norling, "Introduction," *Iron Men, Wooden Women*, xiii.
17. See Greg Dening, *Islands and Beaches: Discourse on a Silent Land: Marquesas 1774–1880* (Chicago: Dorsey Press, 1980); and *Mr Bligh's Bad Language: Passion, Power and Theatre on the Bounty* (Cambridge: Cambridge University Press, 1992).
18. Paul Gilroy, *The Black Atlantic: Modernity and Double Consciousness* (Cambridge, MA: Harvard University Press, 1993), 17. This pioneering study has given rise to a whole field of theoretically informed "Black Atlantic studies," which includes anthologies of original texts of the Black Atlantic, as well as critical studies of Black Atlantic literature and culture. See, for instance, Adam Potkay and Sandra Burr (eds.), *Black Atlantic Writers of the Eighteenth Century: Living the New Exodus in England and the Americas* (Basingstoke: Macmillan, 1995); Alasdair Pettinger (ed.), *Always Elsewhere: Travels of the Black Atlantic* (London: Cassell, 1998); Marcus Wood, *Blind Memory: Visual Representations of Slavery in England and America, 1780–1865* (New York: Routledge, 2000); and Maria Diedrich, Henry Louis Gates, and Carl Pedersen (eds.), *Black Imagination and the Middle Passage* (New York: Oxford University Press, 1999). Most essays in the latter collection follow Gilroy in reading the Middle Passage primarily in metaphorical terms.
19. Gilroy, *The Black Atlantic*, 4.
20. See the macrohistorical studies by, among many others, David Eltis, *Economic Growth and the Ending of the Transatlantic Slave Trade* (New York: Oxford University Press, 1987), Herbert Klein's most recent book *The Atlantic Slave Trade* (Cambridge: Cambridge University Press, 1999); Stanley Engerman and Joseph Inikori (eds.), *The Atlantic Slave Trade*

(Durham, NC: Duke University Press, 1992); and—from a Marxist perspective—Robin Blackburn, *The Overthrow of Colonial Slavery, 1776–1848* (London: Verso, 1988), and *The Making of New World Slavery: From the Baroque to the Modern, 1492–1800* (London: Verso, 1997). Other studies, including James Walvin's *Black Ivory: A History of British Slavery* (London: Fontana, 1993) and Hugh Thomas's *The Slave Trade: The History of the Atlantic Slave Trade, 1440–1870* (Basingstoke: Macmillan, 1998) are more conscious of cultural aspects. Yet none of them focuses on the maritime experience of Atlantic slavery.

21. Martin W. Lewis and Kären E. Wigen, *The Myth of Continents: A Critique of Metageography* (Berkeley: University of California Press, 1997).

22. This is not say that these works have not been impressive scholarly achievements within the terms of their own agenda. See, for example, Haskell Springer (ed.), *America and the Sea* (Athens: University of Georgia Press, 1995) and, for an earlier classic on American sea fiction, Thomas Philbrick, *James Fenimore Cooper and the Development of American Sea Fiction* (Cambridge, MA: Harvard University Press, 1961). Other important works on American and British literature of the sea include Richard Astro (ed.), *Literature and the Sea* (Corvallis: Oregon State University Press, 1976); Patricia Ann Carlson (ed.), *Literature and Lore of the Sea* (Amsterdam: Rodopi, 1986); Bert Bender, *Sea-Brothers: The Tradition of American Sea Fiction from Moby Dick to the Present* (Philadelphia: University of Pennsylvania Press, 1988); John Peck, *Maritime Fiction: Sailors and the Sea in British and American Novels, 1719–1917* (Basingstoke and New York: Palgrave, 2001); and most recently Klein (ed.), *Fictions of the Sea* (2002).

23. Peter Hulme's classic *Colonial Encounters: Europe and the Native Caribbean, 1492–1797* (London: Methuen, 1986) has pioneered other texts that seek to apply the critical terminology of colonial discourse analysis in examining the history of maritime encounters with non-European cultures. They also replace the national perspective of earlier books in defining their geographical scope according to the newly "discovered" non-European cultures. For the Pacific, see Rod Edmond, *Representing the South Pacific: Colonial Discourse from Cook to Gauguin* (Cambridge: Cambridge University Press, 1997); and Vanessa Smith, *Literary Culture and the Pacific: Nineteenth-Century Textual Encounters* (Cambridge: Cambridge University Press, 1998).

24. Fred D'Aguiar, *Feeding the Ghosts* (London: Vintage, 1997), 3. For a reading of this novel in the context of recent historiography on the slave trade, see Carl Pedersen, "The Sea Is Slavery: Middle Passage Narratives," Klein (ed.), *Fictions of the Sea*, 188–202.

25. E. E. Rice, "Introduction," Rice (ed.), *The Sea and History* (Stround: Sutton Publishing, 1996), xi.

CHAPTER 1

Deep Times, Deep Spaces
Civilizing the Sea

GREG DENING

"Like the desert," Gesa Mackenthun and Bernhard Klein write, "the ocean has often been read as an empty space, a cultural and historical void, constantly traversed, circumnavigated and fought over, but rarely inscribed other than symbolically by the self-proclaimed agents of civilization."[1] The Sea tends to have no history, they have suggested. It is a void they would like to fill. I would, too. I would encompass Oceania, the Sea of Islands.

Roland Barthes himself could have been the source of Mackenthun and Klein's challenge. He is asking whether in a world flooded with signifiers, there is somewhere that a semiological science would not reach. "In a single day," he writes while on a beach vacation, "how many really non-signifying fields do we cross? Very few, sometimes none. Here I am before the sea; it is true that it bears no message. But on the beach, what material for semiology! Flags, slogans, signals, sign-boards, clothes, suntan even, which are so many messages for me."[2]

I have to confess that over the years I have had a penchant for beaches as places of history, too. Not the only place for history. I would never say that. But places for special historical insights. In-between places, where every present moment is suffused with the double past of both sides of the beach and complicated by the creative cultures that this mixture makes.

But I am not inclined to Barthes's polarity between the signless sea and the full-of-signs land. Barthes's sense of the sea is a little too close to Freud's notion of "oceanic feeling" as a sensation of eternity, or W. H. Auden's "barbaric vagueness of the sea," or Gaston Bachelard's "substantive nothing-ness of water," or even Jules Michelet's sense of the ocean as sublime slime—wet, fecund femininity.[3]

Claude Lévi-Strauss—a more landlocked thinker, to be sure—makes the same distinction between cultural domains that are historical, touched by time and change, and those that are unhistorical, structured, timeless, unchanging. It is a distinction I would like to oppose. For us who are in a world created by and reflected in Einstein and Picasso, all things are on an "astral plane," only real in their dimensions without number, only objec-tive in their ambiguity and relativity. Historicizing the Sea is an exercise in deep time, shallow time—both: in deep space, shallow space—both.

Polyglot Time: Polyglot Space

So I would like to make my first step a step away from that polarity of an unhistorical sea and a historical land. Historicizing the Sea, we say. Histori-cizing. I note the present participle, historicizing. The subjunctive, "as if" mood. The theater mood. Not the "Historicized Sea." We are making the-ater of the Sea, imbuing the Sea with narrative. We are talking processes. We are talking of the *how* of our history making as much as of the *what*. We are talking tropes and story, fact and fiction, myth and memory, events and agency. Historicizing the Sea is as much a matter of who reads and hears our histories, as who writes and tells them, and what the story is.

Oceania, the Sea of Islands that I would historicize, is a double-visioned place. It has been encompassed these past five hundred years by intruding strangers and encompassed these past three thousand years by the is-landers who have settled and visited all its thousands of islands through its vast spaces. Natives and strangers have drawn their different cultural iden-tities from historicizing the same Sea.[4]

The same Sea? That is the issue, isn't it? By the end of this volume, we will have decapitalized and pluralized our concept of the sea. Not Sea, but seas. A French sea, an American sea, a capitalist sea, an eighteenth-century sea, a Romantic sea, a Viking sea, *moana*—an islanders' sea.

Difference and particularizing is not so much my problem. Time and space are polyglot. So is history. A privileged perspective is a problem, though. It is I, not they, the natives and strangers of yesteryear, who has to encompass Oceania in a multi-timed, multi-spaced, multi-visioned way. They are on my "astral plane," not I on theirs. How do I write a narrative in a unified way of two culturally distinct peoples historicizing the same sea, without privileging a time or a space or a vision that is not there in their historicizations? How do I put a multi-dimensional Oceania on canvas? How do I play Picasso to the Pacific?

Let me reflect a moment on the language of that historicizing. For anthropology, the problem of crossing cultures in space and time is resolved by the creation of a metalanguage—about ritual, symbol, myth, social structure, culture itself. It is a language of human universals that cultures share in their distinctive ways.

History has been shy of such metalanguage, though we easily borrow it and vernacularize it. My narrative strategy is to use that metalanguage in a vernacular way and attach it to a meta-issue—in this case, the issue of cultural identity. As many cultures of natives and strangers historicize their sea, they find their different cultural identities in the same process. They find themselves mirrored in their own historicizations. I try to reveal this mirroring by writing an ethnography of them both historicizing their sea. They do that in theater.

Both land and sea are encompassed by words. Language imprints land and sea with the human spirit, enlarges both with the human spirit. Language encultures land and sea. Language brushes them with metaphor—"South Seas," "Pacific"—fills them with story—"Hawaii" (Sacred Home), "Tahiti" (Distant Place). I would like to reflect on the mystery of this.[5] "In the beginning was the Word," the Judaeo-Christian mythology tells us. Indeed it was. Encompassing begins with the word.

A ship at sea is like an island in the ocean. The horizon is all around. That enclosing horizon seems to fill both a ship and an island with language very intensely. I've had my say on the significance of that in relation to ships.[6] Let me say something about islands.

"Navel of the World," "Center of the World," were the usual Oceanic metaphors for an island. Their gods (*atua/akua*), their ancient heroes, always came from "beyond the horizon." Islanders' penchant for symbols was, and is, for crossing signs—rainbows, feathers, canoes—in-between things, in-between heaven and earth, in-between land and sea, in-between air and soil. Islanders made their cultural identity—they made sense of themselves—in ritual, dance, story, design, and architecture—by making large polarities—Native/Stranger, Land/Sea, Life/Death, Violent Power/Legitimate Authority. They discovered for themselves, by story and talk, the ways in which these polarities were crossed to make themselves who they were.

Islanders read the sea—historicized it—by hearing what they called, in their different dialects, "the language of the sea." The "language of the sea" began at its edges. If the Inuit had thirty words for snow, and the Nuer had twenty-seven words for the color of their cows, the Hawaiians and other islanders had as many words for the shapes and character of the waves that beat against their shores. Waves, in their season and in their weather, had personal names and histories. They told stories, sang songs, made poetry through the generations how these waves had been surfed and beaten.[7] They played with the sea at its edges. They would not have seen the sea as a Turner saw it. They played with it, imposed their signature on it with style.

Maybe I should begin encompassing Oceania with an ethnography of swimming. The first beachcomber to return from Oceania was made swimming instructor to the marines at Cronstadt. Mai, the Raiatean whom Cook brought back from the "Society" Islands on his second voyage, amazed his English hosts with the vigor and energy with which he swam to the horizon from Scarborough beach. Stories of how the islanders could swim for hours, even days, from ships miles out at sea were many. The exhilaration with which they plunged into the sea from the tallest masts of European ships was a sign of a familiarity with the sea that Europeans did not dare have.

The wider sea had an even more complex language, and a recognizable system of signs—of ocean swells, seasonal currents, star risings and settings. That is the point of encompassment, isn't it? To capture the system in the signs, the system in the color of the sea and the shape of its swells, the system in the sun and stars and moon, a system that can be described and correlated, a system that could be verbalized and passed on. Thomas Gladwin's book of genius, *East Is a Big Bird*, catches the rationally different system of Caroline Islands navigation in the metaphor of his title.[8]

I think the most enlightening moment for me of this process of encompassment of Oceania through three thousand years came from a sailor-archaeologist, Geoffrey Irwin. He suggested that the movement of island peoples against the prevailing weather patterns to the outmost reaches of this vast ocean was always predicated on a confidence in their ability to return home. A five-hundred-year stopover, a twenty-generation stopover, allowed a regional encompassment. When the language of the sea could be read so fluently that a return home could be assured, a new stage in Pacific exploration could begin.[9]

One more point about language. If I ask how eighteenth-century strangers and their contemporary third-millennium natives historicized their sea, I need also to ask how I historicize this now bound-together Oceania. For nearly five hundred years, native and strangers have been present in the same sea, have been part of each other's culture-scape. The events of early contact might have been sporadic and disparate, but the exchanged experience and cultural memory of their coming together was more pervasive and permanent. The historicization—the encompassment—of a bound-together Oceania is marked by a process in which the two sides of the cultural divide are changed by one another and discover their separate cultural identity at the same time. *Plus ça change, plus c'est la même chose.*

There was a time forty-five years ago that I felt my twentieth-century person more puritanical and distant from this process. Not now. Outsiders tend to see only discontinuities, write their histories in terms of "befores" and "afters." My aim these days is to see the continuities that insiders see, to discover the metaphorizing processes in cultural change. My confidence that I can do so is born of my sense of the language of the theater I am going to speak about.

That culture is talk and living is story is the discovery of the twentieth century. Clifford Geertz, Jacques Derrida, Michel Foucault, Roland Barthes, Paul Ricoeur, Ludwig Wittgenstein have said it so.

Talk is never bare words, of course. Talk is all the ways words are symbolized. It is voice and gesture, rhythm and timing, color and texture. Talk is tattoo. Talk is body paint, and house columns. Talk is never stream of consciousness, either. It is shaped and dramatized in a dance, a story, a joke. Talk is silence. Talk might seem to be blown away by the wind on the lips, but it never is. It is always archived in some way by the continuities of living. Talk joins past, present, and future.

Words swallow time like black holes. And when words carry space as well as time—giving identity to self and other—boundaries are just as blurred.

As I historicize the sea, as I encompass Oceania, I try to hear the language of the sea in this multi-cultural, multi-spatial, multi-temporal way.

Encompassing Oceania

Let me begin at last. Encompassing Oceania.

The word *compass* and with it *encompass* is one of those words in the *Oxford English Dictionary* with a small discursive introduction puzzling at the word's origins. To "measure," "walk in pace," "stride across" belong to the oldest meanings of *compass* and *encompass*. But surprisingly, so do "contrivance," "artifice," "designing skill," "stratagem." So power is in *encompass*. Something of Colossus astride the globe. There's trickster in the word, too. A touch of fraud and gullibility. There is comfort in it. Reassurance. A sense of completenesss, enfolding.

There are all sorts of ways of encompassing Oceania.

Vasco Núñez de Balboa encompassed Oceania. Standing ankle-deep in the vast plain of stinking mud that the eighteen-foot tide had left in the Gulf of San Miguel on the isthmus of Panama, he tapped the rising sea with his sword and proclaimed that these south seas and all in them from pole to pole belonged to the kings of Castile from that moment till judgment day. That's encompassing with ambit.[10]

Francis Drake encompassed the South Seas when he leaned (*groveled* is his word) far over the southernmost precipice on Horn Island and claimed that no man had gone farther south than he. James Cook said the same on the *Resolution* at 72° South latitude. But his midshipman George Vancouver scrambled out on the bowsprit and shouted, "*Ne plus ultra.*" But Dr. Andreas Sparrman leaning out of the Great Cabin windows caught the *Resolution*'s sternway as she tacked. It was his story that he had reached the farthest south. They were making history we say—the *Guinness Book of Records* type of history, to be sure. But there is much encompassing in such driven energy to be first.[11]

French admirals encompassed Oceania when they bent over diplomatic tables and said that by possessing the Marquesas on the crossroads between Panama and Sydney, Cape Horn and Shanghai, they would force the British to have passports to sail the Pacific.[12]

The United States encompassed Oceania by displacing an island people and exploding two nuclear devices named *Gilda* and *Helen* over their atoll in 1946. They left us forever with an image of a mushroom cloud engulfing Bikini. European fashion designers Jacques Heim and Louis Reard exploited the sexuality of the nuclear moment by inventing what became the fetish of the twentieth century, a swimsuit called first "L'Atome" and then "bikini." *The National Geographic* photographed and described the wave of radioactive water that enveloped the ships at Bikini as a "wet caress, a kiss of death." In historicizing my sea, I'll need to display all the ironies in that.[13]

Global capitalists encompass Oceania in their "Rimspeak." The Pacific Rim is that imaginary space of growth beyond regions of stagnation and market decline. Encompassment in a global economy is the creation of a region outside the ideologically and politically limited boundaries of the state, a space for market and exploitation outside the limits that social ideals and cultural values impose. It is Hermes and Proteus, the trickster and theater gods, who stride the globe in this encompassment, not Colossus.[14]

The Theater of Reenactment

It is Hermes and Proteus about whom I now want to speak. I want to talk about theaters of reenactment that make cultural identity in this double encompassment of Oceania. It is happening in Oceania right now. There are two replica sailing vessels encompassing Oceania, giving cultural identity out of different pasts to very different presents. They are the *Endeavour* and the Polynesian voyaging canoe *Hokule'a*.[15]

I first saw the *Endeavour* replica in 1997 in a place that the original *Endeavour* had never been, Port Phillip Bay of my hometown, Melbourne. I first saw *Hokule'a* in 1975 when Ben Finney was putting her through sea trials off the north shore of Oahu in the Hawaiian islands.

Cultural Icons The *Endeavour* replica, here in Port Philip Bay, Victoria, 1998, and *Hokule'a*, here undergoing sea trials at Kaneohe on the island of Oahu in 1975, are icons of cultural achievements. The *Endeavour* plays out the altruism in pure science and discovery. *Hokule'a* plays out the grandness of the Polynesian discovery and settlement of the Sea of Islands.

I'm not much for reenactments, I have to confess. Reenactment histories tend to hallucinate us into seeing the past as us in funny clothes. Not any "us." An abstracted "us." An "us" reduced to an ideal. An "us" identified with the past as myth.

There hasn't been a man of myth, at least in the encompassment of Oceania, as large as James Cook, and that from the moment of his death in Hawaii. When the famous painting of the *Apotheosis of Captain Cook*, with Cook looking rather nervously at both Britannia and Fame, floated down to the stage at the end of the pantomime *Omai* at Covent Garden in 1785, King George III shed a tear and the audience joined the chorus with gusto to sing:

> The hero of Macedon ran o'er the world
> Yet nothing but death would he give
> 'Twas George's command and the sail was unfurl'd
> And Cook taught mankind how to live.

The humanistic empire and science of Great Britain are identified with and embodied in James Cook, and King George weeps for the goodness of it all.

The second verse goes on to say:

> He came and he saw, not to conquer but to save
> The Caesar of Britain was he
> Who scorned the conditions of making a slave

A Mythic and Historic James Cook A mythic James Cook, represented by Philippe Jacques de Loutherbourg, and looking nervous in the hands of Fame and Britannia, descends on the stage of the pantomime, *Omai,* to the acclamation of all and the tears of George III, December 1785.

A historic James Cook, painted by John Webber, looking too severe for the gentle father he was to his children, in the eyes of Mrs Cook, but looking just right as the "father" of his crew who witnessed his "heivas" of rage on the decks of the *Endeavour.*

> While Britons themselves are so free
> No the Genius of Britain forbids us to grieve
> Since Cook ever honor'd immortal shall live.[16]

As the *Endeavour* replica was launched in Fremantle, Western Australia, there were speeches, of course. They quoted Charles Darwin saying that Cook had "added a hemisphere to the civilised world."[17] This perfect *Endeavour* replica built at a cost of five million dollars was a living creature, they said, imbued with the spirit of Cook. He was "the most moderate, humane, gentle circumnavigator who went upon discovering."[18] The *Endeavour* replica was a symbol of tenacity, skills, endurance, and leadership and of the Australian credo of "Have a go!" It didn't seem to matter that the man who gave the five million was in jail for fraud.

Cook is a man of myth. Cook is a man of anti-myth. Myth and anti-myth are always true. Myth and anti-myth are never true. Off the New South Wales coast where there were Aboriginal first people to see the *Endeavour* replica, in the Bay of Islands and Poverty Bay, New Zealand, where there were Maori eyes to see it, the *Endeavour* replica was not an icon of humanistic empire and science. The theater of the reenactment there was the violence that Cook did in Tonga, Hawaii, Aotearoa (New Zealand), and wherever he put foot on land. The theater is about the resistance that indigenous ancestors would have made if they had known the history that was to follow. The reenactment is the same process, however. The abstraction is "us"—the resistance fighters with a sense of history—in the funny clothes of past ancestors.

I don't mind confessing that I was deeply moved when I first stepped aboard the *Endeavour* replica. Much of my work concerns spaces, symbolic and real, and how they shape human behavior.[19] Seeing Cook's cabin, where he discovered he was a discoverer, seeing the Great Cabin where so much that I respect and admire was done, seeing the quarterdeck where Cook, as his men used to joke behind his back, "did a heiva" (a native Tahitian dance) in transports of rage, seeing the fo'c'sle and knowing the pains and joys of every man who messed there, I know that my narratives are reshaped by my own living experience of the ship's spaces.

Every historian, it seems to me, is engaged in some form of reenactment. I have always felt that the biggest privilege of an historian is to meet the past in manuscript, on paper, with the dust of time still upon it, sometimes stained with tears, and even blood, always touched by the transience of the present moment in which it was written.

So it was a special privilege for me recently—in celebration of the National Library of Australia's hundred years—to be invited to historicize James Cook's own journal on the *Endeavour*. "MS 1" it is cataloged as—in number and in sentiment the foundation document of the National Library, and recently by being nominated as a World Heritage document numbered among the great documents of human history. I have read the journal in transcript many times, of course. But to put on white gloves to open and turn the pages written in Cook's own hand, his first and afterthoughts, his judgments and corrections all there, was indeed special. For my reenactment let me go straight to that text. We never experience the past. We always historicize out of somebody else's history.[20]

Observing the Unobservable

> Saturday 3rd [of June] This day prov'd as favourable to our purpose as we could wish, not a Clowd was to be seen the whole day and the Air was perfectly clear, so that we had every advantage we could desire in Observing the whole of the passage of the Planet Venus over the Suns disk: we very distinctly saw an Atmosphere or dusky shade round the body of the Planet which very much disturbed the times of the Contact particularly the two internal ones. . . . [T]he Thermometer expos'd to the Sun about the middle of the Day rose to a degree of heat we have not before met with.

It was anti-climactic. He wasn't to know that Venus's atmosphere created a penumbra that blurred the moment of Venus's entry and exit of the sun's circumference. It made his and his colleagues' measurements ambiguous by some seconds, which seemed to doom their experiment. It was a moment of pure science that was lost. At that same moment, there were others in South Africa and Mexico as well as Tahiti trying to observe the unobservable, the extent of the universe. What they observed, of course, was the ever-more-finely calibrated measurements of their instruments. But they had to socialize themselves to the "as if" world of their measuring, immerse themselves in special languages, and come out knowing they had seen unseeable distances.

It is the *longue durée* of that encompassment of Oceania that interests me. It is a *longue durée* of science that joins an ancient Greek, Eratosthenes, measuring the size of the earth from the shadows of poles in different places at noon, and Cook making his contribution to measuring the size of the universe from the solar parallax. I would historicize my sea by telling how that *longue durée* has been a story of how Pacific exploration has been a movement from mapping its spaces to measuring its deep time.

Cook in Fort Venus on that famous point of land off Matavai Bay, Tahiti, is my prologue. Cook's tent observatory is behind the palisades. He has his Sheldon pendulum clock there, his Bird quadrant, his Ramsden sextant—the finest astronomical instruments in existence. Fort Venus is more theater than fort, though—theater in the round. The English and the Tahitians perform at one another there, dance at one another. The English dance with their military exercises, their flag raising, and their church services. They display their uniforms, their colors, their order, their violence. The didactics of their theater are always about power and trade, how the power of empire can reach out over distance, can have permanence even without presence; how power is not just a matter of external force, but a binding discipline within the ship as well; how trade isn't exchange or gift, how behavior and work can earn things that will change the relations between people, men and women, chief and servant.

The Tahitians dance with their mocking mime, translating the silences they have no words for, reading new body postures and looks. The Tahitians use the very gateway of the fort as a stage to display their otherness. They choreograph copulations there. They show what wealth and power mean to them, what gender and class.

There is a penumbra around Fort Venus as there is a penumbra around the planet Venus, and Cook's vision is blurred. He can place himself with his science in Tahiti within a few seconds of accuracy by measurement of modern satellite global positioning. But he can't place himself with the same accuracy in his cultural and human relationships. He knows he is seeing difference. He can't really describe it or explain it. He'll be punished for acknowledging difference by a less flexible public, and his sense of differ-

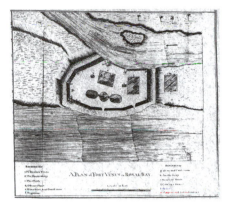
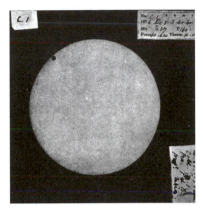

Measuring the Size of the Universe Fort Venus at Matavai was the theater both of Enlightenment science and of the strangeness of native islanders and English intruders to one another. In the tent observatory, Cook observed the Transit of Venus (here photographed in Hawaii in 1874) with the most modern instruments available to him. In the gateway of the fort, on the seaward side, the Tahitians choreographed a copulation for the strangers.

ence will be silenced in him. But it will be with him even at his death in Hawaii.

The prologue to my historicizing my sea, then, is there in Fort Venus, full of stories of power, blurred visions, awkward translations, and tricksters. As any encompassing should be.

Ocean

I think I would call my first chapter "Ocean," my second chapter "Civilizing the Sea." I'd call chapter 1 "Ocean" because I have always been affected by the poetry/science of Rachel Carson's *The Sea around Us*. Maybe you remember her image of the birth of the Pacific Ocean. She imagined the molten liquid surface of the young earth rising into a huge wave through five hundred years of sun tides. This wave, she said, whipped off the earth's surface and became the earth's satellite, the moon. "When the moon was born," she wrote, "there was no ocean." Then the rains came and filled the vast basin left by the birth of the moon. No matter that she was so wrong. The intellectual adventure for me has been to find out why she was wrong. I've gotten to know that a day could be only two and a half hours long for the earth to spin off its moon. I've gotten to know that the biggest encounter in all my encounter histories has been between hydrogen and oxygen. Water takes us back in the deepest of deep time. My "Ocean" is as deep as the Moho line, as high as the Southern Cross, as large as the forces that join them, as old as matter itself.[21]

So how do I historicize this Ocean? I want to say that in the nearly five hundred years since Europe's Discovery of the Sea—*discovery of the sea*, of course, is J. H. Parry's phrase to describe Europe's discovery that the earth's continents were all islands set in one global sea—I want to say that in those five hundred years, the historicizing of the sea—its setting into story and representation—has moved from putting in mind its vast spaces to putting in mind its vast time.[22] Its exploration has moved from enveloping everything that was in it—its vegetation, its rocks and soil, its fauna, the sea itself—within systems of Eurocentered science and cosmology to exploration of its deep time, its *longue durée*. Its historicization has moved from its surface and edges to its floor, from its expanses to its depths.[23]

My mind's eye needs some submarine vehicle to historicize this sea. I need a new Captain Nemo and his *Nautilus*. I need a new *20,000 Leagues Under the Sea*. I need a Jules Verne's brilliant mind of 170 years ago to read the scientific paradigms of my day as he did of his. I need his ability to hear the white noise of a global discourse. Maybe I will have the courage to fictionalize this new exploration in time, the better to travel along the edges of tectonic plates, to catch the origins of life around volcanic vents in the deepest, darkest places on earth. As I enjoy Johann Reinhold Forster puzzling how to measure the temperature of deep layers of the ocean without corrupting his measurements with the temperatures of the upper layers, so I enjoy Francis Beaufort ordering his light, gentle, moderate, fresh, strong, stiff breezes and gales and storms into recognizable, communicable signs, so I enjoy the scientific and engineering miracle of drilling miles deep into the earth's crust from a rolling ship at sea.[24]

To historicize my ocean, I need a hold on paradigms, epistemes, and discourses. I need to plumb the visions of empire. Maybe fiction is the only way I'll get to the truth of it, looking from my submarine down into the depths, up into the imaginary tracks that are left on the ocean's surface, sea-lanes, whales' ways, shearwater flights.

Civilizing the Sea

Chapter 2 would be "Civilizing the Sea." That is because I have always been fascinated by Norbert Elias's *The Civilising Process*, and his reflections on the boundaries around the civilized self and what it costs to make them and cross them. In a dark moment some years ago, as I tried to work with some intransigent naval cliometrics, I came upon a 1950 article by Elias on "The Genesis of the British Naval Profession." In it, he plays on the contradictions between the authority of the captain/squire of a fighting vessel and the authority of the skilled masters of its navigation.[25]

A sailing vessel is a machine energized by natural forces and human vigor. Power so harnessed gives every part of a ship a trembling, beating life that transmits itself to the bodies of the sailors and all their senses. Sailors feel the rhythm, hear it, smell it, see it, have the language to describe it. Their watches might be their hours of vigilance, but they are always awake to the signs of life around them. When life is so dependent on skill and knowledge and the choreography of their movements, true authority is divorced from power. True authority on a ship comes only from experience, not from birth, or gift, or wealth, or Admiralty appointment. A seaman who has gone where others have not been—beyond that point, beyond that cape, beyond that sea—had knowledge into which all others had to be initiated. *To be baptized* was the sailors' phrase for this initiation. It was a ritual for civilizing the sea. It was always a grotesque satire on institutions and roles of power. The satire could be about the sacraments of the state— the accolade of a knight—or the sacraments of the church—baptism by a priest. It could be a statement on kingship and the power over life and death. It was serious play.[26]

In "Civilizing the Sea," I would give consideration to the processes that David Starkey drew our attention to years ago—the processes by which the powers of the state, physically embodied in the king on his throne, is devolved to the outer reaches of his kingdom.[27] There are spaces in that process where central power and the role of law is ambivalent. I borrow Bernard Bailyn's metaphor for such ambivalent spaces, "marchlands"—regressive, bizarre, and wild places, dominated by violence, places where being "civilized" was always compromised by the Realpolitik of the harsh environment, where everybody went a little savage to survive. Marchlands were a place full of the theatricality of derring-do and adventure capitalism. Full of the code of honor and unconscionable violence. The sea of empires, trade, discovery, pirates, and privateers is a marchlands that demands from me an ethnography.[28] Not now.

Double-Visioned History

Forty-five years ago, I made a discovery that changed my life. I discovered that I wanted to encompass Oceania in a double-visioned way. I wanted to write the history of Pacific islands from both sides of the beach. I began to read the voyagers—Cook, Bougainville, Bligh, Vancouver, La Pérouse— then whalers' logs, missionary letters, beachcombers' journals, not so much to tell their stories as to see what their unseeing eyes were seeing, life on the other side of the beach.

Double-visioned history out of one-visioned texts has its epistemological problems, of course. But they were exhilarating times. Innocent ones, too. They were exhilarating because our history knew no boundaries. Every other discipline was an island with its beach that we crossed. They were innocent times because we did not know the politics of our knowledge. Frantz Fanon changed that for us in 1961, but before that it was as if life was a *Times* Literary Crossword Puzzle, full of curiosity without responsibility.

There was an element of the bizarre and extravagant in Pacific studies that distracted us at the time. The Polynesians were "The Lost Tribes of Israel" was one claim. "Easter Island was peopled by St. Brendan and his monks" was another. No, from Outer Space! Thor Heyerdahl's theories of the provenance of Pacific islanders from North and South America were bait to our enthusiastic detective story history.

There was a scholar whose curmudgeonlike character triggered a different sort of pursuit in us. That scholar was Andrew Sharp. In *Ancient Voyagers in the Pacific* (1956), Sharp denied the possibility that the first peoples of the Pacific reached their islands in any other way than by accident. My first academic publication was an attempt to refute his extravagance. This was an exercise in intellectual puritanism on my part. I was offended at his aggressive intransigence on a matter of some ambiguity. I really had no idea how deeply political his argument was. It was an attack on Pacific islanders' sense of identity in their cultural pride in their navigating skills. I did not know it, but I was about to take my first postcolonial step. "One small step for . . ."!

I do all my sailing in libraries. I have no navigating skills. Perhaps that was to my advantage. Other people's skills make one humble. One needs humility to accept that one's knowledge is imperfect, that we "see through a glass darkly."

My seeing through a glass darkly began on a rainy day in the Victorian State Library. I remember that it was rainy because drips from a leak in the huge dome of the reading room were falling into a bucket behind me. The new colony of Victoria, with delusions of grandeur created by gold discoveries, had built the dome in imitation of the British Library's splendid icon. I was following my hunch that Andrew Sharp was as armchair a sailor as I and was looking for more experienced witnesses. I was reading Harold Gatty's *Raft Book*, a pamphlet he had written for airmen shot down into the Pacific Ocean during the Second World War. He was telling them what he had learned from islanders about reaching land through the reflections of green lagoons in clouds, from the changes in wave patterns in the shadow of islands, from birds that flew back to land nests in the evening. I decided to put my double-visioned history ambitions to the test.

I decided to scour my sources for every islander voyage that they reported, whether they were stories of storm-blown survivors of some canoeing disaster, or whether they were planned expeditions in search of land or conquest or trade. The voyages had to be historical, not mythological. There had to be witnesses. They had to have been performed, as far as could possibly be determined, without the aid of navigational instruments or maps or boats imported with the coming of the European strangers.

I discovered 215 of these voyages. I put them on a map, to see their prevailing direction, to determine the distances covered, and their purposes.[29] There were other maps—of the distribution of animal and vegetable foodstuffs that could only have come by canoe, of inhabited islands on which there was evidence of islanders having visited, of the names of other islands given to explorers by the inhabitants of each group. These maps were my first double-visioned encompassment of Oceania. What I learned forty years ago has been far outstripped by brilliant scholarship and practical sailing experience, of course. Nothing I discovered has been gainsaid, I think, but I have admired from a distance the insights into the complexities and subtleties of other navigational systems given us by Thomas Gladwin (*East Is a Big Bird*, 1970), the courage and real experiences of David Lewis (*We, the Navigators*, 1972), the cross-cultural wisdom and practice of Ben Finney (*Hokule'a: The Way to Tahiti*, 1979; *Voyage of Rediscovery*, 1994).

It would be a bore to unravel my thinking of forty years to this point. Let me, then, boldly state my more radical suppositions now as prelude to my final piece of theater. Trust, humility, giving—these are the starting points to seeing someone else's encompassments. The truth is, however, that it is the encounter between natives and strangers that makes this seeing possible. Encounters, according to the prejudice of our established histories of them, are short, sudden, and violent. In fact, encounters are slow, drawn out. They belong to the *longue durée* of living. They never end. In a sense, too, they have no beginning. Encountering otherness, finding cultural identity in the mirror of otherness, seeing the metaphor in something else—all these transforming processes are present in culture. They are rarely episodic. They rarely turn on one event. This creative encountering is a repetitious, reflective thing. It happens not once, but a myriad of times. It is constantly renewed by story, dance, painting. It is re-presented. It is represented in all the social dramas of living. All encountering has continuous theater.

In cultural changes of the encounter, there is rarely a polarity between one way of doing things and another. In cultural changes of the encounter, beliefs, objects, words are not borrowed from one culture by another. They are transformed, re-created. No belief, no object, no word of one culture is nearer the reality it describes or encapsulates than the beliefs, objects, or words of another. Identity in cultural change is continuous. There is no

Mirrors of Cultural Selves The launching of the *Endeavour* replica at Fremantle, Western Australia, in December 1993, and the arrival of *Hokule'a* in Tahiti, June 3, 1976, thirty-three days after leaving Hawaii, were both occasions of ritual when thousands of people discovered who they were in the mirror of an historical reenactment.

loss of authenticity. Culture is as fluent as the language that sustains it. "To arrest the meaning of words once for all, that is what the Terror wants," Jean-François Lyotard once wrote. Writing without the Terror is our post-colonial virtue.[30]

I first saw *Hokule'a* undergoing sea trials in Kaneohe Bay on the north side of Oahu in the Hawaiian islands in 1975. Ben Finney showed her to me. I had first encountered Finney in 1956. He had just written an article on ancient surfboard riding in Hawaii. I thought surfboard research was a pretty good lurk. But it was the beginning for him of a career in which he has wedded theoretical knowledge with practical skill. He calls it "experimental archaeology" these days.[31]

Finney was about to construct a Hawaiian double canoe. It was a replica of King Kamehameha III's royal canoe. He tested her in Californian waters. His purpose was modest: to test whether shallow-rounded hulls would give resistance to leeway, and whether the inverted triangular "crab-claw" sail would drive the canoe into the wind. When Finney brought his canoe to Hawaii from California, Mary Pukena Pukui, one of Hawaii's traditional scholars, called the canoe *Nahelia*, "The Skilled Ones," for the way in which the hulls gracefully rode the swells and into the wind. Already the project was getting larger than itself. The admiration caught in the name was a sign of deeper cultural and political forces beginning to be focused on the question of how the Hawaiians, Tahitians, Maori, and Samoans encompassed Oceania.

By 1975, Finney, now supported and eventually relieved of his leading role by native-born Hawaiians, had turned to the construction of an ocean-going canoe *Hokule'a. Hokule'a* means "Star of Joy," Arcturus, the zenith star of Hawaii's celestial latitude. The overriding ambition of all *Hokule'a*'s great

Brilliant Voyages of Discovery Re-Played The *Hokule'a* and the voyaging canoes that have followed her example have sailed to all points of the Polynesian Triangle—Hawaii, Rapanui (Easter Island), Aotearoa (New Zealand). But the voyages of most significance have been between Hawaii and Tahiti. There can be no doubt that the voyage of discovery and settlement from Havai'iki (Samoa—Tonga— Fiji) to the Marquesas about 2000 years ago, and that from the Marquesas to Hawaii about 1800 years ago, are the most brilliant of voyages of discovery in the Sea of Islands.

voyages was to perform them as much as possible in the way in which they were performed a thousand years ago. *Hokule'a* has voyaged to nearly all parts of the central Polynesian Pacific: Hawaii–Tahiti–Hawaii; Tahiti–Raro-tonga–Aotearoa; Samoa–Aitutaki–Tahiti.[32]

These voyages have been an extraordinary achievement. There is no point in being romantic about them. The thirty years of this odyssey have had their pain and conflict, their tragedies and failures, their political machinations, their greed, their absurdities. But they also have been coura-geous overall triumphs, tapping wellsprings of cultural pride in a sense of continuity with a voyaging tradition. This has not just been in Hawaii, but in Tahiti, Samoa, Aotearoa as well. Everywhere where she has gone, it has been the same. The landfall has been a theater of who island peoples are, who they have been.

Way-Finding

For my theater, let me pick up the homecoming voyage of *Hokule'a* from Tahiti to Hawaii in June 1980. It begins in Matavai Bay, Tahiti, and ends thirty-two days later on the Big Island of Hawaii. Nainoa, a young man of Hawaiian birth, twenty-five years old, is the navigator.[33]

Nainoa apprenticed himself to Mau Piailug, the Micronesian navigator who had taken *Hokule'a* to Tahiti in 1976. Mau gave David Lewis much of his navigator's lore, too. Nainoa does not have a Hawaiian tradition of navigation to call upon. That's gone, or rather is too deeply embedded in mythology and the language of the environment to be of much use. Nainoa has virtually to invent his own system. He does not do it by learning Western celestial navigation. He avoids that. But he has the Bishop Museum Planetarium in Honolulu to set in his mind the night skies. He can simulate the rising and setting of the stars for all seasons in Hawaii and for different latitudes. He creates for himself a star compass and sets it in his mind, as in all systems of oral memory, with a metaphor. His metaphor for *Hokule'a* is "*manu*," a bird with outstretched wings. He has not just a star compass in his mind—different from the ones we know of in Micronesia—but a directional compass in his mind, as well, of thirty-two settings, or "houses" as he calls them, more regular than the traditional settings. He sets himself to remember the rising and setting of stars, sun, and moon in these houses. He also sets himself to calibrate his hand to the two great determinants of his Hawaiian latitudes, the North Star and the Southern Cross. When he is not in the planetarium he is in the seas around Hawaii, experiencing the swells made by the dominant weather patterns and their seasons, the seas created by the changing winds and the movements made by the backlash of the sea against island shores and in the island shadows. His navigational lines, latitudinally, north and south in his system are relatively easy. But his movements east and west along a longitudinal line are far more complex, involving dead reckoning of miles sailed and the relativizing of theorizing and settings in his star compass. That will be the greatest anxiety of his navigation. He has to make landfall upwind of his destination, northeast of Tahiti, southeast of Hawaii. Downwind, if he ends up there, will require tacking.

Let's join him on the last three days of the voyage from Tahiti to Hawaii, May–June 1980. He is tired and anxious. He sleeps hardly at all at night and not more than an hour at a time in the day. For ten days, high clouds obscured the stars. He steered mainly with the sun and the moon. The moon in its crescent carried the sun's shadow vertically near the equator, then more angled as they moved north. The full moon on the horizon gave them a steering target. Dawn was the most important time, not just for the compass point of the sun's rising, but because the angle of the sun made reading swells and seas and the weather of the day come easier. Mau, the Micronesian navigator, had thousands of dawns at sea in his mind. The Southern Cross as it moved lower and to the west brought him the judgment on that third last day that they were 550 miles southeast of Hawaii. But they saw a land dove during the day. How could it have flown that distance between dawn and dusk?

They passed through the equatorial doldrums. They passed through that part of the ocean where the northwest swell of the Northern Hemi-

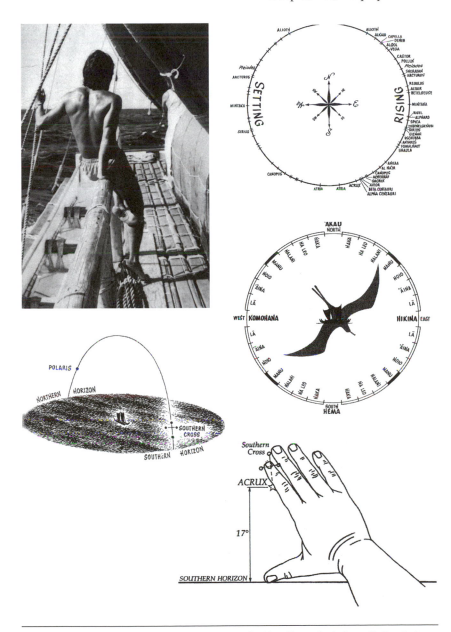

Finding a Way of Way-Finding Nainoa had to invent for himself a method of way-finding that was as accurate and which approached the complexity of the way-finding methods of his ancestors. So he learns the rising and setting of hundreds of stars in all their seasons. He makes a compass in his mind, and a metaphor, *manu*, to work it. He calibrates his hand to the Southern Cross and the southern horizon to give him a latitude. He has Polaris in the north and the Southern Cross in the south to lead him between the hemispheres.

sphere passed over the southeast swell of the Southern Hemisphere and gave the distinctive pitch and roll movement of the canoe. Nainoa learned to feel these different motions of the canoe from Mau Piailug—by lying prone on the decking. Now they are at the most anxious time of their voyage, wondering whether they should trust their calculations and turn westward in the Hawaiian latitudes. In way-finding—the term they preferred to use, rather than *navigation*—each day and night is a new calculation, a new assessment. It is important to note that. What seemed undeniable in Sharp's argument was that errors were cumulative and, once committed, drove canoes into oblivion. But the discovery over all of *Hokule'a*'s voyaging was that errors were random and tended to counter one another. Still, that did not relieve the tension at moments of critical commitment.

Tropical birds are plenty, but these are no sure sign of the direction of land. But there are *manu ku*, land doves, too. They know land was near. They catch the angle of the North Star against the horizon and get a clear sighting of the Southern Cross. These convince them that their latitude calculations were right. On the second-to-last day Nainoa said they were 210 miles from the Big Island, but nervously changed his calculations to 300 miles.

All day on the last day, the clouds on the horizon seem stationary. Clouds at sea move. Clouds over land stay still. There is something different about the setting sun. They can't say what—its coloring, perhaps—as it catches the air around and above Hawaii. They alter their course a little in its direction. It is in the right house of Nainoa's compass for land.

Then a stationary white cloud opens up and reveals the long gentle slope of Mauna Kea on Hawaii. Nainoa says to himself: "The way-finding at this moment seems to be out of my hands and beyond my control. I'm the one given the opportunity of feeling the emotions of way-finding, not yet ready to have a complete understanding of what is happening. It is a moment of self-perspective, of one person in a vast ocean given an opportunity of looking through a window into my heritage."[34]

I think he is correct. All over Polynesia, island peoples saw themselves in their canoes—in the canoe's making, in its parts, in its launching, in its voyaging. The canoe was an icon of all sorts of continuities of identity, an icon of a conjoining of past and present. I don't have difficulty in believing that island peoples can recognize themselves in *Hokule'a* and embroider that recognition with all sorts of rebirths of traditional arts and crafts, with dance, poetry, and song. Whatever the transformations of modernity that masquerade as discontinuities—religion, science, politics—the theater of *Hokule'a*'s reenactment is directed to that recognition, a new and an old encompassment in one.

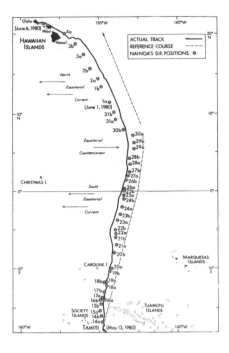

Home-Coming Nainoa finds his way home to Hawaii June 4, 1980. A tracing of his voyage, noting where he thought himself to be and where he actually was, shows that his errors were random and corrected themselves. There are few scholars these days who doubt that the principal Polynesian voyages of discovery and settlement were deliberate.

Looming

Looming is a word from the sea. *Glim* is, too, though in our daily usage we have transformed *glim* into *glimpse* and *glimmer*. On the horizons of the sea—as we see them from the decks of a ship or from the beach—things loom through the glim. For a moment, in the glim's shimmering light and haze, we see beyond the horizon, beyond the ordinary limits of our vision.

Sailors, whose lives are ordinarily spent at the center of the circle of the sea's horizons, are the philosophers of "looming." They tell us how sometimes the looming is distorted. Ships beyond the horizon appear upside down, skewed on their masts or angled as if they were sinking. But sometimes a whole coastal landscape beyond the horizon is crystal clear, hung in the sky above the sea.[35]

In historicizing the sea, it seems to me, we need always to catch the loomings beyond the many horizons in our lives—of gender, age, color, class, profession, nation. Nothing looms through their glim, I think, unless we are prepared to give a little of ourselves first.

Notes

1. In the *Call for Papers* for the conference "Sea Changes: Historicizing the Ocean, c. 1500– c. 1900" (University of Greifswald, Germany, July 20–4, 2000), where most of the essays collected in this volume were originally given as conference papers.

2. Roland Barthes, *Mythologies* [French original 1957], trans. Annette Lavers (London: Jonathan Cape, 1972), 112.

3. Sigmund Freud, *Civilization and Its Discontents* [German original 1930], trans. James Strachey (New York: W. W. Norton, 1962), 11; W. H. Auden, *The Enchafèd Flood; or The Romantic Iconography of the Sea* (New York: Random House, 1950), 6–7; Gaston Bachelard, *Water and Dreams* [French original 1942], trans. Edith R. Farrell (Dallas: Pegasus, 1983), 6, 152–3; and Jules Michelet, *La Mer* (Lausanne: L'Age d'Homme, 1980), 76, 193–4, quoted in Christopher L. Connery, "The Oceanic Feeling and the Regional Imaginary," Rob Wilson and Wimal Dissanayake (eds.), *Global/Local: Cultural Production and the Transnational Imaginary* (Durham, NC: Duke University Press, 1996), 284–311: 292–3.

4. See Epeli Hau'ofa et al. (eds.), *A New Oceania: Rediscovering Our Sea of Islands* (Suva: School of Social and Economic Development, University of the South Pacific, 1993); and Epeli Hau'ofa, "The Ocean in Us," *The Contemporary Pacific* 10 (1998), 391–410.

5. Greg Dening, "Time Searchers," *The Australian's Review of Books* 7, no. 4 (1999), 11–2.

6. Greg Dening, *Mr Bligh's Bad Language: Passion, Power and Theatre on the Bounty* (Cambridge: Cambridge University Press, 1992), 55–88.

7. Ben Finney and James B. Houston, *Surfing: A History of the Ancient Hawaiian Sport* (San Francisco: Pomegranate Artbooks, 1996).

8. Thomas Gladwin, *East Is a Big Bird* (Cambridge, MA: Harvard University Press, 1970).

9. Geoffrey Irwin, *The Prehistoric Exploration and Colonisation of the Pacific* (Cambridge: Cambridge University Press, 1992).

10. Simon Winchester, *Pacific Rising* (New York: Prentice Hall, 1991), 65–80.

11. Greg Dening, *The Death of William Gooch: History's Anthropology* (Honolulu: University of Hawaii Press, 1995), 31–2.

12. Greg Dening, *Islands and Beaches: Discourse on a Silent Land: Marquesas 1774–1880* (Melbourne: Melbourne University Press, 1980), 205–15.

13. Jonathan M. Weisgall, *Operation Crossroads: The Atomic Tests at Bikini Atoll* (Annapolis: Naval Institute Press, 1994), 263–5; and Teresia K. Teaiwa, "bikinis and other s/pacific n/oceans," *The Contemporary Pacific* 6, no. 1 (1994), 87–109.

14. *Rimspeak* is Bruce Cuming's phrase, quoted in Connery, "The Oceanic Feeling," 285. Jean Christoph Agnew, *Worlds Apart: The Market and the Theater in Anglo-American Thought, 1550–1750* (Cambridge: Cambridge University Press, 1986), 18–27, explains the symbolism of Hermes and Proteus.

15. Peter Petroff and John Ferguson, *Sailing Endeavour* (Sydney: Maritime Heritage Press, 1994); and Ben R. Finney, *Hokule'a: The Way to Tahiti* (New York: Dodd, Mead, 1979).

16. John O'Keeffe, *Omai, or a Trip Round the World* [1785], Pantomime Programme, Canberra: Australian National Library, ADD NLA Manuscript, R Bq Misc 1991. See Greg Dening, "Possessing Tahiti," *Archaeology in Oceania* 21 (1986), 103–18; and "O Mai, 'This is Mai': A Masque of a Sort," Michelle Hetherington (ed.), *Cook and Omai: The Cult of the South Seas* (Canberra: National Library of Australia, 2000), 51–6.

17. Petroff and Ferguson, *Sailing Endeavour*, 6.

18. *Ibid.*

19. For the most exact description of the spaces of the *Endeavour*, see Ray Parkin, *H.M. Bark Endeavour* (Melbourne: Melbourne University Press, 1997).

20. James Cook, "Holograph Journal," Manuscript 1, National Library of Australia. Entry for June 3, 1769. Cook's observations on the Transit of Venus are to be found in *The Journals of Captain James Cook: The Voyage of the Endeavour 1768–1771*, ed. J. C. Beaglehole (Cambridge: Hakluyt Society, 1968), 97–9. Cook's *Endeavour Journal* is also to be found on CD-ROM: *Endeavour: Captain Cook's Journal 1768–71* (Canberra: National Library of Australia, n.d.). See Greg Dening, "MS1—Cook, J.—Holograph Journal," Peter Cochrane (ed.), *Remarkable Occurrences: The National Library of Australia's First 100 Years, 1901–2001* (Canberra: National Library of Australia, 2001), 1–21.

21. Rachel Carson, *The Sea around Us* (New York: Mentor, 1989), 20–1.

22. J. H. Parry, *The Discovery of the Sea: An Illustrated History of Men, Ships and the Sea in the Fifteenth and Sixteenth Centuries* (New York: Dial Press, 1974).

23. Robert Kunzig, *The Restless Sea: Exploring the World beneath the Waves* (New York: W. W. Norton, 1999); Ellen J. Prager, *The Oceans* (New York: McGraw Hill, 2000); and Kenneth J. Hsu, *Challenger at Sea: A Ship That Revolutionised Earth Science* (Princeton, NJ: Princeton University Press, 1992).

24. Jules Verne, *20,000 Leagues Under the Sea* [French original 1869–70], trans. Walter James Miller and Frederick Paul Walter (Annapolis: Naval Institute Press, 1993); Michel de Certeau, "Writing the Sea: Jules Verne," *Heterologies: Discourse on the Other*, trans. Brian Massumi (Minneapolis: University of Minnesota Press, 1986), 137–49; and Johann Reinhold Forster, "Remarks on Water and the Ocean," *Observations Made during a Voyage round the World*, ed. Nicholas Thomas et al. (Honolulu: University of Hawaii Press, 1996), 45–78.

25. Norbert Elias, "Studies on the Genesis of the Naval Profession," *British Journal of Sociology* 1 (1950), 291–301.

26. Henning Henningsen, *Crossing the Equator: Sailor's Baptisms and Other Initiation Rites* (Copenhagen: Munksgaard, 1961); and Harry Miller Lydenberg, *Crossing the Line* (New York: New York Public Library, 1957).

27. David Starkey, "Representations through Intimacy," Ioan Lewis (ed.), *Symbols and Sentiments: Cross-cultural Studies in Symbolism* (London: Academic Press, 1977), 187–224.

28. Bernard Bailyn, *The Peopling of British North America: An Introduction* (New York: Vintage, 1986), 112–3; and Greg Dening, "Theatricalities of Derring-Do," *Readings/Writings* (Melbourne: Melbourne University Press, 1998), 159–76.

29. Greg Dening, "The Geographical Knowledge of the Polynesians and the Nature of Inter-Island Contact" [1962], Jack Golson (ed.), *Polynesian Navigation* (Wellington: Polynesian Society, 3rd ed. 1972), 102–53.

30. Lyotard quoted in Michel de Certeau, *The Practice of Everyday Life* [French original 1974], trans. Steven Rendall (Berkeley: University of California Press, 1988), 168.

31. Ben Finney, "Surfing in Ancient Hawaii," *Journal of the Polynesian Society* 68 (1959), 327–47.

32. Ben Finney, *Voyage of Rediscovery: A Cultural Odyssey through Polynesia* (Berkeley: University of California Press, 1994).

33. Will Kyselka, *An Ocean in Mind* (Honolulu: University of Hawaii Press, 1987).

34. Nainoa quoted in Kyselka, *An Ocean in Mind*, 221–2.

35. John Stilgoe, *Alongshore* (New Haven, CT: Yale University Press, 1994), 23–5.

CHAPTER 2

Costume Changes

Passing at Sea and on the Beach

VANESSA SMITH

The ocean crossing discussed in this chapter is both a voyage and a change of identity. I will examine the passage of a sea voyage as the shifting locus of acts of passing, focusing my discussion upon two individual stories from the first French maritime expedition to the Pacific. Passing is a word predominantly associated with motion, with procession or journeying, but has more recently been adopted to describe successful attempts to be held or accepted as a member of a religious, ethnic, racial, class, or gender category or group other than one's own. The notion of the journey remains implicit in this rendering. Recent theory figures race and gender passing in terms of a movement across boundaries, a destabilizing of what are presumed to be fixed categories; or, as Marjorie Garber expresses it, "a borderline that becomes permeable, that permits of border crossings from one (apparently distinct) category to another."[1] Passing may be prompted by genetic predisposition, which influences factors such as skin tone or build, but it will always also involve explicit practices of mimicry and disguise, such as transvestism or speech alteration. In thinking about some instances of passing that occurred around or aboard a ship's voyage, crossing the permeable borders of an unmapped ocean, I want to reanchor this metaphor to a specific political context: to focus on the kinds of role playing that voyages of imperial exploration licensed, and those it sought to contain.

Divested of Command

In Bougainville's account of his 1766–9 voyage around the world, the moment of arrival in Tahiti is accompanied by reciprocal scenes of undressing. The ship's anchoring was obstructed by *peraguas* full of beguiling women: "Most of these fair females were naked; for the men and the old women that accompanied them, had stripped them of the garments which they generally dress themselves in."[2] The spectacle threatens discipline aboard ship, for as Bougainville explains,

> It was very difficult, amidst such a sight, to keep at their work four hundred young French sailors, who had seen no women for six months. In spite of all our precautions, a young girl came on board, and placed herself upon the quarter-deck, near one of the hatch-ways, which was open, in order to give air to those who were heaving at the capstern below it. The girl carelessly dropt a cloth, which covered her, and appeared to the eyes of all beholders, such as Venus shewed herself to the Phrygian shepherd, having, indeed, the celestial form of that goddess. . . . At last our cares succeeded in keeping these bewitched fellows in order, though it was no less difficult to keep the command of ourselves. (Forster 218–9; Bougainville 190–1)

The striptease by a single Tahitian female threatens to unman the vessel. Bougainville's admission that the scene disturbs the self-command of the officers as much as the discipline of the crew enacts, even as it repudiates, a loss of authority, as hierarchy is seen to dissolve. The crew's unmanning is subsequently literalized in a cautionary tale, which occurs as soon as an individual leaves the safety of the shipboard community:

> One single Frenchman, who was my cook, having found means to escape against my orders, soon returned more dead than alive. He had hardly set his feet on shore, with the fair whom he had chosen, when he was immediately surrounded by a croud of Indians, who undressed him from head to feet. He thought he was utterly lost, not knowing where the exclamations of those people would end, who were tumultuously examining every part of his body. After having considered him well, they returned him his clothes, put into his pockets whatever they had taken out of them, and brought the girl to him, desiring him to content those desires [en le present de contenter les desires] which had brought him on shore with her. All their persuasive arguments had no effect; they were obliged to bring the poor cook on board, who told me, that I might reprimand him as much as I pleased, but that I could never frighten him so much, as he had just now been frightened on shore. (Forster 219; Bougainville 191)

Just as a single girl escapes the crowd of the Tahitians for the ship, so a single crew member escapes the ship for the shore, but where she, naked, presents a spectacle of consummate femininity, he, naked, is emasculated. The errant Frenchman, a cook rather than a sailor, is already a feminized figure in the shipboard world: a ship's domestic rather than an exemplary seaman proves least commandable among the crew. Both scenes of undressing represent Tahiti as a nirvana of licensed licentiousness; permissible permissiveness. Society condones libido: young women are undressed and presented by their mothers and husbands; a crowd undresses the hapless cook and presents him with the object of his desire.[3] But it is precisely this perfect concord between the desired and the acceptable—a potential for ideal consummation signaled, in J. R. Forster's English translation, by the shift of *desire* from verb to noun, "desiring him to content those desires"—that renders the latter subject impotent, producing "no effect." The cook must return to the haven of the ship, where the lesson he has received on shore serves to deprive his commander's reprimands of all potency, once again divesting command of its force.

The Moment of Discovery

This hinged scene of divestment, even as it works to set up the crew as guileless lotus-eaters, is also, as we have seen, a highly constructed account whose juxtaposition of two undressings constitutes a prefatory admission of the limitations to satisfaction offered by this desirable locus. Yet Bougainville's presentation is as interesting for what it conceals as for what it exposes. For, as we later learn, the arrival of the French ships at Tahiti resulted in another unveiling, and the explicit unmanning of a member of the French expedition. It is not until Bougainville's narrative has left Tahiti in its wake and entered the archipelago of the New Hebrides, named, with Homeric wishful thinking, the Great Cyclades by the French expedition, that this third scene of divestment is analeptically invoked. As Forster translates Bougainville's account:

> Whilst we were amidst the great Cyclades, some business called me on board the Etoile, and I had an opportunity of verifying a very singular fact. For some time there was a report in both ships, that the servant of M. de Commerçon, named Baré, was a woman. His shape, voice, beardless chin, and scrupulous attention of not changing his linen, or making the natural discharges in the presence of any one, besides several other signs, had given rise to, and kept up this suspicion. But how was it possible to discover the woman in the indefatigable Baré, who was already an expert botanist, had followed his master in all his botanical walks, amidst the snows and frozen mountains of the straits of Magalhaens, and had even on such troublesome excursions carried provisions, arms, and herbals, with so much courage and strength, that the naturalist had called him his beast of burden? A scene which passed at Taiti changed this suspicion into certainty. M. de Commerçon went on shore to botanize there; Baré had hardly set his feet on shore with the herbal under his arm, when the men of Taiti surrounded him, cried out, It is a woman, and wanted to give her the honours customary in the isle. The Chevalier de Bournand, who was upon guard on shore, was obliged to come to her assistance, and escort her to the boat. After that period it was difficult to prevent the sailors from alarming her modesty. When I came on board the Etoile, Baré, with her face bathed in tears, owned to me that she was a woman; she said that she had deceived her master

at Rochefort, by offering to serve him in men's cloaths at the very moment
when he was embarking; that she had already before served a Geneva gentleman at Paris, in quality of a valet; that being born in Burgundy, and become an
orphan, the loss of a law-suit had brought her to a distressed situation, and inspired her with the resolution to disguise her sex; that she well knew when she
embarked that we were going round the world, and that such a voyage had
raised her curiosity. She will be the first woman that ever made it, and I must
do her the justice to affirm that she has always behaved on board with the most
scrupulous modesty. She is neither ugly nor handsome, and is no more than
twenty-six or twenty-seven years of age. It must be owned, that if the two ships
had been wrecked on any desart isle in the ocean, Baré's fate would have been a
very singular one. (Forster 300–1; Bougainville 253–4)

What Bougainville appears to deny the reader here is a striptease. The
story of Baré's gradual exposure is presented in one go, rather than glimpsed,
titillatingly, through the course of the narrative, in anticipation of final revelation. Yet the neat, summary account offered to the reader is one of considerable tension, in which the effort of distinguishing masculine from
feminine proves to be as much a discursive as a physical exercise. Bougainville
announces that he has been able to "verify a singular fact" from multiple "report[s]" and "suspicion[s]" proliferating among the ships' crews. The commander has extricated a masculine certainty and facticity from the feminine
babel of rumor. In Forster's English translation, the moment of discovery, at
which Baré's identity is revealed, announces itself through grammatical confusion rather than clarification, with a shift of pronoun mid-sentence effectively obscuring the subject at the moment of revelation: "the men of Taiti
surrounded *him*, cried out, *It* is a woman, and wanted to give *her* the honours
customary in the isle" (my italics). Bougainville's original reads, "les Taitiens
l'entourent, crient que c'est une femme & veulent lui faire les honneurs de
l'île." Forster's translation appears to be functioning exegetically here, to fore-
ground the transformation taking place in perceptions of Baré's gender. This
cleft sentence in turn cleaves narrative genre: Baré's story, formerly an account of loyal masculine servitude, now proceeds as a feminine sentimental
narrative, yet one in which she figures, hermaphroditically, as both distressed
female and the masculine hero who rescues her.[4] Bougainville's description
of Baré's physical appearance registers the discursive confusion produced
by the revelation of her sexual identity. He offers simply the brief, negatively
constructed statement "she is neither ugly nor handsome," his stymied prose
stuck in the neither/nor produced by her act of cross-dressing.

Opposite Camps

Two things seem to me to be significant about this moment of discovery,
and the reflection it offers to the project of discovery represented by the
voyage as a whole. One is what is discovered, and the other is who discov-

ers. What is discovered is an act of impersonation: Baré is a female in drag. In the world of contemporary scholarship, drag means different things. For historians, "female tars" are a perfect case study for the normalizing enterprise of close historical research. Through the lens of history, we are enabled to view the transvestite exception as, if not the rule, then the familiar, defusing the excitement of critical theorists who, in an opposite camp, regard drag as a form of subversion that foregrounds the performativity of gender roles or introduces a third term to challenge the binary construction of gender. The historian's assertion that cross-dressing aboard ship was a commonplace has itself become commonplace. Suzanne Stark writes, moderately, that "there are verified accounts of more than twenty women who joined the Royal Navy or Marines dressed as men in the period from the late seventeenth to the early nineteenth century." Stark also refers to disclosure as a moment of discovery, claiming that "[s]ome of them served for years before their true gender was discovered. Undoubtedly there were others whose male disguise was never penetrated, and whose stories have therefore gone unrecorded."[5] Her reference to penetration puns on the link between gendered and sexual identities that drag inevitably foregrounds. Rudolf Dekker and Lotte van de Pol cite 119 cases of cross-dressing Dutch women who served in the army and navy during the seventeenth and eighteenth centuries, and also appeal to the potentially vast number of successful passings to which these discovered acts of transvestism attest, but whose very effectiveness renders them invisible to record.[6] Daniel Cohen claims that "hundreds, if not thousands, of cross-dressing women (along with underaged boys) served in European and North American armies and navies between the sixteenth and nineteenth centuries,"[7] a contention that is obfuscated (was it hundreds or thousands? did the category include the underage boys, a claim that would itself be political, since it would convert the issue from one of cross-dressing to one of dressing-up?) in the interest of polemic. Cohen is in part engaging in a piece of historical one-upmanship directed at recent interventions in the theoretics of drag by feminist critics Judith Butler and Marjorie Garber. For Garber, "one of the most important aspects of cross-dressing is the way in which it offers a challenge to easy notions of binarity, putting into question the categories of 'female' and 'male,' whether they are considered essential or constructed, biological or cultural."[8] Butler is interested in drag as a form of gender parody, arguing that "*[i]n imitating gender, drag implicitly reveals the imitative structure of gender itself—as well as its contingency.*"[9] Cohen recuperates such acts of subversion as the prerogative of his own historical territory: "While Butler's insights may rightly pass for 'cutting edge' in the late twentieth-century academy, they would have been dull commonplaces to the authors, protagonists, and readers of early modern Female Warrior narratives."[10]

In reading the disclosure of Baré's act of cross-dressing, I want, to some extent, to resist both these interpretations. Rather than neutralizing her particular example by referring to a range of female transvestite impersonations on board ship, I want to focus, with Bougainville, on what was exceptional about this instance. Throughout the course of Bougainville's voyage, disclosure is repeatedly associated with the recognition of the supplementary status of French discovery. After leaving Tahiti, Bougainville is informed "that about eight months before our arrival at [the] island, an English ship had touched there" (Forster 273; Bougainville 232), a precedence confirmed by the appearance of venereal diseases among the ship's crew—a manifestation that serves in turn to render primacy a dubious honor (Forster 286; Bougainville 241–2). Exploring the coastline of New Ireland, Bougainville reports,

> A sailor, belonging to my barge, being in search of shells, found buried in the sand, a piece of a plate of lead, on which we read these remains of English words,
> HOR'D HERE
> ICK MAJESTY's
> (Forster 327; Bougainville 275)

Bougainville identifies the remnants as belonging to the English vessel *Swallow*: his "exploration" of the island from this point becomes centered as much on uncovering signs of the English presence as on mapping the island.[11] At the same time, the sign of British discovery—destroyed, Bougainville surmises, by savages—attests, punningly, once again, to the mutual implication of imperial precedence and infection, since the remaining letters might be read more simply and phonetically as traces of the words "WHOR'D HERE" and "SICK MAJESTY's" than as fragments of the staked claim "ANCHOR'D HERE" and "BRITANNICK MAJESTY's SHIP."[12] By contrast with these scenes of forfeited originality, the discovery of Baré's female identity involves an incontrovertible claim to precedence. As Bougainville observes, "[s]he will be the first woman that ever made it." The captain allows himself to be undeceived, acknowledging his own role as dupe in order to register one of the most significant inaugural aspects of his voyage: Baré's primacy as a woman in the history of circumnavigation.

Breeches of Etiquette

This brings me to the second issue I raised, which I would argue in turn complicates some recent theoretical observations on the logic of passing: the question of who actually discovers Baré; who sees through her clothes. Because it is, of course, Tahitians. In a kind of Emperor's New Clothes scenario, what has been suspected and hinted at on board ship is articulated, rendered incontrovertible and apparent, by the native on the beach. As the comparison with the Emperor's New Clothes tale suggests, there is a patronizing element to this representation: the innocent and unsocialized child/native peels away the trappings to see clearly what then becomes obvious to all. And there is also an explicit connection made between this perception of sexual difference and the natives' purportedly excessive sexual appetites—a theme I will return to at the end of the chapter. But these provisos registered, placing the act of discovery in the mouths of Tahitians is also an acknowledgment of native authority. To indicate how unique this concession of insight is, I want to contrast it with a more typical European representation of a Polynesian encounter with European disguise.

When William Bligh visited Tahiti in 1788 on the ill-fated *Bounty* voyage, his anxious regard for etiquette did not prevent him from indulging in a prank at the expense of his native hosts. As he recounts in *A Voyage to the South Sea*:

> The ship's barber had brought with him from London, a painted head, such as the hair-dressers have in their shops, to shew the different fashions of dressing-hair; and it being made with regular features, and well coloured, I desired him to dress it, which he did with much neatness, and with a stick, and a quantity of cloth, he formed a body. It was then reported to the natives that we had an English woman on board, and the quarter-deck was cleared of the croud, that she might make her appearance. Being handed up the ladder, and carried to the after-part of the deck, there was a general shout of "*Huaheine no Brittanne myty.*" Huaheine signifies woman, and myty, good. Many of them thought it was living, and asked if it was my wife. One old woman ran with presents of cloth and bread-fruit, and laid them at her feet; at last they found out the cheat; but continued all delighted with it, except the old lady, who felt herself mortified, and took back her presents, for which she was laughed at exceedingly. Tinah and all the chiefs enjoyed the joke, and, after making many enquiries about the British women, they strictly enjoined me, when I came again, to bring a ship full of them.[13]

In this scenario, a woman is assembled for, rather than exposed by, the Tahitian gaze. Once again, pronouns shift in the recounting, but where in Bougainville's story of Baré's disclosure native perception forces the narrator to alter course mid-sentence, transforming "he" to "she," here the encounter with the Tahitian audience is pointedly a moment of misrecognition. Between, rather than mid-sentence, on the deck of the ship rather than the shore of the island, the "she" destined to make her appearance becomes "it" in the reflection of the native gaze. The joke here is preeminently at the expense of the native: in a literal as well as a metaphorical sense. Despite the protestations of general good humor, the jest cuts across Pacific etiquette, and makes a mockery of the reciprocal contract of gift-giving. A Tahitian woman loses face to a British woman who is all face and, a rare occurrence in the history of prestation, retracts the gift, undoing customary practice in the face of the superior British joke. Her act of bewildered hospitality is surely not, however, the last laugh of this anecdote: the chiefs suggest that this dummy is the template of British womanhood, implying that the entire female English population is more literally "mortified" than the embarrassed Tahitian "old lady."

Seeing through Clothes

What, then, does it mean for Jeanne Baré to have been exposed through Tahitian eyes? Is this just another version of the Bligh story, except that the same lascivious natives, who see sex wherever they look, happen to get it right in this one instance? The moment of specular identification between the racial and gendered other would seem to constitute a primal scene for recent theorizations of passing. In her introduction to a recent collection of essays, *Passing and the Fictions of Identity*, Elaine K. Ginsberg argues for the "similarities of black-to-white race passing and female-to-male gender passing as sources of cultural anxiety, for both 'not-white' and 'woman' are sites of difference that affirm the priority of 'white' and 'man' in the hegemonic ideology."[14] While the unmasking of the cross-dressing French female by the Tahitian native seems, obligingly for Ginsberg's argument, to map gender onto racial politics, a reading of the discovery of Baré's identity in these terms would exclude more than it explains. In particular, it obfuscates the complex exchange of subject positions and identifications that the scene initiates. Amy Robinson has astutely questioned the emphasis on insider (that is, private and prediscursive) knowledge as the key to recognition of the passing subject ("'it takes one to know one'"), asking "what purpose is served by naming as intuition a complex system of cultural literacy?" She points out that what the in-group member may possess is not so much the secret of essential identity as insight into "the apparatus of passing—literally the machinery that enables the performance." So, "'it takes one to know one' . . . signifies a position that identifies a performance, not one that claims ontological knowledge of the identity of the performer."[15] Yet this kind of insider knowledge into the techniques of a performance—and in particular the technique of costume change[16]—is precisely what is unavailable in situations of cross-cultural encounter. As the Bligh anecdote I just quoted and countless other accounts of native misconstrual and misappropriation of European garb are made to attest, cultural encounter enacts *unfamiliarity*; an exposure of the workings of cultural performance through misapprehension rather than recognition. The Tahitians who recognize Jeanne Baré's femininity are unfamiliar with the codes of European femininity that are contradicted by this "first" female's masculine appearance. Their "reading" of her passing cannot, at this juncture in culture contact, be figured as superinformed. Moreover, to figure the Tahitians as readers, even in the service of an interpretation that "not only envisions identity politics as a skill of reading but chronicles the process by which the hegemonic reader is always already posited as dupe,"[17] is to privilege the act of reading in describing a culture that would not have recognized reading as a practice.

What occurs in this scene is not, in fact, the silent exchange, the secret recognition, that Robinson has identified with in-group identification of the passing subject. Rather, it is a moment of betrayal, of exposure. Bougainville's own analeptic strategy in relating Baré's story serves to highlight this. He waits until the scene of her personal confession to announce the existence of suspicions concerning her identity, which we then learn have earlier been cast among the crew and are at this juncture merely voiced by the Tahitians. He chivalrously closes the gap between exposure and disclosure. The Tahitian, on the other hand, articulates what the white male crew has suppressed: the dupe it has allowed in order that sexuality, so destructive to ship's discipline as we saw with the Tahitian arrival scene, may not be allowed to disrupt the smooth course of the ship while at sea.[18] Where Robinson would argue that such identifications of the passing subject constitute a sophisticated hermeneutic, rather than naively essentialist practice, the child/native who points his finger at the female's new clothes becomes paradoxically, through the act of identification, the kind of reader that the European always sees: the naive reader, the innocent literalist, the stater of the obvious.[19]

The Tahitian intervention, then, is conflictingly ideologized. On the one hand, it is the native's duty to peel back civil disguise and expose falsity. On the other, it is by this very gesture to reposition him- or herself as savage. The fissured role of the noble savage, required by Enlightenment philosophy simultaneously to expose and affirm the civil contract, is brought into explicit focus when enacted in relation to the disguised Jeanne Baré. For at the moment Baré is revealed as false by the Tahitian gaze, she is rendered virtuous, a female in distress, who instantly becomes a focus for fears of Tahitian sexual excess. And the capacity to "see through clothes"—to identify the female body within the male costume—becomes, not a sign of innocent, unsocialized perception, but of hypersexualized voyeurism.[20]

"A Proper Sample"

The second significant first traveler of Bougainville's voyage, "Aotourou," the Tahitian who returns to Paris with the expedition, plays out this revisionist scenario during the course of his voyage and visit. Aotourou is represented in Bougainville's account as importunate to travel aboard the European vessel from the day of its arrival at Tahiti (Forster 262; Bougainville 223), when he came intrepidly aboard ship. As Charles-Félix-Pierre Fesche, volunteer aboard the *Boudeuse*, recorded, Aotourou sent away his *peragua* and remained aboard during the three days that the *Etoile* beat about in sight of the island before dropping anchor, revealing a singular comfort with the shipboard world.[21] Once the ship set sail from Tahiti, he displayed cognizance of the principles of navigation by the stars and a quick comprehension of the mechanics of the ship: at one point, attempting to steer toward some islands he knew to be bountiful and friendly, he "ran to get hold of the wheel of the helm, the use of which he had already found out, and endeavoured in spite of the helm's man to change [course], and steer directly upon the star, which he pointed at" (Forster 276; Bougainville 234).

It was not as a sailor, however, that Aotourou would serve Bougainville's expedition. Rather, it was hoped he could play the dual and potentially contradictory role of local informant during the course of the voyage, and exotic specimen in the metropolis. He was to conform to type, first as same and then as other: to be useful in both generic and specific capacities. Among the islands of the Pacific, Bougainville explains, Aotourou was expected to pass as native at each port of call:

> As we were forced to sail through an unknown ocean, and sure to owe all the assistance and refreshments on which our life depended, to the humanity of the people we should meet with, it was of great consequence to us to take a man on board from one of the most considerable islands in this ocean. It was to be supposed that he spoke the same language as his neighbours, that his manners were the same, and that his credit with them would be decisive in our favour, when he should inform them of our proceedings towards his country-men, and our behaviour to him. (Forster 262; Bougainville 223–4)

As Pacific islander, Aotourou is required to speak "the same" language, to display "the same" manners, and thus serve as litmus and guarantor of a common humanity. Yet when the opportunity arises for Aotourou to perform as native, difference rather than similarity is affirmed, on both sides of the beach. Arriving at an island in the region of the Solomons, the French encounter a *peragua* of islanders "naked, excepting their natural parts, [who] shewed us cocoa-nuts and roots. Our Taiti-man stripped naked as they were, and spoke his language to them, but they did not understand him: they are no more of the same nation here" (Forster 280; Bougainville 237). Aotourou dresses down for the encounter, but his impersonation of savagery goes unrecognized. He in turn asserts distinction rather than displaying sympathy: "Aotourou expressed the greatest contempt for these islanders" (Forster 282; Bougainville 239).

Although Bougainville here seems oblivious to the distinctions among Pacific societies, at other points in his narrative he invokes what was later to become a familiar color hierarchy in descriptions of Pacific islanders, subsequently reified in the nineteenth century as a division between

Melanesians and Polynesians. He notes, for instance, that "we have in general observed in the course of this voyage, that the black men are much more ill natured than those whose colour comes close to white" (Forster 320; Bougainville 269) (a comment that supports Bronwyn Douglas's thesis that among later eighteenth-century voyagers, "relative approval or disapproval of people encountered in the islands of what would later be 'Melanesia' registered a complex set of responses, which filtered emotion roused by physical appearance through a screen of native behaviour"[22]). Bougainville's assumption that Aotourou might pass as native in the western Pacific may have had its basis in his depiction of the islander as belonging to a darker and in his opinion physically inferior order of Tahitians. He writes:

> The inhabitants of Taiti consist of two races of men, very different from each other, but speaking the same language, having the same customs, and seemingly mixing without distinction. The first, which is the most numerous one, produces men of the greatest size; it is very common to see them measure six (Paris) feet and upwards in height. I never saw men better made, and whose limbs were more proportionate: in order to paint a Hercules or a Mars, one could no where find such beautiful models. Nothing distinguishes their features from those of Europeans: and if they were cloathed; if they lived less in the open air, and were less exposed to the sun at noon, they would be as white as ourselves: their hair in general is black. The second race are a middle size, have frizzled hair as hard as bristles, and both in colour and features they differ but little from mulattoes. The Taiti man who embarked with us, is of this second race, though his father is chief of a district: but he possesses in understanding what he wants in beauty. (Forster 249; Bougainville 214)

Bougainville's sheepish sense that the specimen he has brought back to Paris doesn't measure up is equally founded on this assessment. On the one hand, Aotourou does not represent the majority of Tahitians: he comes from a less significant "race" that Bougainville's description renders aberrant. More significantly, his physical type is not one that, like the majority of Tahitians, could pass as white. He is neither in the ideal classical nor the familiar European mold. I will look at the significance of Aotourou's failed passing in metropolitan Paris in the final section of this chapter, but here I would like simply to draw attention to the tropological status that apologies for purportedly inadequate human specimens acquire within the exploration literature. Compare James Cook's comments on Omai, or Mai, the Raiatean who accompanied his second expedition back to England in 1774:

> Before we quitted this island, Captain Furneaux agreed to receive on board his ship a young man named Omai, a native of Ulietea . . . I at first rather wondered that Captain Furneaux would encumber himself with this man, who, in my opinion, was not a proper sample of the inhabitants of these happy islands,

> not having any advantage of birth, or acquired rank; not being eminent in
> shape, figure or complexion. For their people of the first rank are much fairer,
> and usually better behaved, and more intelligent than the middling class of
> people, among whom Omai is to be ranked.[23]

Cook makes a more explicit equation than Bougainville between complexion and social status, but his consciousness that his party may have failed to procure a "proper sample" echoes Bougainville's more reserved commentary. Both Aotourou and Omai occupy a position adjacent, rather than central to, Tahitian culture. Omai is a Raiatean, whose journey was most probably motivated by a desire to obtain prestige and power in an ongoing struggle to reclaim his ancestral lands from Boraborean enemies.[24] Aotourou explained his smaller stature and darker complexion by claiming he was the offspring of a captive woman, and David Chappell speculates that "if he really was the offspring of a war captive, he may have been regarded as expendable as an ambassador."[25] Both "samples," then, are figured to differing degrees as passing for, rather than representative of, the Tahitian model.

"A Genteel Dressing"

Once he reaches Paris, Aotourou is apprehended not merely as specimen but as spectacle: he is not allowed to pass unnoticed. Bougainville fulminates, "[t]he desire of seeing him has been very violent; idle curiosity, which has served only to give false ideas to men whose constant practice it is to traduce others, who never went beyond the capital, never examine any thing, and who being influenced by errors of all sorts, never cast an impartial eye upon any object, and yet pretend to decide with majesterial severity, and without appeal!" (Forster 263; Bougainville 224). Aotourou is assessed and found wanting by pseudo-connoisseurs, practitioners of an idle rather than scientific curiosity. Yet as on the beach, so in the metropolis, the Tahitian exposes a European "violent" desire disguised as enlightened objectivity.

The "desire of seeing" that accompanies the apparition of the Noble Savage in metropolitan society is a complex one, as narcissistic as it is curious; comprised of both recognition and repudiation. His performance here is more explicitly to combine the roles of exotic specimen and natural aristocrat. The shifts of register required to accommodate this conflicted identity are apparent in the report of a Royal Society Fellow, Sir John Callum, who writes of Omai, the guest of Sir Joseph Banks at a Society dinner: "He walks erect, and has acquired a tolerably genteel Bow," neatly referencing the diminution of stature required for the evolution of *homo erectus* into civilized socialite.[26] Other commentaries attempt to naturalize the act of passing. Thus Fanny Burney, in her long account of her first meeting with Omai, focuses on cross-cultural performances such as the bow, and also the toast, table manners, and care and appropriateness of dress, as signifiers of natural rather than acquired civility. She notes Omai's lack of self-consciousness in his new costume: "He never looked at his dress, though it was on for the first time,"[27] and writes:

> He makes *remarkably* good Bows—not for *him*, but for *any body*, however long under a Dancing Master's care. Indeed he seems to Shame Education, for his manners are so extremely graceful, & he is so polite, attentive, & easy, that you would have thought he came from some foreign Court.

Her Rousseauesque rejection of the finesses of elite education becomes more explicit as Burney concludes her account with a reflection on the relative merits of the overeducated Stanhope and the uneducated Tahitian:

> [T]he first with all the advantage of Lord Chesterfield's instruction, brought up at a great school, introduced at fifteen to a Court, taught all possible accomplishments from an infant, and having all the care, expence, labour, and benefit of the best education that any man can receive,—proved after it all a meer *pedantic booby*;—the second with no tutor but Nature, changes, after he has grown up, his dress, his way of life, his diet, his country and his friends;—and appears in a *new world* like a man who had all his life studied *the Graces*, and attended with unremitting application and diligence to form his manners, and to render his appearance and behaviour *politely easy*, and thoroughly *well bred*! I think this shows how much more *nature* can do without *art*, than *art* with all her refinement unassisted by *nature*.[28]

Burney makes a heavy lesson of her repudiation of educated over "natural" behavior, but her comments make clear the complexity of the particular role the Society Islander was required to perform in the metropolitan salon. Rather than passing by effectively mimicking the costume and social behavior of those around him, he served at once to exceed and undermine the social model, offering a reflection of subtle and telling difference rather than similitude. The distinction he was to represent was that between cultivation and nature, between inculcated and natural grace (an opposition that reflected parallel representations of Tahiti as a place of natural bounty against Europe's ordered agricultural landscapes).

As distorting rather than simply affirming mirrors of polished society, Omai, and to a lesser extent Aotourou, were to survive and flourish in a literature of satirical commentary long after their departures from Europe. When the actor-playwright David Garrick planned a farce upon contemporary fashion in the 1780s, for instance, he proposed that "Omaih was to be my Arlequin Sauvage—a fine character to give our fine folks a genteel dressing."[29] His comment puns on the relationship between passing and satire. Omai is able to give "fine folks . . . a genteel dressing" not by dressing up to pass as genteel, but by offering his natural gentility as a reflection for their cultivated distinction. Ironically, in the case of Aotourou and Omai, this paradigm involved the suppression of a more effective pass, in which two men who were outsiders to Tahitian culture became received within European courts and salons as representatives of Tahiti's "natural" aristocracy.[30]

Bougainville's disturbed acknowledgment of the "violent . . . desire of seeing" provoked by Aotourou's arrival in Paris incorporates the recognition, however, that the reflection thrown back by the Pacific islander in the European capital is not merely the sophisticated self-analysis of satire, but a more primitive and visceral response to difference, akin to that his ships' crews met in Tahiti. Perhaps in resistance to this implication, he attempts to assemble an anecdote of Aotourou's successful passing on the streets of Paris: a story of urban navigation. He claims that:

> though Atourou could hardly blabber some words of our language, yet he went out by himself every day, and passed through the whole town without once missing or losing his way. He often made some purchases, and hardly ever paid for things beyond their real value. The only shew which pleased him, was the opera, for he was excessively fond of dancing. He knew perfectly well upon what days this kind of entertainment was played; he went thither by himself, paid at the door the same as every body else, and his favourite place was in the galleries behind the boxes. (Forster 265–6; Bougainville 226)

In this anecdote, Aotourou is spectator rather than spectacle, mingling with rather than mirroring French society. Bougainville emphasizes his assimilation: his ability to steer his way through town, to value correctly and conduct financial transactions, to appear "the same as every body else" when he assumes the role of the viewer rather than the viewed.

Yet it remains equally crucial to Aotourou's representation that he is not allowed to pass. He is necessarily a figure of difference, a difference that is represented most immediately in sexual terms. His very interest in the Paris Opera is less a sign of his cosmopolitanism than shorthand for a purported lasciviousness. Other representations of Aotourou in Paris focus on the Tahitian's sex drive as promoting misapprehension rather than heightened appreciation. In April 1769, the traveler and *philosophe* La Condamine came to observe Aotourou in Bougainville's apartments in Paris. Here he witnessed a tableau of unveiling, performed by the Tahitian:

> Jai vu notre insulaire [faire des signes très énergiques] qui n'avoient rien d'équivoque à l'aspect d'un tableau qui représentoit une Vénus presque nue; il fit semblant d'abord d'écarter le linge qui la couvroit très légèrement. Ici je me trouve embarrassé à décrire les autres signes que fit le jeune sauvage. . . .
>
> [I saw our islander [make very energetic signs] which were in no way ambiguous, at the sight of a picture which represented an almost naked Venus: he made as if to move aside the linen which very lightly covered her. Here I

find myself embarrassed to describe the other signs that the young savage made. . . .][31]

The Tahitian who saw through Jeanne Baré's disguise,[32] who exposed the secret, or the blindness, of Bougainville and his crew, and who was later to offer a mirror for satirical reflection upon polished European society is here depicted more typically as an at once naive and oversexed interpreter of a European representation, whose overweening desire prevents him from discerning the difference between reality and its likeness. As Neil Rennie summarizes, La Condamine detailed "an elaborate mime of smelling, tasting, grimacing and smiling" performed by the Pacific islander in front of the painting, which he interpreted to signify "Aotourou's prodigious ability to diagnose female venereal infection by smell and taste."[33] His account of Aotourou's mimicry of connoisseurship is designed to expose the savage, not the savant. Natives don't, after all, see through clothes: they smell through them. The anecdote may have offered a consoling footnote to those Frenchmen who felt themselves exposed by sexual revelations in the harbor and on the beach in Tahiti.

Notes

1. Marjorie Garber, *Vested Interests: Cross-Dressing and Cultural Anxiety* (New York and London: Routledge, 1992), 16. The word transvestism has similar associations, as Elizabeth McMahon points out: "As announced by its prefix, *transvestism* has been constructed as occupying the interstitial position of betwixt and between. In relation to traditions of representation, the transvestic figure is variously in transit, of transience, and an agent of transport across discrete categories of classification." Elizabeth McMahon, "Australia Crossed Over: Images of Cross-Dressing in Australian Art and Culture," *Art and Australia* 34, no. 3 (1997), 372–9: 375.
2. Louis de Bougainville, *A Voyage Round the World, performed by order of his most Christian Majesty, in the years 1766, 1767, 1768, and 1769*, trans. John Reinhold Forster (London: J. Nourse, 1772; reprinted Amsterdam: N. Israel, 1967), 218. Compare Louis Antoine de Bougainville, *Voyage autour du monde, par le frégate de roi la Boudeuse et la flûte l'étoile; en 1766, 1767, 1768 & 1769* (Paris: Saillant and Nyon, 1771), 190. Forster's translation has been used throughout this essay, with Bougainville's original French quoted only in instances where the nuances of translation have potentially influenced my interpretation. Subsequent references in the text are to both editions, cited as Forster and Bougainville, respectively.
3. Such scenes, in which mothers are complicit in the unveiling of their daughters for foreign crews, recur in the literature of contact in Tahiti, producing an unsettled European response in which gratification is tinged with compromise. Compare Forster 228 (Bougainville 197–8); and James Cook, *The Journals of Captain James Cook on His Voyages of Discovery I: The Voyage of the Endeavour 1768–1771*, ed. J. C. Beaglehole (Cambridge: Hakluyt Society and Cambridge University Press, 1955), 93–4. See also Neil Rennie's "The Point Venus Scene," Margarette Lincoln (ed.), *Science and Exploration in the Pacific: European Voyages to the Southern Oceans in the Eighteenth Century* (Suffolk and Rochester, NY: Boydell and Brewer, 1998), 135–46.
4. Compare Daniel A. Cohen's introduction to his edition of *The Female Marine and Related Works: Narratives of Cross-Dressing and Urban Vice in America's Early Republic* (Amherst: University of Massachusetts Press, 1997), 1–45, where he argues that "ambiguity in genre is paralleled by the multiple uncertainties and misperceptions experienced by characters within the plot itself" (8).
5. Suzanne J. Stark, *Female Tars: Women Aboard Ship in the Age of Sail* (London: Pimlico, 1998), 82.

6. Rudolf M. Dekker and Lotte C. van de Pol, *The Tradition of Female Transvestism in Early Modern Europe* (London: Macmillan, 1989), 3. Compare also Julie Wheelwright, *Amazons and Military Maids: Women Who Dressed as Men in the Pursuit of Life, Liberty and Happiness* (London: Pandora, 1989), 8. By contrast, Linda Grant de Pauw makes the more conservative claim that "[m]ost [women] went [to sea] in clearly defined feminine roles: wife, laundress, cook, nurse, or prostitute. A much smaller number of women assumed male roles and served as sailors before the mast or in positions of command. Seafaring women were a minority among both women and seafarers." *Seafaring Women* (Boston: Houghton Mifflin, 1982), 18.

7. Cohen, *The Female Marine*, 9.

8. Garber, *Vested Interests*, 10.

9. Judith Butler, *Gender Trouble: Feminism and the Subversion of Identity* (New York and London: Routledge, 1990), 137.

10. Cohen, *The Female Marine*, 14. Cohen deftly reserves himself a foot in both camps here: he is both the late twentieth-century academic and the reader of early modern Female Warrior narratives.

11. This had been the first act of possession performed by Carteret on his blighted voyage across the Pacific. On September 7, 1767, Carteret's journal reports: "We nailed a piece of board on a high Tree on which were engraved the Engl. Colours, Capt. & Ships Name, time of comming & sailing from and Name of the Cove." Carteret had christened the spot "English Cove." Philip Carteret, *Carteret's Voyage round the World 1766–1769*, vol. 1, ed. Helen Wallis (Cambridge: Hakluyt Society, 1965), 183–4.

12. The words are, of course, more explicitly reified as signs within the French text of Bougainville's voyage, where they stand out from the body of the text: "Un matelot de mon canot, cherchant des coquilles, y trouva enterré dans le sable un morceau d'une plaque de plomb, sur lequel on lisoit ce reste de mots Anglois:
    HOR'D HERE
    ICK MAJESTY'S"

13. William Bligh, *A Voyage to the South Sea, undertaken by command of his majesty, for the purpose of conveying the bread-fruit tree to the West Indies, in His Majesty's ship the Bounty, commanded by Lieutenant William Bligh* (London: George Nicol, 1792; facs. ed. Melbourne: Hutchinson, 1979), 85.

14. Elaine K. Ginsberg (ed.), *Passing and the Fictions of Identity* (Durham, NC, and London: Duke University Press, 1996), 5.

15. Amy Robinson, "It Takes One to Know One: Passing and Communities of Common Interest," *Critical Inquiry* 20, no. 4 (1994), 715–36: 720, 721, 722.

16. As Robinson notes, passing in drag makes this logic particularly explicit: "passing in drag shifts the presumption of identity from the internal coherence of mimesis to an explicitly social field of mediated meaning." *Ibid.*, 728.

17. *Ibid.*, 731.

18. Bougainville's account of the revelation of Baré's identity concludes by speculating on Baré's fate had the ship been wrecked on a "desart isle," leaving the reader to contemplate the situation of the solitary woman among a group of men freed from the regulatory context of the ship: a prospect that requires no alien native presence to register a hint of threat. It is clear that Baré's "exposure" itself constituted another performance on her part. Despite her protestations of M. de Commerçon's innocence, she had in fact previously served as his housekeeper and mistress, and was later the beneficiary of his will. See "Journal de François Vivez (Manuscrit de Versailles)," Étienne Taillemite (ed.), *Bougainville et ses compagnons autour de monde 1766–1769* (Paris: Imprimerie Nationale, 1977), tome 2, 237; and the comically reticent but nonetheless revealing account by S. Pasfield Oliver, *The Life of Philibert Commerçon* (London: John Murray, 1909), 85, 87. Oliver imitates Bougainville's chivalric reserve with reference to the disclosure of Baré's identity, concluding: "It is best, after a lapse of a hundred and sixty years or so, to add no comment whatever to this extraordinary story" (139).

19. I have discussed European representations of Pacific islanders as naive readers of European texts and material culture at length in *Literary Culture and the Pacific: Nineteenth-Century Textual Encounters* (Cambridge: Cambridge University Press, 1998).

20. As Anne Hollander has pointed out, however, the desire to penetrate the disguise of clothing also has a Romantic literary heritage: "Nothing is more common than the metaphorical men-

tion of clothing, first of all to indicate a simple screen that hides the truth or, more subtly, a distracting display that demands attention but confounds true perception. These notions invoke dress in its erotic function, as something that seems to promise something else, a mystery that promotes in the viewer the desire to remove it, get behind it, through it, or under it." *Seeing through Clothes* [1975] (Berkeley: University of California Press, 1993), 445–7. Representations of hypersexualized savagery must compete with a proto-Romanticized equation of nakedness with the natural and clothing with the false values of civil society.

21. "Journal de Charles-Félix-Pierre Fesche," Taillemite (ed.), *Bougainville et ses compagnons*, tome 2, 92.

22. Bronwyn Douglas, "Art as Ethno-historical Text: Science, Representation and Indigenous Presence in Eighteenth and Nineteenth Century Oceanic Voyage Literature," Nicholas Thomas and Diane Losche (eds.), *Double Vision: Art Histories and Colonial Histories in the Pacific* (Cambridge: Cambridge University Press, 1999), 65–99: 72. Compare Nicholas Thomas, "The Force of Ethnology: Origins and Significance of the Melanesia/Polynesia Division," *Current Anthropology* 30 (1989), 27–41.

23. James Cook, *A Voyage towards the South Pole* (London: W. Strahan & T. Cadell, 1777), vol. 1, 169–70, quoted in E. H. McCormick, *Omai: Pacific Envoy* (Auckland: Auckland University Press, 1977), 182.

24. Paul Turnbull, "Mai, the Other Beyond the Exotic Stranger," Michelle Hetherington et al. (eds.), *Cook and Omai: The Cult of the South Seas* (Canberra: National Library of Australia, 2001), 43–9.

25. David A. Chappell, *Double Ghosts: Oceanian Voyagers on Euroamerican Ships* (Armonk, NY: M. E. Sharpe, 1997), 29.

26. Callum to Tyson, January 2, 1775, Suffolk Record Office, Bury St. Edmunds, quoted in Michael Alexander, *Omai: Noble Savage* (London: Harvill, 1977), 101.

27. Fanny Burney to Samuel Crisp, quoted in *ibid.*, 90.

28. Fanny Burney to Samuel Crisp, quoted in McCormick, *Omai: Pacific Envoy*, 125–8.

29. Quoted in Alexander Cook, "The Art of Ventriloquism: European Imagination and the Pacific," Hetherington et al. (eds.), *Cook and Omai*, 38. As Cook points out, "a host of . . . writers . . . used Omai as a lash with which to whip the vices of Europe. They wrote pamphlets and poems in his voice. Sometimes the naïve observer, sometimes the knowing sage, he proved an ideal commentator to highlight the hypocrisy and absurdity of metropolitan culture" (39).

30. This was later mirrored by a comparable imposition practised by beachcombers in the early nineteenth-century Pacific, who served as representatives of metropolitan society and culture in the islands, even though they were typically outcasts from that society: absconding sailors or convicts. See Smith, *Literary Culture and the Pacific*, 19.

31. La Condamine, "Observations," MS, quoted in Neil Rennie, *Far Fetched Facts: The Literature of Travel and the Idea of the South Seas* (Oxford: Oxford University Press, 1995), 110 (my translation).

32. In at least one account from Bougainville's voyage, Aotourou is represented as the first islander to point out that Baré is a woman, when he comes on board the *Etoile*, and prior to the more comprehensive recognition scene that takes place upon Tahitian soil. "Journal de François Vivez," 240.

33. Rennie, *Far Fetched Facts*, 110.

CHAPTER 3

The Global Economy and the Sulu Zone
Connections, Commodities, and Culture

JAMES FRANCIS WARREN

Introduction: Space and Time

The aim of this paper is to explore ethnic, cultural, and material changes in the transformative history of oceans and seas, commodities and populations, mariners and ships, raiders and refugees, in Southeast Asia, with particular reference to the Sulu-Mindanao region, or the "Sulu Zone" (figure 3.1).[1] The oceans and seas of Asia, east by south, from Canton to Makassar, and from Singapore to the Birds Head coast of New Guinea, crossed by Iranun and Balangingi raiding and slaving ships, Southeast Asian merchant vessels and colonial warships, have been the sites of extraordinary conflicts and changes often associated with the formation of ethnic groups and boundaries, political struggles and national histories. Examining the profound changes that were taking place in the Sulu-Mindanao region and elsewhere, this paper charts an ethnohistorical framework for understanding the emerging interconnected patterns of global commerce, long-distance maritime raiding, and the formation and maintenance of ethnic identity. I begin by tracing the evolution of Iranun maritime raiding from its late eighteenth-century origins to support the English supplies of tea from China, into the nineteenth-century systematic, regional-based slaving and marauding activity.[2] I then draw out the implications of that evolution for colonial systems of domination, development, and discourse in

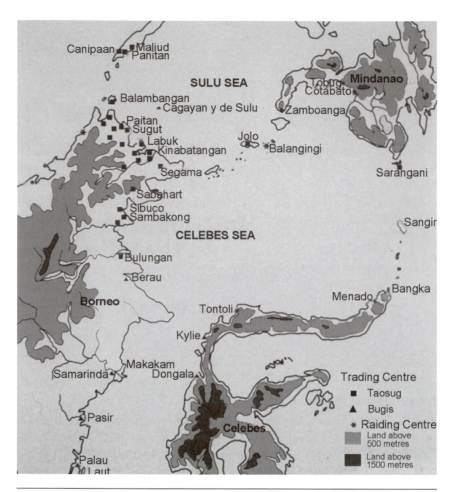

Fig. 3.1 Sulu and Celebes Seas. The Sulu Zone constituted a Southeast Asian economic region with a multi-ethnic, pre-colonial, Malayo-Muslim state and an ethnically heterogeneous set of societies of diverse political backgrounds and alignments. These diverse ethnic groups could be set within a strategic hierarchy of kinship-orientated stateless societies: maritime, nomadic fishers and forest-dwellers. In terms of world commerce and economic growth, the "Sulu Zone" was not an important economic region until the end of the eighteenth century.

the context of transoceanic trade, cross-cultural commerce, and empire building.

For several centuries, the Sulu-Mindanao region has been known for "piracy"; in the early nineteenth century, entire ethnic groups—Iranun and Balangingi—specialized in the state-sanctioned maritime raiding, attacking Southeast Asian coastal settlements and trading vessels sailing

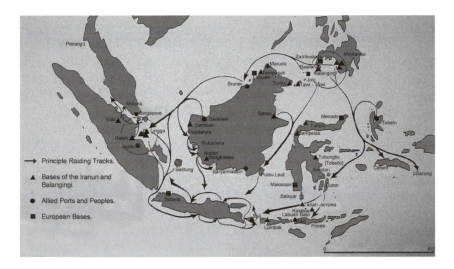

Fig. 3.2 Iranun maritime raiding and the Malay Archipelago in the first half of the nineteenth century.

for the fabled Spice Islands, or for Singapore, Manila, and Batavia (figure 3.2). When people think of slavery in Southeast Asia, they rightly imagine tens of thousands of peoples stolen from their villages across the region and sent directly to work the large fisheries and wilderness reserves of the Sulu Sultanate. The insatiable demands of the sultanate for labor to harvest and procure exotic natural commodities, such as sea cucumbers and birds' nests, reached a peak in the first half of the nineteenth century as the China trade flourished.[3] In this new globalized world, Jolo, Balangingi, Canton, and London were all intimately interconnected. A major feature of this emerging global economy was that more than two hundred years ago, Europe and the then emerging markets of East and Southeast Asia were tangled in a commercial and political web that was in many ways just as global as today's world economy. Yet another characteristic of late eighteenth- and nineteenth-century globalization was that it went hand in hand with degeneration and fragmentation. Even as economies of traditional trading states such as Sulu's integrated, others—for example, the sultanates of Brunei and Cotabato—disintegrated, while regional populations across Southeast Asia were fragmented, scattered, and relocated in the process. This paper takes note of the massive forced migrations of the unfortunate mass of captives and slaves caught in the cogs of the Sulu economy, which shaped the destiny and demographic origins of the Iranun and Balangingi, and the overall population trends and settlement patterns of much of the Philippines and eastern Indonesia well into the end of the nineteenth century.

In contemporary ethnohistorical studies of Southeast Asia, the "zone" and/or "border" have recently become chosen metaphors for theorizing the historically complex and contradictory ways in which cultural difference and ethnic diversity have been articulated in social relations and in political and economic practice across time. This paper aims to explore global cultural interconnections and interdependencies in the Southeast Asian world of the late eighteenth and nineteenth centuries with particular reference to the "Sulu Zone."[4] The paper also aims to enhance critical understanding and discussion of historiographical methods and models used in the problematizing of economic and cultural "border zones" in a changing global-local context. My emphasis is on a "zone" created through the intersections of geography, culture, and history centered on the Sulu and Celebes Seas, as well as China's and the West's complicated place within this "zone."

As cross-cultural flows of trade goods, technology, people, and information intensified in speed and volume in late eighteenth-century Southeast Asia, the localized borders of states and economic regions were becoming ever more porous. Did the world capitalist economy at that time create "borderless worlds"? Or did borders—cultural, national, or otherwise—prove to be more resistant and tenacious or vulnerable to the European presence and economic expansion? As some borders broke down, others were erected, both among and within nations, states, and empires. For example, while Sulu desperately wanted to become a part of the East Asian global-regional economy and Britain's "push into Asia," Chinese exclusivism and xenophobia were on the rise in the region. The southern Chinese border was forced to open to the West in the 1840s, but new "borders" had already been forged or imposed in the Sulu region and elsewhere in eastern Indonesia because of the China connection and economic conditions in that particular area. While captive labor power from all across Southeast Asia was introduced into the Zone's space, comprising the sultanate's fisheries and tropical forests, the boundaries of its economy, culture, and ecology were increasingly blurred by the rhetoric and practice of global trade, cultural pluralism, and Western imperialism.

A "zone," like that of the Sulu Sultanate, was not just a "spatial" site of economic, cross-cultural, and symbolic contact. Such a "zone" was both a meeting ground and arena of potential antagonism and conflict in which peoples geographically and historically separated came into contact with one another and often established ongoing relations. It was a "zone" where two or more cultures rubbed up against one another due to events going on beyond its geographical borders, where people of different origins and ethnicity came to occupy the "contact" space and/or historical territory, where lower, middle, and upper classes touched, involving possible conditions of coercion, inequality, and conflict. How were such "zones" or "border worlds," geographically and culturally defined, affirmed and contested, and transgressed? What impact did the China tea trade and the world capitalist economy have on both the making, physical and symbolic, and unmaking, of Taosug society and culture and the "Sulu Zone" from the late eighteenth to the end of the nineteenth century? The ethnohistorically based arguments, evidentiary examples, and other presentations in this paper tackle these questions from a variety of theoretical, historical, and empirical perspectives based on my earlier research on the world of the Sulu Sultanate. Together they vividly illuminate how contemporary culture and society were determined by "globalization," including the continuous flow of cross-cultural trade and interactions both within and among several large geo-economic "cores" and smaller "zones," involving, in this case, China, Britain, and the Sulu Sultanate, as well as thousands of separate smaller places.

The Sulu Zone constituted a Southeast Asian economic region with a multi-ethnic, precolonial Malayo-Muslim state, and an ethnically heterogeneous set of societies of diverse political backgrounds and alignments that could be set within a stratified hierarchy of kinship-oriented stateless societies, maritime nomadic fishers, and forest dwellers.[5] In terms of the international trade economy, the Sulu Zone was not an important economic region until the end of the eighteenth century. The key articulating unit in this seemingly small, inconsequential economic network was a strong regional sultanate. In the case of Sulu, it was set in a political and ecological framework that served to integrate the economic activity and resources of ethnically diverse and often politically divided groups and smaller subregions that would supply the larger markets in China and the West with exotic marine and forest commodities.

The Sultanate's entrepôt, at Jolo, integrated supply and distribution of manufactured and exported industrial goods such as textiles, weapons, porcelain, and opium emanating from powerful state systems—in particular the core areas of Europe and China. In terms of economic multi-functionality, the Sulu Zone did not manufacture or export industrial products on any scale.[6] However, the Zone and all of its subregions became part of the world capitalist economy with an international monetary system based on silver and gold. Tea, slaves, and opium were to play a critically important regional role in a global economic equation involving ever-expanding markets, patterns of consumption, and events going on beyond its geographical borders. The Sulu Sultanate is an important case study of an island entrepôt state that suddenly grew over several decades from being a secondary principality based on fishing and "piracy," located on the eastern edge of island Southeast Asia, into one of the most powerful and important precolonial trading states of the entire Malayo-Muslim "zone" of Southeast Asia (present-day Indonesia, Malaysia, and the southern Philippines).

Two factors governed the aims of the international trade economy between the West and China, namely, the location of marine and forest products for the Canton market and the potential ways to acquire them, using the strategies of cross-cultural trade and access from the seas. Given available nautical technology and the application of naval strength, the seas were the natural avenues for Western traders and travelers to intrude into the affairs of Southeast Asia, as they were in Northeast Asia. Three waterborne routes led into the heart of the Sulu Zone. The Chinese began with the Sulu Sea, an extension southward from their trade entrepôts in the Philippines, but they also navigated across the South China Sea through the Palawan passage, while the Bugis mariners sailed north through the Celebes Sea into the Zone. In this context, if the traditional political boundaries are ignored, and these seas are viewed as unifying rather than divisive agents—"great connectors" strategically extending across the region's key shipping routes—a strong case could be made for regarding the Zone as one of the final, albeit critically important peripheries of the world capitalist economy in eastern Asia.

Having examined the spatial system, I now want to speak briefly of a "regional time." The creation of a "zone" delineated both by space and by time, whose essence and demarcation came with the spread of commodities, technology, ideas, and practices of the world capitalist economy and Western imperialism, were two halves of the same process. The Sulu Zone as a regional "spatial" system and social order, like the economy it represented, was not atemporal. My framing and interpretation of the Zone as a spatial system rested on the axiom that it was "inherently unstable and generally dynamic,"[7] and that it was thrust onto the global stage at a specific moment or era in "regional time." Leach's remarkable work on state and community structures in highland Burma aimed at tracing the pattern of the shifting balance between two representations of political order and social phenomena over some 150 years. Similarly, for me, the Zone was also "a process in time."[8] In other words, it was a recognition that all ethnic groups and communities were being shaped and reshaped by the interplay between internal social and cultural forms and ongoing, external courses of action. In a very real sense, the peoples of the Zone were in fact "products" of large-scale processes of global socioeconomic change that had made them what they were and continued to make them what they would become in reaction to the uncontrollable and rapid impact of these forces.

The holism of the Zone as a "spatial system" was posited, both as a model and a necessary analytic fiction, not given. The invisible connections, linking the process of structural change and the dynamic movement of local systems and networks of this Zone to the wider economic and political world(s) of which it was becoming a part, had to be traced and explained in "regional time."

Commodities and the Search for Labor

This late eighteenth-century intrusion of the world capitalist economy was not resisted by the Taosug, who made their society relatively open to outside influences and social change, but largely on their terms. The coastal traders were mostly aristocrats who recognized the advantage in accepting and "borrowing" foreign technology, new ideas, luxury imports, and trade goods. The impact of this maritime expansion and growing influence of the outside world on Taosug political organization was significant. The rapid increase in trade goods and revenues, and the control and dissemination of improved firearms to mobile marauding communities residing in the Zone, encouraged the development of a more coercive, bureaucratically organized economy and state.[9]

What the Europeans and Chinese sought at Jolo and from the fisheries and forests of the Zone was, above all, *tripang*, pearls and birds' nests. Between 1768 and 1848, hundreds of vessels visited Jolo, almost all of them trading over either one or two seasons. *Tripang* was obtained, at first, in return for cloth, clothing, iron, and other metals; soon after for gunpowder, muskets, and cannon. The Taosug traders were mostly coastal *datus* or "chiefs" who mobilized their factions and contacts throughout the Zone to deliver the products, and whose power and wealth grew together with the development of the trade. I must note here, however, that this rapid trade expansion did not entirely dovetail with preexisting Sulu circuits of exchange, as their basic structure was altered somewhat by global-regional trade, Islam, and the way slavery could be used to bring in more commodities. Of particular importance for Sulu were guns and gunpowder and other imported manufactures, textiles, and also opium, which contributed to the sultanate's centralizing coercive power and integration of the economy with other social institutions. Taosug merchants or chiefs on the coast, and their descendants, developed an extensive redistributive trade in which they wrested the function of the collection and distribution of commodities for the China tea trade from traditional competitors—the sultanates of Brunei and Cotabato.

Critical regional transitions began in the late eighteenth century with Britain's involvement in the intra-Asian trade. British merchants in the search for wealth bartered arms, textiles, opium, and specie (silver) for an enormous variety of local commodities to balance the economic drain of their China trade. As British power increased in the late eighteenth century, trading settlements and outposts along the coasts of Southeast Asia developed rapidly, and along with places like Penang and Balambangan came the unfolding of the China trade and the search for profitable commodities.[10] This quest for *tripang*, birds' nests, pearls, and other desirable commodities, was to have a profound impact upon the various peoples of the Zone and their way of life and much of the rest of the eastern archipelago, constituting one of the most dramatic and fascinating episodes in the history of China's tea trade and the world capitalist economy.

By 1700, tea had become, along with coffee and cocoa, one of the "great nonalcoholic drinks" for all those Europeans with a sound grasp of epidemiological principles and fear of waterborne diseases and pestilence. Within a century, the English, rightly reluctant to go beyond the bounds of epidemiological common sense, were each annually consuming two and a half pounds of tea and seventeen pounds of sugar.[11] The right lessons and examples from history about global economic-cultural interconnections and interdependencies tend to explain patterns and events that have been formally glossed over. For example, sugar "demanded" slaves and the Atlantic slave trade. Similarly, tea, inextricably bound to sugar as product and fate, would also inadvertently "demand" slaves in the Sulu Zone and the advent of Iranun and Balangingi slave raiding. Since the British primarily wanted sea cucumbers, sharks' fins, pearls, and birds' nests for the trade in China tea, the issue of the nature of productive relations in Sulu or slavery suddenly became primary. The demand for local commodities in return for imports affected the allocation of labor power and the demand for people throughout the Zone. In this globalizing context, tea was more than simply the major commodity in the development of trade between China and Britain. It was also a plant that was instrumental in the rise and transformation of the Sulu Sultanate as a regional power, permanently influencing the economic organization and integration of the Zone.

The increase in the production of sea cucumbers had direct repercussions throughout the Zone, where it highlighted the importance of the labor power of maritime nomadic fishers and slaves in the local regional economy and further altered the balance of power between sedentary coastal trading populations and these maritime nomadic "masters" of the seas. As the sultanate organized its economy around the collection and distribution of marine and jungle produce, there was a greater need for large-scale recruitment of labor power to do the intensive work of procurement. I estimate that sixty-eight thousand workers labored each year in the Sulu

Zone's *tripang* fisheries to provide the popular Chinese exotica—a standard banquet fare that appeared in so many menus, sometimes braised with geese's feet or abalone. The Taosug, with their retainers and slaves, collected about ten thousand *piculs* of *tripang* in any one season in the first half of the nineteenth century (one *picul* is equivalent to 133.33 pounds). Birds' nests for the Qing cuisine had to be obtained in the wilderness of Borneo. As the English traders increasingly procured *tripang* and birds' nests from Taosug *datus* in Sulu, demand for workers harvesting the commodities outstripped supply. Slaving activity developed to meet the accentuated demands of external trade. The Taosug *datus* turned to slave raiding to address the shortage of labor, and Jolo became the nerve center for coordination of long-distance maritime slave raiding.

Lanun: A Terrifying Presence

The Iranun and Balangingi Samal, the slave raiders of the Sulu Zone, met the need for a reliable source of workers. *Iranun* is from the Magindanao word *I-Lanaw-en*, or "People from the Lake," suggesting that they originally came from around Lanao Lake in southwestern Mindanao. The Balangingi Samal lived along with Iranun and other Samal-speaking groups in a dozen or more villages scattered along the southern Mindanao coast, the southern shore of Basilan, and on the islands of the Samalese cluster. The Taosug *datus* supplied the Iranun and Balangingi with provisions for the long-distance raiding. Within three decades (1768–98), their raids encompassed all of insular Southeast Asia. From the end of the eighteenth century to the middle of the nineteenth, Southeast Asia felt the full force of the slave traders of the Sulu Zone. Well-organized fleets of large, swift *prahus* carried out these large-scale operations.

Lanun. The name struck fear into the hearts and minds of riverine and coastal populations across Southeast Asia nearly two centuries ago. Recently, ethnohistorical research has also shown that where Iranun or Lanun maritime raiding is concerned, old traditions die hard. The terrors of the sudden harsh presence of these well-armed alien raiders live on in the oral recollections, reminiscences, popular folk epics, and dramas of the victims' descendants in the Philippines, Indonesia, and Malaysia to this day.[12] Only in one part of the globe, in the latter part of the eighteenth century, did Europeans find "piracy" flourishing extensively, pursued as a vocation or calling, not by individuals, as was the case with most of those who had followed the profession of buccaneering in the West, but by entire communities and states with whom it came to be regarded as the most honorable course of life—a profession.

The Iranun were frequently the enemies of every community and nation stretching from the Birds Head coast of New Guinea and the Moluccas (among the most productive spice islands of the Netherlands East Indies) to mainland Southeast Asia. More than two centuries ago, a Buginese writer chronicled that "Lanun" in double-decked *prahus* up to ninety or one hundred feet long, rowed by perhaps one hundred slaves and armed with intricately wrought swivel cannon cast in bronze, were plundering villages and robbing Malay fishers in the Straits of Malacca and the Riau Islands. Among other victims of their marauding were the coastal inhabitants and fishers of Thailand and Vietnam.[13] They would also raid in the Philippines, where the central and northern sections of the archipelago were under the control of Spain.[14] Iranun squadrons regularly plundered villages and captured slaves. Their exploits and conquests had the immediate effect of both disrupting and destroying traditional trade routes. Chinese junks and traders were driven off from states such as Brunei and Cotabato, the erstwhile masters of the Iranun robbing parts of the archipelago of the traditional trade and exchange of spices, birds' nests, camphor, rattans, and other items.[15] The Iranun earned a fearsome reputation in an era of extensive world commerce and economic growth between the West and China. Writing in the late 1840s, the Dominican chronicler and public intellectual Francisco Gainza described the fearless maritime populations that lived along the eastern shore of Illana Bay, southern Mindanao, who called themselves "Iranun":

> This large population, designated by some geographers with the name of the Illana [Iranun] Confederation, in reality does not form a single political body except to defend its independence when it is found threatened. . . . They live loaded with weapons; they reside in dwellings artfully encircled by barricades . . . and they maintain their bellicose spirit by continuously engaging in robbery and theft. Through piracy they strive to gather slaves for aggrandizement and to provide their subsistence. . . . In short, this particular society can only be considered a great lair of robbers, or a nursery for destructive and ferocious men.[16]

For late eighteenth- and nineteenth-century Europeans, the problems of Iranun and Balangingi marauding and slave raiding were complicated by diverse modes of operation and geography. Whatever the exact cause(s) for the sudden advent of large-scale, long-range Iranun maritime raiding, the geographical setting and opportunity or timing were right for these emergent seafaring peoples. The innumerable islands of Southeast Asia had been home to generations of people of "Malay" origin, who had progressively converted to Islam from the fifteenth century and engaged in trading, raiding, and warfare before the arrival of Europeans in the sixteenth century. Early Western explorers, travelers, and merchants recorded their exploits. More than two centuries later, at the height of the China tea trade, marauding and maritime slave raiding were still going strong, stronger than ever before. The greatest threat to seaborne traders and the coastal populace came from the Iranun who operated from the mangrove-lined inlets, bays, and reef-strewn islets in the waters round the southern Philippines and Borneo, especially the Sulu and Celebes Seas. They preyed on an increasingly rich shipping trade of the Spanish, Dutch, and English, and Bugis and Chinese merchants, and seized their cargoes of tin, opium, spices, munitions, and slaves as the merchants headed to and from the trading centers of Manila, Makassar, Batavia, and Penang.[17]

Expeditions sent against the raiders promised no lasting results because the points to which they could retire were innumerable and often off the charts. The Spanish officer Don Jose Maria Halcon, providing naval intelligence about Iranun and Balangingi "piracy" to an English officer at Manila in 1838, compared their haunts to extensive "nests or banks of rats" where they could fly from one refuge to another, with impunity.[18] Europeans, he believed, could never succeed in annihilating them. A decade earlier, Edward Presgrave, registrar of imports and exports at the newly founded British settlement of Singapore, astutely pointed out one of the major reasons why Iranun maritime raiding was concentrated in that particular region of the world. He noted, with some trepidation, "that piracy does exist to a very great extent even in the neighbourhood of our settlement is notorious . . . the most casual view of a chart of these seas is sufficient to convince anyone that no corner of the globe is more favourably adapted for the secure and successful practice of piracy."[19] Hence, geography as destiny was a sinister friend, albeit an ally, of the Iranun and Balangingi.

Access to foreign maritime technology also facilitated slave raiding. Chinese compasses, European mariners' charts, and brass telescopes were all widely used to great advantage as "weapons of war" by the sea raiders. Guns and gunpowder further intensified slave raiding. Acquisition of cannon, gunpowder, flintlock rifles, and shot from European China traders in return for exotic commodities led to increased traffic in slaves, warfare, and ever-increasing levels of arms imports into Sulu after the last quarter of the eighteenth century. In the first quarter of the nineteenth century, the supply of firearms to the Zone escalated dramatically with the entry of New England Yankee traders and whalers from the United States, who sold arms freely to the Taosug and Samal. The Taosug demanded the highest-quality firearms and weapons, prompting traders and manufacturers to custom-produce them on consignment. English industrial technology in Sheffield, Birmingham, and Manchester developed beautiful, dependable *kris* and firearms for the Taosug. Equipped with the latest firearms, the slave raiders were universally feared by coastal and riverine people throughout Southeast Asia. Large settlements were targets of fleets of forty to fifty *prahus*. The boats carried two and a half to three thousand armed men as well as heavy artillery.

The Iranun burst quite suddenly into Southeast Asian history in the second half of the eighteenth century with a series of terrifying raids and attacks on the coasts and shipping of the Philippines, the Straits of Malacca, and the islands beyond Sulawesi. Their primary targets were unprotected coastal settlements and trading boats that traveled throughout Southeast Asia bringing valuable commodities from China and the West back to the most remote parts of the archipelago. It is estimated that during the last quarter of this century (1774–98) of maritime raiding and slaving against the Dutch and Spanish, between 150 and 200 raiding ships set out from the Mindanao-Sulu area each year. The sheer size of the vessels—the largest *lanong* measuring upward of 130 feet in length—and the scale of the expeditions dwarfed most previous efforts, marking a significant turning point in the naval strategy of Malay maritime raiding as it had been traditionally understood.[20] Rescued captives interrogated by colonial officials had often been traumatized by the violence they had witnessed during the sea attacks and settlement raids along the coastline. The oral traditions of their descendants still speak of "the terror." They tell of the terrifying landing on the beach and the way that the slave raiders ended years, perhaps even decades, of anonymity that hid their ancestors from the war at sea and the machinations of the global economy. Barnes, in his classic study of Lamalera, a remote community on the south coast of the island of Lembata, near the eastern end of Flores, notes that the village is really a "twin settlement," with the lower one (Lamalera Bawah) on the beach and an upper one (Lamalera Atas) on a nearby cliff for protection from earlier Iranun maritime slave raids. Such villages in eyrie-like settings were usually palisaded, but in this case (as at Tira, the site of Southon's fieldwork in Buton) the main defense was inaccessibility. Heersink also notes that on Salayer, most of the nineteenth-century settlements were situated in the interior. Here the northern and southern extremities of the island were the least safe, and suffered most from Iranun "piracy," while the alluvial west coast became the prominent zone of security and trade.[21] New evidence has also emerged supporting the widespread fear and dread of the Iranun in the Java Sea. Stenross, researching the traditional sailing boats of Madura, recently accidentally came across people with terrifying memories of the Iranun still intact on the north coast, in a small isolated village. In Tamberu, he found—while discussing photographs of Bajau grave markers shaped like miniature boats—evidence of centuries-old oral traditions about the "Lanun" that signify tales of cultural confrontations and conflicts. These confrontations originated in the violent intimacies of the encounter between expansive Iranun and struggling, oppressed coastal people. Obviously, the fear of the Iranun went a long way since their maritime raiding tracks crossed regional and ethnic boundaries like no other before, not bypassing even a tiny village like Tamberu, reaching extremes of pain and alienation among the Madurese coastal inhabitants there. The number of people plucked by the Sulu Sultanate from the shores of Southeast Asia in a span of one hundred years was staggering. Between two and three hundred thousand slaves were moved in Iranun and Samal vessels to the Sulu Sultanate in the period 1770–1870. A substantial number of the slaves were traded like commodities. The elderly and infirm were sold to tribes in Borneo for human sacrifice. Those left behind were absorbed into Sulu society.

Colonialism's Pirates

The Iranun were considered, in the minds of ordinary Filipinos and Malays, to be well organized, numerous, fierce, and ruthless. Their massive fleets and inshore scouring operations were hallmarks of the Iranun. Flotillas of *lanong* attacked large trading ships and regional centers, while Iranun slave raiders, hundreds strong, harried small settlements along the coasts of the Philippines and Sulawesi. These raids left such a feeling of dread among the local populace that anything threatening or evil became synonymous in the minds of mothers and children with the "Lanun" and *moros*—the notorious "pirate tribes of Mindanao and Sulu."[22] The lesson to be learned everywhere across Southeast Asia was deep and powerful, especially for ordinary Christian converts whose belief system was essentially Animist, but whose world under colonial rule was rapidly becoming "modern." On Luzon or Sulawesi, the Tagalog or Menadonese might see clearly what they might become if they did not live according to their highest evangelized nature. Iranun warriors and seafarers became important for the European colonial mind, not for who they were in and of themselves, but rather for what they showed "civilized" colonized men and women they were not and must not be. Stemming from profound differences between the cultures of Spain and England and the culture of the Iranun, as well as from Spanish and English colonial self-interest, convictions of superiority, and a chronic disinclination to view Iranun motives and actions from any perspective but their own, these myopic imperial images and beliefs signified by the signs "*moro*" and "*Illanun*" defamed and dehumanized the Muslim inhabitants of Sulu and Mindanao. In the European mind and imagination, the Iranun were reduced to something sinister and faceless, akin to the barbarians who resisted Roman rule and Christianity—barbarians who had to be cleared from the seas of Southeast Asia rather than the lands of Caesar's empire. Not only did the pejorative images associated with the labels "*moro*" and "*Illanun*," as ethnic pseudo-nyms, contribute to further misinformation, misunderstanding, and hostility, but they also justified and made more acceptable—as their lasting legacy does to this day—the final aggression and injustice.

Moro came to symbolize all that was dangerous, dark, and cruel about the tragic confrontation, and the Iranun's adherence to Islam. For the Spanish, the colonial enterprise in the Philippines was in many ways a religious enterprise. For the British, sea tenure and empire were also finally to be demonstrated from a different sort of theology—capitalism and industrial technology. But the fundamental characteristic and central focus of the centuries-long mutual conflict and uneasiness had always been the fact that almost everything that mattered to the Iranun had come to be defined and measured by the seas—the seas that in so many ways were invented, "discovered," and eventually ruled by the Spanish and English. The central fact of domination and empire was the fundamental attitude and belief that the Iranun possessed their seas only as a natural right, since that possession, in the minds of the Spanish and English, existed prior to and outside of a properly civilized state. What followed, then, was that the sea was technically *vacuum domicilium* and that the Spanish and English, who would control the sea and make it productive for Christ and world commerce, who would give it order and regulate interregional trade, were obliged to take over and exterminate the *moros* and *Illanun* of the "eastern seas" in order that *laissez-faire* trade and colonial Christian enterprise could be carried out successfully. This extreme posture and situation had always been incomprehensible to the Iranun of Sulu and Mindanao, and it was also clear that the central focus of these cultures in conflict had always been in the sea. The sea, which, in more ways than one, was discovered by Spain and Britain, functioned as a political instrument, a commodity, an empire lifeline, a national prerogative and aspiration. The Iranun were defined by it, measured by their domination and use of it, and were to be dispossessed of it. But in the latter half of the nineteenth century, even as the last Iranun villages and raiding vessels were burned or broken up, the denigrating image of the *moro* and *Illanun* as slave raider and savage pirate now began to hold new moral meaning for both the European and Christian Filipino imagination. The myth of the "savage" now both evoked and guaranteed the final success of the larger sacred-secular drama of colonization, conquest, and annexation and the vision of the Filipino people's own place in it, just before the dawn of the twentieth century.

Certainly no ethnohistory of the Iranun and Balangingi since the late eighteenth century, no description of the meaning and constitution of their "cultures," and no anthropologically informed historical analysis of the transformation of their societies can be undertaken without reference to the advent of the China tea trade and the rise of the Sulu Sultanate. Both these processes played an integral role in Iranun and Balangingi slave raiding, which was so forcefully felt by most indigenous groups in island Southeast Asia. Yet, despite their major historical importance, the Iranun and Balangingi, the infamous *moros*, remain among the least known and most misunderstood ethnic groups in the modern history of Southeast Asia.

While there are occasional references to them in earlier histories, travel accounts and official reports, recent historians have had to burrow deeper and deeper into the sources at the Archivo de Indias, the Rijksarchief, the Public Records Office, and various archives in Southeast Asia, especially the Philippine National Archive, in order to reconstruct a detailed ethnohistorical account of these maritime peoples and their relationships to one another. As I have shown in *The Sulu Zone 1768–1898*, sources are of critical importance, but they are of little value unless the historian knows what to do with them.[23] The main impetus for fashioning a new understanding of the Iranun and Balangingi past has been the radical change in perspective that some historians have adopted to study the region's recent history and its continuing integration within the world capitalist economy. These changes in perspective attempt to combine the historiographical approaches and ideas of the Annales historians with the conceptual framework of world-system theorists and solid ethnography.[24] Here, I pay particular attention to the pathbreaking book written by Eric Wolf in the early 1980s, *Europe and the People without History*.[25] Wolf argues that no community or nation is or has been an island, and the world, a totality of interconnected processes or systems, is not and never has been a sum of self-contained human groups and cultures. The modern world-system, as it developed, never confined global capitalism to the political limitations of single states or empires. Wolf's postulations, if accepted, imply that an analysis of global capitalism, not limited to the study of single states or empires, will be more complete and, in certain ways, less static. The point is that history consists of the interaction of variously structured and geographically distributed social entities that mutually reshape each other. The transformation of Britain and China and the rise of the Iranun in modern Southeast Asian history cannot be separated: each is the other's history.

The complexities of relations in the struggle over power and autonomy on the seas, between the maritime Islamic world of the Iranun and the conflicting interests and machinations of the Western powers bent on controlling the oceans and sea-lanes, demonstrates how a pathology of physical and cultural violence associated with global macro-contact wars and empire building in various parts of Southeast Asia led to widespread conflicts and regional tragedies. The enormous increase in global trade that affected state formation, statecraft, and economic integration made it absolutely imperative to import captives from outside the Sulu Zone to meet labor power requirements. As commodities from China, Europe, and North America flowed to Sulu, the Taosug aristocrats thrived, and there emerged the Iranun—strong, skilled maritime people who were the scourge of Southeast Asia, as they raided in one-hundred-foot-long sailing ships. The sea and tropical forests were the life force of the Sultanate, where tens of thousands of captives and slaves labored annually to collect and process exotic commodities for the China trade. The rising demand for captives and slaves from across Southeast Asia reshaped the character of the political economies of Sulu and China and, as part of the same process, gave birth to the advent of highly specialized mobile communities of maritime raiders. Thus, the history of slaving and the slave trade and the rise of the Iranun must be framed as part of a unitary historical process, which explains the major factors contributing to the formation and maintenance of their ethnic identity. The intrusive roles played in the Iranun's sudden development and expansion by the global economy and singular entangled commodities, particularly tea, sea cucumbers, birds' nests, and firearms, result from this historical process. Maritime raiding, or what the Spanish, British, and Dutch labeled "piracy," was not a manifestation of savagery and dependence; rather, it was the result of phenomenal economic growth and strength. The state-sanctioned system of maritime raiding and slaving in Sulu was part of a vital effort to partake in and control a rapidly increasing volume of global commerce triggered by the advent of Europeans in the China trade in the late eighteenth century. Accusations of cultural decadence and barbarism that were repeatedly directed against the Sulu Sultanate and the Iranun by leading European participants in that trade are both ironic and incorrect when approached from the perspective of a unitary historical process.

The Sulu Sultanate was successful because it achieved global scale in particular types of commodity production, integrating labor acquisition and allocation—slaving and slavery—commodity production, marketing, and other functions on a global-regional scale. The losers in this contest were traditional states and ethnic groups that neither achieved nor specialized on a global-regional scale, but relied on an entrenched position in their local markets for the bulk of their power and profits. This essentially market-determined commercial encounter in the latter part of the eighteenth century, as the tangled fateful relationship between Britain, China, and Sulu was established, transformed the population and history of Southeast Asia. In their remorseless search for captives and slaves, the Iranun and Balangingi brought the "illegible" maritime spaces, "border arcs" and moving frontiers of the margins of the Malayo-Muslim world, and the various colonial peripheries, home to the centers, striking back at the empire's heart(s) around Batavia and Singapore, in the Straits of Malacca and

Manila Bay, and beyond, reaching right across the top of northern Australia.[26] These fearsome alien marauders originated from areas beyond the pale—unknown "illegible" sites still well outside the reach of colonial dominion. The Iranun and Balangingi profited from the expanding China trade, which they supplied with captives and slaves taken on the high seas and along the shores of Southeast Asia, in return for weapons and luxury goods. These sea raiders—the lords of the eastern seas—were the "shapers," a set of ethnic groups that specialized in long-distance maritime raiding but did it on a regional scale.

To what extent did the English discovery of tea, as one of the great, universal nonalcoholic drinks, accelerate the decline of China, contribute sharply to the rise of Sulu slave raiding, and create a widespread catastrophe with the trade of opium for tea throughout eastern Asia? The argument, as you now know, runs roughly as follows. The end of the eighteenth century was an age of "economic revolution" in the Zone in which labor demands grew larger and larger. To meet the unprecedented needs of the Chinese markets, Taosug rulers had to find more and more labor power. Sulu's "principle number one" was specialization. It found, for the populations of the Zone, a few key areas where the Sultanate set out to be the best in the local-regional context, the best in Southeast Asia, and then, also, the best in the world. Those areas were highly focused local specializations relating to Taosug social organization of slave raiding as a permanent activity, and their local extractive industries, bringing key people and social groups together to build economic relationships, in order to then facilitate the process by which they carried on the redistributive economy. The slave raiders also in turn helped to enforce the collection of exotic commodities, thus establishing a coercion-extraction cycle that was an intended consequence of competition for resources and power by this go-ahead state in the global economic arena.

The mingling of commodities served not only as a motor of change but as a realized sign, signifying that two or more worlds met, as well. This meeting of commodities and peoples highlighted in different ways the interconnectedness of the modern world. These commodities led to a continuous redefinition of belonging to a place as either "here" or "there" and/or as markers of social identity. Lives and cultures blended wherever commodities changed hands in the Zone. The sultanate's trade had started along the coast of northeast Borneo when Europeans and Taosug found that each had key items of global commerce that the other wanted. The Sulu and Samal desired European firearms, knives, kettles, and textiles. The Europeans valued the Zone's natural products, especially birds' nests, sea cucumbers, and pearls. They traded, and both parties thought they were often getting a bargain. But their worlds and lives had been altered in the process, sometimes irrevocably so. After 1768, the consequence of "globalization" accelerated by the world capitalist economy was that

areas—from remote maritime villages and tribal longhouses in the Zone
to entire continents—were "caught up in processes which linked them to
events that, though geographically distant [were] culturally, economically,
politically, strategically, and ecologically quite near [and] the distinction
between 'here' and 'there' [broke] down."[27]

The large-scale progressive intake of captive peoples from various parts
of Southeast Asia and beyond also reflected Sulu's moving closer to Europe
and China, economically and culturally. In the pages of my original volume on the Sulu Zone, the world has changed through the intersections of
the global economy centered on the Sulu and Celebes Seas, as well as the
sultanate's critical place within it. Here, ordinary Southeast Asian farmers
and fishers are traumatically uprooted and forced to live in a distant economic region: a world made up of winners responding to new economic
opportunities of "globalization," and losers—those forced to live in ways
unanticipated before that moment of capture and enslavement. Trade
debts in Jolo are paid off by slaves serving Taosug masters in the fisheries
and forests of the Zone. The point is that tens of thousands of ordinary
Southeast Asians lived among maritime peoples completely removed from
those with whom they had been born and grew up. They found themselves
abroad in the land- and seascape of the Zone, first, because advanced
technologies and new social alignments made long-distance slave raiding
relatively easy, and second, because revolutionary economic historical developments forcefully landed them in an unintended place—the Zone. European traders joined with Taosug *datus* to spark one of the largest
population movements in recent Southeast Asian history, with hundreds
of thousands of individuals sent into slavery across the Zone. By the start
of the nineteenth century, slave identities in the Zone were being shaped
and changed by the forces of "globalization" as distinctions of ethnicity
and culture blurred and broke down, and thousands of "outsiders" were
being incorporated into the lower reaches of a rapidly expanding trading
society. All this ethnic edging up against one another and establishing ongoing relations involving conditions of slavery had been for the sake of a
widely consumed, mildly addictive commodity that had become a necessity in the European diet and way of life—tea. Sulu provides an exceptional
case study of *how* a collective identity was established, made real, and took
on a particular cultural content.[28]

Notes

1. James Francis Warren, *The Sulu Zone, the World Capitalist Economy and the Historical
    Imagination* (Amsterdam: VU Press, 1998), 9–13; James Francis Warren, *The Sulu Zone
    1768–1898: The Dynamics of External Trade, Slavery and Ethnicity in the Transformation
    of a Southeast Asian Maritime State* (Singapore: Singapore University Press, 1981),
    xix–xxvi.

2. Warren, *The Sulu Zone 1768–1898*, 149–214.

3. Warren, *The Sulu Zone, the World Capitalist Economy and the Historical Imagination*, 39–45.

4. Compare Howard Dick, "Indonesian Economic History Inside Out," *Review of Indonesian and Malaysian Affairs* 27 (1993), 1–12: 6; and Warren, *The Sulu Zone 1768–1898*.

5. Warren, *The Sulu Zone 1768–1898*, xix–xxvi.

6. In terms of the geographical concept of "central-place" theory and its implications for hierarchy and multi-functionality, see the pioneering historical analysis of G. William Skinner, "Marketing and Social Structure in Rural China," *Journal of Asian Studies* 24 (1964), 3–44; and G. William Skinner (ed.), *The City in Late Imperial China* (Stanford, CA: Stanford University Press, 1977).

7. John Comaroff and Jean Comaroff, *Ethnography and the Historical Imagination* (Boulder, CO: Westview Press, 1992), 22.

8. E. R. Leach, *Political Systems of Highland Burma: A Study of Kachin Social Structure* (London: London School of Economics and Political Science, 1954), 4, 212.

9. Victor Lieberman, "An Age of Commerce in Southeast Asia? Problems of Regional Coherence—A Review Article," *The Journal of Asian Studies* 54, no. 3 (1995), 796–807: 797.

10. James Francis Warren, "Balambangan and the Rise of the Sulu Sultanate 1772–1775," *Journal of the Malaysian Branch Royal Asiatic Society* 50, no. 1 (1977), 73–93.

11. Henry Hobhouse, *Seeds of Change: Five Plants That Transformed Mankind* (London: Paper Mac, 1992), 115.

12. Compare Charles O. Frake, "Abu Sayaff Displays of Violence and the Proliferation of Contested Identities among Philippines Muslims," *American Anthropologist* 100, no. 1 (1998), 41–54; Benedict Sandin, *The Sea Dayaks of Borneo Before White Rajah Rule* (London: Macmillan, 1967), 63–5, 127; and Warren, *The Sulu Zone, the World Capitalist Economy and the Historical Imagination*, 44.

13. See Raja Ali Haji Ibn Ahmad, *The Precious Gift Tuhfat Al-Nafis* (Kuala Lumpur: Oxford University Press, 1982).

14. Compare Warren, *The Sulu Zone 1768–1898*, 147–56, 165–81.

15. *Ibid.*, 152–3.

16. Emilio Bernaldez, *Resana historico de la guerra a Sur de Filipinas, sostenida por las armas Espanoles contra los piratas de aquel archipielago, desde la conquista hasta nuestros dias* (Madrid: Imprenta del Memorial de Ingenieros, 1857), 46–7.

17. For an important study of how Southeast Asia became a crucial part of a global commercial system between the fifteenth and mid–seventeenth centuries, see Anthony Reid, *Southeast Asia in the Age of Commerce 1450–1680, Vol. 2: Expansion and Crisis* (New Haven, CT: Yale University Press, 1993).

18. Blake to Maitland, August 13, 1838. *East India Company and India Board Records*, Board's Collection. B.C. 86974, 4.

19. E. Presgrave to K. Murchison, Resident Councilor at Singapore, *Report on Piracy in the Straits Settlements*, December 5, 1828. India Office Records, Board's Collections (IOR). IOR, F/4/1724 (69433).

20. Warren, *The Sulu Zone 1768–1898*, 147–8, 256–8.

21. Compare Robert Barnes, *Sea Hunters of Indonesia: Fishers and Weavers of Lamalera* (New York: Oxford University Press, 1996), 44; and Christiaan Heersink, "Environmental Adaptations in Southern Sulawesi," Victor T. King (ed.), *Environmental Challenges in South-East Asia* (London: Curzon, 1988), 103–4.

22. See Charles O. Frake, "The Genesis of Kinds of People in the Sulu Archipelago," Frake (ed.), *Language and Cultural Description* (Stanford, CA: Stanford University Press, 1980), 314–18; and Frake, "Aber Sayaff," 42–3.

23. Warren, *The Sulu Zone 1768–1898*, 51–8.

24. See Peter Burke, *The French Historical Revolution: The Annales School 1929–1989* (Stanford, CA: Stanford University Press, 1990); Paul Baran, *The Political Economy of Growth* (New York: Monthly Review Press, 1957); Andre Gunder Frank, *World Accumulation, 1492–1789* (London: Macmillan, 1978); and Immanuel Wallerstein, *The Modern World System: Capitalist Agriculture and the Origins of the European World Economy in the Sixteenth Century* (New York: Academic Press, 1974).

25. Eric R. Wolf, *Europe and the People without History* (Berkeley: University of California Press, 1982).

26. Jim Scott uses the term *illegible* to define nonstate spaces where people can move about with impunity, just out of reach of the state. Nonstate spaces generally include swamps, marshes, deltas, reef-girdled islets, mountains, et ectera. See James Scott, "The State and People Who Move Around," *IIAS Newsletter* 19 (1999), 3, 45.

27. Kenneth Prewitt, "Presidential Items," *Items (Social Science Research Council)* 50, no. 1 (1996), 15–18: 15.

28. Comaroff and Comaroff, *Ethnography and the Historical Imagination*, 44.

CHAPTER 4

Ahab's Boat

Non-European Seamen in Western Ships of Exploration and Commerce

DAVID A. CHAPPELL

> With a start all glared at dark Ahab, who was surrounded by five dusky phan-
> toms . . . of that vivid, tiger-yellow complexion peculiar to some of the aborig-
> inal natives of the Manillas. . . . Ahab cried out to the white-turbaned old man
> at their head, "All ready there, Fedallah?" "Ready," was the half-hissed reply.
> "Lower away then; d'ye hear?"[1]

Herman Melville, in his nineteenth-century novel *Moby-Dick*, wrote,
"Upon the good conduct of the harpooneers, the success of a whaling voyage largely depends."[2] What is striking is that Melville put all the *Pequod*'s
harpoons in the hands of non-Europeans: Queequeg the Pacific islander,
Tashtego the Massachusetts Indian, and Daggoo the African. In fact, he
manned the captain's own whaleboat entirely with "Manila-men," a catchall
category that included Chinese, Malays, Oceanians, and mixed-race Asian
seamen.[3] In the end, the white whale kills Ahab and drowns all his Manila-
men, including their harpooner, Fedallah, also described as a Parsee, or
South Asian. Moby Dick finally wrecks the ship, but not before Queequeg,
Tashtego, and Daggoo climb to the top of each mast. "[T]he pagan harpooneers," Melville wrote, "still maintained their sinking lookouts on the
sea."[4] This dramatic scene challenges the triumphalist tale of European seafarers heroically globalizing the world[5] and offers us instead an image of in-
terdependency with alien "others," whose skills made voyaging so far from

home possible and, if your captain was not fatally obsessed with a particular whale, even profitable. Melville's fiction was not far from fact.

This paper will address the important role played in European maritime expansion by sailors indigenous to the regions being explored. It will suggest that globalization was from the start a two-way process, despite inequalities, and that non-Western seamen counterexplored the ships, sea routes, and home ports of Europeans who arrived in their waters after 1500. In fact, studies of the early modern world economy suggest that Europeans used their naval war technology and their financial windfalls from the Americas to graft themselves onto a preexisting Afro-Asian trading network, which was founded on ancient knowledge of the monsoon winds and centered on China and the Muslim world.[6] This interpretation implies that Europeans would likely need help from local seamen in Africa, Asia, and the Pacific as they sailed farther and farther away from home to distant, unfamiliar ports of call—much as Nepalese guides and porters enable Western climbers of Mount Everest to reach its peak. We know, for example, that Vasco da Gama, though financed partly by a Portuguese crusading order, relied on a Muslim to pilot his caravel from Malindi, on the Swahili coast of East Africa, to Calicut in India, where Muslim merchants and Hindu courtiers laughed at his paltry gifts for the local ruler.[7]

Despite their rapid conquest of strategic ports around the Indian Ocean, economically "the Portuguese were but another component, another competitor on the local scene and in no way able to supplant their predecessors, be they Southeast Asians, Tamils, Gujaratis, or Chinese."[8] As European vessels ventured outside the Atlantic into the shipping circuits of other peoples, most notably those engaged in what Gang Deng calls the Pan-Asian Trading Ring from the Indian Ocean to the Sea of Japan,[9] they needed not only guides but also crew replacements. Kenneth McPherson points out that despite a long history of Iberian antipathy toward Muslims,

> [w]hen the Portuguese attempted to establish a maritime empire in the Indian Ocean they were desperately short of manpower. Seamen were recruited from all the ports of Europe, as well as from many parts of the Indian Ocean, with the result that African and Asian Muslims crewed Portuguese vessels from Sofala to Nagasaki.[10]

Over time, European vessels far from home came to depend on regional pools of maritime labor to make their commercial voyages profitable. We can map out such dependency if we divide the sea route from Europe to China into segments. Along the West African coast, European ships used mixed Afro-Portuguese from the Cape Verde Islands and Kru mariners from Liberia to man surfboats and to serve as intermediaries between ship and shore. In the Indian Ocean, varieties of local seamen competed with or participated in European shipping, most notably the so-called lascars of India who served on British East India Company ships. In Southeast Asia, "Manila-men" served on the transpacific Spanish galleons as well as on Dutch and other European vessels. The Pacific Ocean, in fact, became a maritime melting pot as the China trade and whaling drew more and more foreign ships into the region. Melville's Tashtego archetype represents those Gay Head Indians from Massachusetts who often served as harpooners on New England whaling ships,[11] and since the main whaling grounds in the nineteenth century were in the Pacific, so-called kanakas like Melville's Queequeg made up perhaps a fifth or more of the crews of American whalers.[12]

These are only a few of the best-known examples of participation by local sailors in European vessels abroad. To explore this topic further, let me briefly touch on four categories of non-European seamen: Manila-men, lascars, kanakas, and Kru, who together constitute the unsung working class of Western trading and whaling ships in their waters. Like the Indian Ocean, the South China Sea had a long maritime tradition that predated the arrival of Europeans. Its maze of island archipelagoes and seacoasts generated the Malay term *orang laut*, or "sea people," who might sail in locally made *jongs*, or "junks," as far as China, India and Arabia. En route, they passed incoming Chinese, Indian, and Arab tradeships, and cosmopolitan port cultures emerged at places like Melaka, a Malay state on the strategic strait that connects South and East Asian sea-lanes.[13] After the Spanish established colonial ports in Manila and Acapulco in the sixteenth century, a hybridized new category of seafarers emerged. "Manila-men" served on Spanish galleons, often under the label "*Indios*," and crisscrossed the Pacific in the annual China trade for two hundred years, arriving in Mexico by the thousands. Some even reached Europe.[14]

Many were conscripted as greenhands who had to learn the ropes under rather harsh masters. Yet complaints about the incompetence of conscripts coexist in the Spanish records with praise for the seafaring skills of those Philippine islanders (including immigrant Chinese and mixed-race subjects) who learned Western nautical ways quickly and sometimes rose in rank to *steer* the ships—a rather appropriative image. As one Spaniard wrote, "[t]here is hardly an Indian who has sailed the seas who does not understand the mariner's compass, and therefore on this trade route there are some very skilful and dextrous helmsmen."[15] But Manila-men were paid about half of what Spanish sailors earned, and captains often neglected to pay them at all, giving them vouchers instead, which in desperation the crews in port might sell for a fraction of their value. The death rate among *Indios* in colder latitudes was high, their food rations were only half what Spaniards ate, and they were treated, according to one Spanish official, "like dogs."[16] It comes as no surprise, then, that many deserted in America. In 1618, one galleon lost seventy-four of her seventy-five *Indios* to desertion in Mexico, where local Native Americans hired them to brew palm wine![17]

Both Portuguese and Spanish shipping relied a great deal on foreign manpower. Despite government attempts to limit their numbers, alien sailors were both cheaper and more readily available in rival European and Asian ports.[18] As European trade overseas became more competitive, Manila-men served under a variety of flags. The nickname *Dutch* came to be applied to any mixed crew, because Dutch East India Company vessels used so many foreign sailors, including Malagasy and Malay slaves.[19] British and American fur traders who traveled between China and the northwest coast of America experienced chronic labor shortages because of deaths and desertion and hired regional replacements. Given their subaltern status, the loyalty of Manila-men in a crisis depended on the circumstances. Like many shipmates away from home, they might defend the vessel, as a Spaniard noted: "When placed on a ship from which they cannot escape, they fight with spirit and courage."[20] Yet Amasa Delano claimed that the British would not insure a vessel with even five or six Manila-men in its crew, because they sometimes collaborated with Malay pirates. In 1789, a Filipino named Anthony was killed by Hawaiians who stole a ship's boat, so the American captain allowed his vengeful Manila crew to unleash devastating cannon fire on local canoes that came out to trade; a year later, Hawaiians killed that captain's son, on another ship, along with his mostly Manila crew. In about 1800, a seal-hunting ship mistreated some Maoris in New Zealand, so they killed the whole crew except for a Filipino called Tommy Manilla. He settled down, married a local woman, and lived to old age, telling stories of the battle that changed his destiny.[21]

Ranajit Guha has argued that European expansionists in Asia might achieve domination over indigenous subjects through force or persuasion, but they could only achieve true hegemony, in the sense of immanent power, with a significant degree of local collaboration. The alternative response was resistance, which James Scott has shown may take many forms, from overt rebellion to more subtle noncooperation such as sabotage or work slowdowns.[22] "Lazy natives," then, were actually opting to do alien work on their own terms. Like resistance, collaboration was a multi-faceted strategy of response to domination that created an ambivalent space for subversive agency by supposedly subaltern natives, who could mediate the directives of their overlords in quietly empowering ways and ultimately manipulate the colonizer.[23] The above data on the Manila-men demonstrate such themes in the relations between European employers and their indigenous seamen. Clearly, there was coercion (but many European sailors were also "crimped," and brutalized, especially in wartime[24]), and also economic exploitation, relative to what European shipmates considered normal. But how did even "half" pay resonate in only partly monetarized societies where wages might be even lower than they were on foreign ships? What status symbols could Asian seamen acquire from their service at sea? Moreover, the fear of conspiracy or mutiny, the displacement of skills and control over firepower to able and vengeful crews, even the selective survival and opportunities for desertion on foreign shores reveal a slippery grasp by would-be colonizers over the aliens in their midst, whose sheer numbers, Delano said, could compromise the enterprise.

Some Manila-men, like Melville's Fedallah, were actually "seafaring Lascars" from South Asia.[25] After all, workers from the Indian subcontinent had labored in ports and on the ships plying their ocean for centuries before Europeans arrived, having long ago cracked the code of the monsoon winds.[26] After rounding Africa and entering what the Arabs called the *bahr al Hindi*, the Portuguese soon began employing Indians in similar tasks, circulating widely the local word *kuli* ("coolie") as a term for "wage-laborer." Another South Asian term for "worker" was *lascar*, derived from the Persian-Urdu word for "army or camp follower," which Europeans applied to native soldiers in their employ and later to hired sailors on their ships.[27] The Danes were among the first to recruit Indian seamen, from their colony in Fredericknagore, for as early as 1780 a Danish royal edict ordered captains to return their lascars home. By 1782, English officials shared that concern, because penniless Indian sailors were perceived as a problem in London.[28] In the early years, relatively few lascars served in British East India Company vessels, because the Navigation Acts restricted their numbers, but by the 1780s, crew shortages during the American and French Revolutions opened a floodgate of Indian seamen, until in the 1840s three thousand arrived in England every year. Missionaries finally opened an Asiatic sailors' home, which joined other boardinghouses in East London in catering to non-European seamen, including Manila-men, Pacific kanakas, and Africans.[29]

Rozina Visram has discussed the plight of lascars stranded in England, arguing that the East India Company tended to blame the Indian seamen themselves, or their compatriot overseers, for the fact that perhaps two hundred died in London every year. Hilton Docker, the company's physician, accused the Society for the Protection of Asiatic Sailors of "personal ignorance of the characters of the Native seamen"[30] and commended their confinement in a barracks and the harsh discipline enforced by Indian overseers (which included locking recalcitrants in coffin-sized cupboards). Otherwise, he claimed, the lascars would not only be victimized for the few possessions they had but also would become a threat to the public if "let loose" because of their abject poverty. Because of the frequently long waiting period until a ship could take them home, the Company and Society made some effort to provide them with temporary employment, only to incur the wrath of unemployed English and Irish laborers. Despite repeated Parliamentary inquiries and attempts to punish the Company if lascars were not returned home, the problem persisted until in 1857 (the year of the Indian Mutiny that terminated Company rule) the Strangers' Home was founded for Asiatics, Africans, and South Sea islanders. Non-Europeans who landed in other English ports were escorted to this facility in London until they could ship out. Many succumbed to the cold weather, and lascars being shipped home were often rounded up by force from the streets and, though technically passengers, forced to work their passage.[31]

Lascars endured gendered racial prejudice at sea, as Laura Tabili has argued. Like Chinese and Africans, they were assigned tasks on the basis of stereotypes. The work of stewards and cooks was considered effeminate and hence suited for "smaller" races than manly Englishmen, and menial work below deck on steamships, stoking the boilers in tropical heat, was also fit only for nonwhites, who were presumed able to work longer hours on less food and to sleep anywhere. The rise of British seamen's unions in the late nineteenth century narrowed work assignments even further and finally militated against hiring nonwhites at all. In Asian waters, however, the very prejudice against them gave lascars an ironic job security, if not decent working conditions. Sailors from different parts of India were categorized in ethnically essentialist terms, with some supposedly abler to stand cold and others easier to discipline. They were even praised as less drunken and intractable than their white shipmates, from whom they were kept segregated.[32]

Like other regionally recruited sailors, lascars were exploited physically and financially by their European employers, but Indian agency was also a factor. Indigenous recruiters controlled local hiring despite all British attempts at reform. A *ghat-serang* provided gangs of lascars who worked under their own shipboard supervisors, called *serangs*, creating a tendency toward larger crews, since the *ghat-serang* padded his contracts with relatives and debtors. Lascars were generally paid about one-fifth to one-third what their white counterparts earned, though their pay was often reduced by the bribes they paid to the *ghat-serang* and their work supervisors. Opinions about the quality of their food and clothing vary; though most sources say it was poor, lascars had their own cooks. By the 1820s, low-paid lascars often made up the majority of East India Company crews, and as the fleet declined in the 1840s, they almost monopolized labor on its vessels. When the transition was made to steam-powered ships not long afterward, lascars were especially sought after for work in the hot engine rooms. Employers used divide-and-rule tactics to control these native crews, by recruiting Muslim Pathans and Punjabis to work below deck, Christians from southwest India as messhands, and Hindu Bengalis as deckhands.[33]

Yet the category "lascar" was apparently as flexible as "Manila-men," suggesting the ultimate inadequacy of European efforts to camouflage their own dependency with manageable mental typologies. By 1855, the British merchant service employed about "12,000 lascars," half of whom arrived in England every year. Of those, 60 percent were Indians, 20 percent Malays, 10 percent Chinese, and 10 percent African or Arabian. Joseph Salter, a reformer in the 1870s, visited ships in London harbor and cited a dozen ethnic and regional categories among the non-European seamen, of whom Indians were simply the largest group.[34] Despite all the evidence for exploitation and mistreatment, Indian and other Asiatic seamen traveled on European vessels around the globe, muddling spatial distinctions between powerful cores and dominated peripheries in the Eurocentric world-system. Melville puts both "Lascars and Malays" on Regent Street in New Bedford, Massachusetts, while Visram notes that some lascars and Chinese seamen married European wives and set up their own boarding-houses in London, which reformers regarded as gambling and opium dens.[35] Lascars also made it into the Pacific, serving with *bêche-de-mer* stations in Micronesia and with sandalwood ships in the South Seas.[36] In 1826, a beachcomber on Tikopia known as Joe the Lascar provided Peter Dillon with the clue he needed to solve the forty-year mystery of the shipwreck of the French explorer *La Pérouse*.[37] Lascars, then, played a role in history making as well as profit making, carved out a space for themselves in the global maritime circuit, and, as we have seen, put down roots overseas. Though their employers feared they would be a threat to the "public," confining their circulation to their regions of origin failed.

Some Manila-men turned out not to be "Asians" but rather castaways in the Philippines from islands farther east, in Micronesia, the northwest portion of Oceania.[38] Like the Indian Ocean, the Pacific was already a map of seaways before Europeans arrived. Direct maritime links between Native American and Pacific islander seafarers are still a matter of intriguing speculation,[39] but the evidence for long-distance navigating skills and regular exchange networks among the inhabitants of Oceania is abundant.[40] As early as the 1520s, the Spanish began to kidnap islanders as guides and laborers, and by 1767 the British enlisted the first voluntary recruit on an exploring vessel, dubbing him "Joseph Freewill" to celebrate the occasion. Thereafter, French and British explorers in the Age of Enlightenment brought back specimens of what they regarded as "noble savagery" to Paris and London, where they created a sensation but often died of disease. The most impressive voyager on a British exploring ship was Tupaia, who traveled as a guide with Captain James Cook in 1769–70, from Tahiti through the central Pacific to New Zealand, Australia, and Java, where unfortunately he, too, died of disease. Tupaia was a trained navigator who drew a map of islands for Cook. He also acted as interpreter between Cook and the Maori of New Zealand, who named children after Tupaia and asked after him when Cook returned later on his second Pacific voyage. In fact, it could be argued that Tupaia's cross-cultural role was so important to Cook's contact with the Maori that he, not Cook, was the true explorer. As Sir Joseph Banks said of Tupaia among the Maori, "whenever he began to preach as we called it he was sure of a numerous audience who attended with most profound silence."[41] The episode is reminiscent of da Gama's Muslim pilot to India.

Oceanian visitors to the European-dominated power centers of world shipping made sharp comments to their white mentors that provide us with precious insights—however indirect, because they are not in the first person—into subversive perceptions by Pacific islanders of the West. A Hawaiian chief who had been to London proudly told an English visitor that "he saw plenty of poor people in England, but we see none here, that they got plenty of poi, taro and fish and none want for anything." Similarly, Maori chief Te Pahi lectured the English governor of Sydney about punishing convicts for stealing potatoes, because in Aotearoa (New Zealand) anyone who needed food received it. King Tupou of Tonga saw so many beggars in Sydney, many of whom were indigenous Aborigines, that he vowed never to sell any land to non-Tongans. Another comment on individualistic notions of private property came from a Micronesian who visited London and voiced surprise that people there lived in stacks of strangely isolated "boxes," some of which they put on wheels to get from one cubical hideaway to another. Maori chiefs Hongi Hika and Te Pehi Kupe were frank about why they voyaged to London: they only wanted guns with which to defeat their enemies and were unimpressed with most of the other gifts they got.[42] Such criticism or disdain of supposedly superior European civilization would have gladdened the heart of Jean-Jacques Rousseau, who cited similar reactions by Africans and Native Americans.[43]

As China traders and whalers followed the explorers' accounts to commercial resources, more Oceanians shipped out on foreign vessels, sometimes as victims of kidnapping but increasingly as volunteers seeking their fortune overseas, carrying on their ancestral voyaging traditions in new vehicles. They had to endure initiations into the shipboard life of their hosts, taking new names, dressing in strange clothes, learning new words, and experiencing exotic customs, such as the rite of Neptune when a greenhand first crossed the equator. In 1854, an American whale ship hired a Hope (Arorae) Islander, who was quickly adopted by his shipmates: "The old man sent him forward and told us to use him well and learn him something. One gave him a shirt, another a hat, pants, etc. We then cut his hair, put a knife in his pocket, Christened him Hope and had him metamorphosed into a Yankee sailor."[44] Many Oceanians on English ships were

called George, because of the monarchy, and nicknames given by crew-
mates often stuck, including Jim Crow for a Maori who earned his job not
only by successfully steering the ship but also by clowning. In fact, mimicry
seems to have been a common asset for many Oceanians seeking acceptance on foreign vessels, as when an American quickly taught two Hawaiian recruits "the English names of the ship's rigging, masts, spars, etc.,
which they learned very readily."[45] But as Homi Bhabha has said, mimicry
is a double-edged strategem for the "not quite/not white" that can be
subversive.[46] Kadu of Woleai imitated the walk of his captain, Otto von
Kotzebue, so well that the crew's amusement finally forced the commander
to ban such antics, and Richard Henry Dana reported that Hawaiian seamen sometimes poked fun at their white coworkers in chants.[47]

Kanakas,[48] as working Oceanian sailors were called by their employers,
did not always succeed in adapting to the cramped life in the forecastle;
some deserted, others mutinied, and many died. One recruit called Sam
Kanaka, a typical shipboard name, panicked when he could not communi-
cate effectively with his shipmates. The captain wrote, "[h]is eyes had a
rather wild and worried expression. . . . He soon began to get excited and
talked quite fast in his own tongue. I tried to calm him but he suddenly
grabbed me by the wrist and gave me such a wild look that I wrenched
myself free." Poor Sam wound up getting into a fight with his shipmates,
stabbed two, and was finally shot as he jumped from bunk to bunk shouting
words they could not understand.[49] Kanakas often started out as "waisters,"
meaning those who worked amidship doing whatever unskilled labor was
required. Such men earned low pay as seasonal hires who might be put
ashore on any generic island before their ship left the Pacific. The newspapers of nineteenth-century New England are filled with accounts of mutinies by Pacific islanders when they felt they were mistreated. On whale
ships, if they were not paid a customary share of the profits and remained
on board when the boat crews were out chasing whales, they might try to
seize the vessel. Gilbertese succeeded at this on the American whaler *John*
and vowed to sail the ship to a beach "where no white man lived."[50]

But some kanakas managed to earn promotions as harpooners, which
doubled their pay, and as boatswains, mates, or even captains of their own
schooners in coastal New Zealand. A literate Maori named James Earl Bailey
rose to chief mate on an Australian whale ship, and Hawaiian "Admiral"
John Hall captained schooners in the local interisland shipping service for
many years, amusing his passengers with the story of how he had been
sacked from the king's fleet.[51] As in the case of lascars and Manila-men, attempts to confine kanakas to their region failed. Typically, the British tried
to keep them from being stranded in Sydney by ordering ship captains to
see that kanakas were returned home, but more kept coming, especially

Maori from New Zealand. Hawaiian monarchs required ship captains to post bonds guaranteeing the safe return of recruits, and American missionaries warned against taking kanakas beyond Cape Horn, because of the ill health Polynesians encountered in strange climates. Nevertheless, hundreds still arrived in New England. They decorate New Bedford harbor in the opening pages of *Moby-Dick*, where Melville claimed that "actual cannibals stand chatting on the street corners."[52] Some Hawaiians, such as Henry Opukahaia, converted to Christianity in New England and inspired the first American missionaries to sail to the Pacific. But another Hawaiian called Tama disembarked from a Boston ship in the Marquesas and soon undermined the efforts of a local missionary. Tama told his native hosts that he had seen, firsthand, that white men had no gods.[53]

The shipboard category "kanaka" was at least as heterogeneous as "lascar" or "Manila-men," since Oceanian peoples speak more than one thousand languages and vary significantly in cultures and physical appearance. The intrusion of foreign vessels into their ancient, self-contained seafaring world, however, created new circuits of common experience for those who engaged their services as kanakas, an identity formation that expanded during the massive plantation labor trade of the late nineteenth century.[54] When they shared watches, manned boats together, or worked as unskilled "waisters," they joined a pan-Pacific society of "kanakadom." Learning shipboard terms could also form subaltern bonds between kanakas and other non-Europeans, as when Jo Bob of Rarotonga (Cook Islands) taught pidgin words to a black Portuguese from the Cape Verde Islands on night watch.[55] Those who disembarked from ships to become beachcombers on strange islands played a similar role to that of white or Asian beachcombers in the Pacific, namely as cultural mediators between ship and shore. Tama, for example, became a war leader for a Marquesan chief, another Hawaiian called Tuitui used his pidgin English to help a Tongan chief lure ships into ambushes, and still another Hawaiian piloted foreign vessels into Pago Pago harbor in Samoa. On Pohnpei in Micronesia, beachcombers from within and without Oceania created a near monopoly over commercial exchange between ships and shore.[56] Returnees to their own islands also demonstrated such appropriation by serving their chiefs as interpreters, trade advisers, founders of syncretic religious sects, war leaders, and pilots. In *Typee*, Melville hints at a circuit of what he labeled "tabooed kannakas" who used their travel experiences to become middlemen in trade by building local partnerships through gift exchanges.[57] Clearly, not only Manila-men could turn the liminal deck to their own purposes and even pose a threat to European domination.

Africans, too, worked on early modern European ships. Although information about their long-distance voyaging across the Atlantic is mostly speculative,[58] West Africans fished and traded along their coasts in canoes that could be as long as seventy feet and carry sixty men with cargo, and East Africans sailed the Indian Ocean monsoon winds.[59] As early as the late 1400s, Africans in the Cape Verde Islands and nearby mainland worked with Portuguese explorers and tradeships as *grumetes* (apprentices), visited the Mediterranean, intermarried with local Europeans to form a hybrid creole population along the West African coast, and ultimately created a maritime "Black Atlantic" that linked Africa, Europe, and the Americas in ways that a monolithic notion of the tragic slave trade's Middle Passage cannot encompass adequately.[60] Except for coastal stations where Europeans specialized in trading guns and other manufactured goods for war captives—thus making slave labor readily available for a wide range of uses, from domestic servants to exports—free Africans often found wage-earning niches as boatmen, interpreters, and cargo handlers. Some adopted quasi-European lifestyles, and as early as the 1600s were making a living as sailors on transatlantic voyages. When England began to suppress the slave trade in the late eighteenth and early nineteenth centuries, however, a new era began of paying opportunities for African seamen on foreign vessels.[61]

Most notable in West Africa were the Kru of Liberia, who served on British vessels beginning in the 1780s, when English abolitionists founded a protected port in Freetown, Sierra Leone. The origin of the ethnic term *Kru* appears to be a mix of local usage, for seamen hired out by an enterprising chief named Kulu, and the English term *crew*.[62] To distinguish themselves from enslaved Africans, the Kru tattooed a blue stripe down their forehead to the tip of their nose, and they enlisted in gangs led by their own foremen, bringing their canoes aboard to transport people and goods over the surf. Because West Africa has few natural harbors and a strong coastal current, Kru surfboats were often the only safe link between ship and shore; the boatmen paddled in unison, keeping time to chants led by their boatswain, and were valued for their ability to rescue cargo (and Europeans) if a wave capsized the canoe. The Dutch and French also hired African boatmen, not only for their maritime skills but also because equatorial heat and malaria made the Guinea coast a "white man's grave." In the 1830s, before quinine was developed as a preventive and cure for malaria, European ships might lose three-quarters of their white crews to fever attacks, as many as a fifth of them fatal, so that hiring African sailors became a logistical necessity.[63] The transition to steam-powered vessels in the mid-1800s reinforced this employment pattern, because the hot engine rooms, only a few degrees above the equator, were deemed unsuitable work environments for white crews.[64]

But like their counterparts in Oceania, African seamen also played important roles as brokers in trade. Many acted as interpreters for ships plying the Guinea coast and helped to bargain for ivory, gold, and palm oil, and like seasonally hired Pacific islanders, the Kru were usually let off down the African coast, near the Congo River, when their ship was finished trading. The alternative was for the ship to sail home before prevailing easterlies, which took it out into the Atlantic and to England, where its Kru would join lascars and Malays in the Strangers' Home. Most discharged Kru paddled their way back up the African coast in their canoes to Liberia, exchanging their hardware and cloth wages for local products, until they reached their home village as celebrated travelers. Because the Kru came from one main area, present-day eastern Liberia, they provide the most complete picture of a local society linked to shipping out. Their ethnic group was decentralized politically, as individuals competed for titles in an age-grade system and owed allegiance to a cluster of villages through marriage, trade, and migration. The greater a man's retinue, the greater his prestige, so that status was acquired through generosity. When a Kru mariner came home, he donned a dress suit for his first public appearance and paraded before the crowd, shooting off his gun. His new wealth and fame enabled him to pay off debts, acquire wives and land, earn promotions, and recruit younger dependent men for future voyages. Veteran Kru went out to foreign vessels in their canoes with work gangs and written recommendations to show ship captains. Some returned with syncretic religious ideas or modern weapons to resist colonial conquest, adapting their experiences to their own agendas.[65]

Twenty years ago, Eric Wolf argued that analyses of the process of global integration that accelerated when Europeans extended their power and influence overseas "must take account of the conjoint participation of western and non-western peoples," because "the common people were as much agents in the historical process as they were its victims and silent witnesses."[66] In the Pacific, Greg Dening has written of the "ambivalent space" on the decks of ships in strange ports, and of the cultural beaches that seamen cross going between ship and shore.[67] The above examples show that the expansion of European shipping was indeed a two-way process of cross-cultural contact, as seafarers from African, Asian, and Pacific waters joined the enterprise and counterexplored the new global maritime circuits. Despite the obvious inequalities embedded in their relationships with European and American employers (or kidnappers), individually and collectively non-Europeans could extract from that fluid frontier profits and meanings all their own, from status as cultural brokers to the acquisition of titles.

Their feedback often helped their home societies to adjust to the changes washing up on their beaches, thereby mediating the process of modernization. Oceanians made telling critiques of European civilization, and kanaka returnees or beachcombers became interpreters, boat pilots, war leaders, and preachers, forming subversive spaces between ship and shore. Kru turned their skills against foreign domination, as did Manila-men who cooperated with Malay pirates, or Oceanians who conspired in ship seizures. Lascars played such an important role in British shipping that those "muscles of empire" developed a growing seamen's union movement in the first half of the twentieth century.[68] Such groups defied attempts to be easily categorized or confined regionally,[69] retained significant degrees of indigenous agency, and ultimately reminded European colonialists that they were only visitors in ancient seafaring worlds. In a sense, they were forerunners of the large-scale migration from Third World countries to industrial cores today, reversing the roles of indigenous and immigrant. One example of the way that non-Europeans could appropriate the new global adventure was a Hawaiian in the 1820s who took the name Sir Joseph Banks, after serving in the China trade. In 1831, he bought his own Western-style schooner and set off for Tahiti, saying, "I like take the sun, sail out o' sight o' land, and go to any part o' the world."[70] Tupaia might have been proud.

Notes

1. Herman Melville, *Moby-Dick* (New York: Bantam, 1967), 205–6.
2. *Ibid.*, 139. Technically, such men were boat steerers, because after harpooning the whale, they changed places at the rudder with the mate in command of the boat, who made the final kill.
3. Rhys Richards, "'Manilla-Men' and Pacific Commerce," *Solidarity* 95 (1983), 47–57.
4. Melville, *Moby-Dick*, 520.
5. See, for example, J. H. Parry, *The Discovery of the Sea: An Illustrated History of Men, Ships and the Sea in the Fifteenth and Sixteenth Centuries* (New York: Dial Press; London: Weidenfeld and Nicolson, 1974).
6. Andre Gunder Frank, *Re-Orient* (Berkeley: University of California Press, 1998); and Eric Wolf, *Europe and the People without History* (Berkeley: University of California Press, 1982), 237.
7. K. N. Chaudhuri, *Trade and Civilisation in the Indian Ocean* (New York: Cambridge University Press, 1985), 63; and Charles Verlinden, "The Big Leap Under Dom João II: From the Atlantic to the Indian Ocean," John Hattendorf (ed.), *Maritime History, Vol. 1: The Age of Discovery* (Malabar, FL: Krieger, 1996), 80–1.
8. Pierre-Yves Manguin, "The Vanishing *Jong*: Insular Southeast Asian Fleets in Trade and War," Anthony Reid (ed.), *Southeast Asia in the Early Modern Era: Trade Power and Belief* (Ithaca, NY: Cornell University Press, 1993), 201.
9. Gang Deng, *Chinese Maritime Activities and Socioeconomic Development, c. 2100 B.C.–1900 A.D.* (Westport, CT: Greenwood, 1997), 159.
10. Kenneth McPherson, *The Indian Ocean: A History of People and the Sea* (Delhi: Oxford University Press, 1993), 187–9.
11. Samuel Eliot Morison, *The Maritime History of Massachusetts* (Boston: Houghton Mifflin, 1921), 158.
12. David Chappell, *Double Ghosts: Oceanian Voyagers on Euroamerican Ships* (Armonk, NY: M. E. Sharpe, Inc., 1997), 4.
13. Reid, *Southeast Asia in the Early Modern Period*, chapters 3 and 8; and Kenneth Hall, *Maritime Trade and State Development in Early Southeast Asia* (Honolulu: University of Hawaii Press, 1985). *Orang utan*, in Malay, means "jungle person."

14. O. H. K. Spate, *The Spanish Lake* (Canberra: Australian National University Press, 1979), 223; and Joseph Salter, *The Asiatic in England* (London: Seeley, Jackson and Halliday, 1873), 154. Chinese brought silks and porcelain to Manila and formed a community there, including sailors.
15. Quoted in William Schurz, *The Manila Galleons* (New York: Dutton, 1959), 211.
16. *Ibid.*, 212.
17. *Ibid.*, 211.
18. Pablo Perez-Mallaina, *Spain's Men of the Sea* (Baltimore: Johns Hopkins University Press, 1998), 55–61; and A. J. R. Russell-Wood, *The Portuguese Empire* (Baltimore: Johns Hopkins University Press, 1998), 41–55.
19. C. R. Boxer, *The Dutch Seaborne Empire* (New York: Penguin, 1990), 79–81.
20. Quoted in Schurz, *The Manila Galleons*, 211.
21. Richards, "'Manilla-Men' and Pacific Commerce," 48–52.
22. Ranajit Guha, *Dominance without Hegemony* (Cambridge, MA: Harvard University Press, 1997); and James Scott, *Weapons of the Weak: Everyday Forms of Peasant Resistance* (New Haven, CT: Yale University Press, 1985).
23. Brij Lal, Doug Munro, and Edward Beechert (eds.), *Plantation Workers: Resistance and Accommodation* (Honolulu: University of Hawaii Press, 1993), introduction.
24. Marcus Rediker, *Between the Devil and the Deep Blue Sea: Merchant Seamen, Pirates, and the Anglo-American Maritime World, 1700–1750* (New York: Cambridge University Press, 1987).
25. Schurz, *The Manila Galleons*, 210.
26. K. M. Panikkar, *India and the Indian Ocean: An Essay on the Influence of Sea Power in Indian History* (London: Allen and Unwin, 1951).
27. Hugh Tinker, *A New System of Slavery* (New York: Oxford University Press, 1974), 41–2; and Conrad Dixon, "Lascars: The Forgotten Seaman," Rosemary Ommer and Gerald Panting (eds.), *Working Men Who Got Wet* (St. John's: Memorial University of Newfoundland, 1980), 265.
28. Dixon, "Lascars: The Forgotten Seaman," 265.
29. Joseph Salter, *Asiatic in England*, 3; and Rozina Visram, *Ayahs, Lascars and Princes: The Story of Indians in Britain, 1700–1947* (London: Pluto Press, 1986), 34.
30. Visram, *Ayahs, Lascars and Princes*, 41.
31. *Ibid.*, chapter 3 and 204; and Paul Gordon and Danny Reilly, "Guest Workers of the Sea: Racism in British Shipping," *Race & Class* 28, no. 2 (autumn 1986), 73–82.
32. Laura Tabili, "A Maritime Race," Margaret Creighton and Lisa Norling (eds.), *Iron Men, Wooden Women: Gender and Seafaring in the Atlantic World, 1700–1920* (Baltimore: Johns Hopkins University Press, 1996), 169–88.
33. Dixon, "Lascars: The Forgotten Seaman"; and Tabili, "A Maritime Race," 176.
34. Visram, *Ayahs, Lascars and Princes*, 52–3; and Salter, *Asiatic in England*.
35. Melville, *Moby-Dick*, 39; Visram, *Ayahs, Lascars and Princes*, 51.
36. Dorothy Shineberg (ed.), *The Trading Voyages of Andrew Cheyne* (Honolulu: University of Hawaii Press, 1971), 290.
37. Peter Dillon, *Narrative and Successful Result of a Voyage in the South Seas* (London: Hurst, Chance, 1829), vol. 1, 33; and J. W. Davidson, *Peter Dillon* (New York: Oxford University Press, 1975), 75, 131.
38. Shineberg, *Trading Voyages*, 333–7.
39. Thor Heyerdahl, "Tucume and the Maritime Heritage of Peru's North Coast," Thor Heyerdahl, Daniel Sandweiss, and Alfredo Narvaez, *Pyramids of Tucume: The Quest for Peru's Forgotten City* (London: Thames and Hudson, 1995), 29–33; and Peter Buck, *Vikings of the Pacific* (Chicago: University of Chicago Press, 1959), 322.
40. Douglas Oliver, *Oceania* (Honolulu: University of Hawaii Press, 1989), vol. 1, chapter 12; and Ben Finney, *Voyage of Rediscovery* (Berkeley: University of California Press, 1994).
41. Quoted in Chappell, *Double Ghosts*, 74.
42. *Ibid.*, 166–7.
43. Jean-Jacques Rousseau, *The First and Second Discourses*, ed. Roger Masters (New York: St. Martin's Press, 1964), 224–6.
44. Log of the *Sea Shell*, Warren, Log George Wheldon, October 2, 1854; C. S. Stewart, *A Visit to the South Seas in the US Ship Vincennes, During the Years 1829 and 1830* (New York: Praeger, 1970).

45. J. C. Mullett, *A Five Years' Whaling Voyage, 1848–1853* (Fairfield, WA: Galleon, 1977), 44–6.

46. Homi Bhabha, *The Location of Culture* (New York: Routledge, 1994), 92.

47. Chappell, *Double Ghosts*, chapter 4, 61–2.

48. A Hawaiian word meaning "person" that spread widely in shipboard and plantation pidgin.

49. Harold Williams (ed.), *One Whaling Family* (Boston: Houghton Mifflin, 1964), 292–6.

50. R. Gerard Ward (ed.), *American Activities in the Central Pacific* (Ridgewood, NJ: Gregg Press, 1966), vol. 6, 141–51.

51. Mifflin Thomas, *Schooner from Windward* (Honolulu: University of Hawaii Press, 1983), 26–61.

52. Melville, *Moby-Dick*, 39.

53. Chappell, *Double Ghosts*, 80.

54. Clive Moore, *Kanaka: A History of the Melanesian Mackay* (Port Moresby: University of Papua New Guinea, 1985); and Peter Corris, *Port, Passage and Plantation* (Melbourne: University of Melbourne Press, 1973). Some 120,000 Oceanians worked on overseas plantations.

55. Chappell, *Double Ghosts*, 51.

56. David Chappell, "Secret Sharers: Indigenous Beachcombers in the Pacific Islands," *Pacific Studies* 17, no. 2 (June 1994), 1–22.

57. Herman Melville, *Typee: A Peep at Polynesian Life* (New York: Penguin, 1972), 120, 192–203, 328–33.

58. Ivan Van Sertima, *They Came Before Columbus* (New York: Random House, 1976).

59. Walter Rodney, *A History of the Upper Guinea Coast* (New York: Monthly Review Press, 1970), 16–8; and John Middleton, *The World of the Swahili* (New Haven, CT: Yale University Press, 1992).

60. W. Jeffrey Bolster, *Black Jacks: African American Seamen in the Age of Sail* (Cambridge, MA: Harvard University Press, 1997), 9–10, 47–67. See also Paul Gilroy, *The Black Atlantic: Modernity and Double Consciousness* (Cambridge, MA: Harvard University Press, 1993).

61. George Brooks, *The Kru Mariner* (Newark: University of Delaware Press, 1972), 1–3; and Bolster, *Black Jacks*, 9.

62. David Chappell, "Kru and Kanaka: Participation by African and Pacific Island Sailors in Euroamerican Maritime Frontiers," *International Journal of Maritime History* 6, no. 2 (December 1994), 91–2.

63. W. F. W. Owen, *Narrative of Voyages to Explore the Shores of Africa, Arabia and Madagascar* (New York: n.p., 1833), 104.

64. Tabili, "A Maritime Race," 178.

65. Chappell, "Kru and Kanaka," 93–4, 111.

66. Wolf, *Europe and the People without History*, ix–x.

67. Greg Dening, *The Bounty* (Melbourne: Melbourne University Press, 1988), 31; and *Islands and Beaches* (Honolulu: University of Hawaii Press, 1980), 34.

68. F. Broeze, "The Muscles of Empire," *Indian Economic and Social History Review* 18, no. 1 (1981), 43–67.

69. For example, after many years of double-crewing—that is, sending home lascars as "passengers" on ships leaving England while the vessel was nominally worked by British seamen (to conform to the Navigation Acts)—the laws were changed in 1849, in effect declaring the lascars "British for purposes of shipping," and enabling them to be employed officially for both legs of the run to India. As late as 1970, however, England was still trying to prohibit black seamen, from Africa or India, from being discharged in its ports, a testimony to the impossibility of preventing it for more than two hundred years. Gordon and Reilly, "Guest Workers of the Sea," 74.

70. Quoted in Chappell, *Double Ghosts*, 152.

CHAPTER **5**

Staying Afloat
Literary Shipboard Encounters
from Columbus to Equiano

BERNHARD KLEIN

I

Sunday, 16 December [1492] . . . [C]oming from the coast of the island of Española and sailing close-hauled because presently at the hour of terce the wind blew from the E, in mid gulf he encountered a canoe with a solitary Indian in it, and the Admiral was amazed at the way he managed to remain afloat [cómo se podía tener sobre el agua] with the strong wind. He had him and his canoe brought aboard the ship and flattered him with some presents of glass beads, hawk's bells and brass rings. . . .[1]

That Columbus should have been surprised about the seafaring skills of the maritime people he encountered on this, his first voyage to the Indies, is strictly in keeping with his attitude throughout his logbook[2] of viewing the natives as tabula rasa, as lacking the inscription of culture and civilization on their bodies and souls—a mental reflex only reinforced by the nakedness he observed all around him. The surprise is feigned to some degree—even Columbus notes often enough the existence and assistance of the local guides who made the foreign space of the Caribbean Sea accessible to him. Recent studies have increased our understanding of the dependence of early Western explorers and seafarers in foreign waters on indigenous knowledge and navigational skills; even J. H. Parry, for whom the early modern "discovery of the sea"[3] was a strictly European achievement, acknowledges that "most of the European explorers relied heavily . . . upon local knowledge and skill."[4] In the previous essay of this volume, David Chappell has impressively reconstructed some of the crucial roles indigenous seafarers were to play on Western ships from the sixteenth century onward, and described the changes these maritime encounters have brought to their lives.[5] Such insights still need frequent retelling, if only to correct the falsely triumphalist image of Europe's unchallenged maritime superiority.

In this essay I want to exploit the image of the tiny canoe, manned by a single native, next to the full-rigged, well-found Spanish *nao*[6] to make a slightly different point. On the one hand, the symbolic story it tells is familiar enough. The classic colonial encounter is here structured on various levels around the discursive opposition between raw nature and refined civilization: naked Indians versus clothed Spaniards, a primitive canoe versus the sophisticated deep-sea vessel, coasting versus navigation, and so on. To fall for trinkets such as "glass beads, hawk's bells and brass rings" is a relapse into childish ignorance made doubly pitiful by inviting direct comparison with the skill and courage of European seafarers who have mastered the space and time of the Atlantic, who can note with accuracy their position far from home at this "hour of terce [when] the wind blew from the E." The "Indian," in this episode, emerges as the atemporal, prehistoric, prelapsarian creature the discipline of anthropology was later to invent as one of the founding fictions of modernity.

But on the other hand, the moment of direct encounter—when the Indian and his canoe were "brought aboard the ship"—can be made to tell a different story. The indigenous canoe may be swallowed here by the Spanish ship just as the people and the culture of the Caribbean were soon to be swallowed by Europe, but the reverse angle would rather bring into focus an already hybrid shipboard community made still more hybrid by the arrival in their midst of a "solitary Indian" from Hispaniola: Columbus had already taken on board a number of other natives from different islands in the few weeks since his arrival, several members of the nominally Catholic expedition were probably Marranos, including Luís de Torres, a speaker of Hebrew, Arabic, and Chaldean[7] (the Admiral had to keep open his options on how to converse with the Great Khan), Columbus himself hailed from Genoa, not from Spain, and although his crew was largely Spanish (from Andalusía and the north), "there also were sailors from Portugal, Italy and Flanders, and possibly one or two from the Levant and North Africa"[8] (and the sizable Spanish contingent actually made the crew untypical, for such relative national homogeneity was not customary on comparable fifteenth-century ships[9]). The cultural proliferation on board the *Santa María* is all the more notable in view of the opening reference in Columbus's journal to an early modern instance of ethnic cleansing: the expulsion of Jews[10] and Muslims from Spain in 1492, which was one significant step toward maintaining (in fact, creating) the imperial fiction of an all-white, all-Christian Europe. The community of the ship—if we accept for a moment the *Santa María* as both parody and paradigm—disputes that fiction by turning what was legally a territorial extension of Spain into its multi-cultural opposite.

In terms of its spatial properties, the ship thus assumes the guise of a heterotopia (in Foucault's coinage), a place, space, or countersite "in which the real sites, all the other real sites that can be found within the culture, are simultaneously represented, contested, and inverted."[11] Such sites are social reflectors that function as "a kind of effectively enacted utopia"[12] because in contradistinction to the "no-place" or "good place" that Thomas More first imagined in 1516, these are real rather than virtual sites. Their function in relation to the world they reflect or represent, Foucault suggests, is either to create a space of illusion (exposing all other spaces as even more illusory) or a space of compensation (presenting as perfect and well ordered what is actually imperfect and disordered), but the function of the ship, "the heterotopia *par excellence*,"[13] would rather seem to create a space of cultural expansion and imaginative possibility—in the sense of suggesting and making possible historical alternatives and unexplored choices:

> [I]f we think, after all, that the boat is a floating piece of space, a place without a place, that exists by itself, that is closed in on itself and at the same time is given over to the infinity of the sea and that, from port to port, from tack to tack, from brothel to brothel, it goes as far as the colonies in search of the most precious treasures they conceal in their gardens, you will understand why the boat has not only been for our civilization, from the sixteenth century until the present, the great instrument of economic development . . . but has simultaneously been the greatest reserve of the imagination. . . . In civilizations without boats, dreams dry up, espionage takes the place of adventure, and the police take the place of pirates.[14]

In its baroque opulence, this language is clearly infected by the romance of the sea, a mode of imagining the maritime world that Auden claims was a "revolutionary change" in style and sensibility only at the end of the eighteenth century.[15] The point I find more significant, though, than the charge of anachronism is the suggestion that ships can be read as spaces that enable an inversion or contestation of the world they would claim not only to re-create in fact and spirit but even to export wholesale to distant shores.

One of the most famous literary heterotopias of maritime provenance encompassed by this conceptual agenda was published within a year of Columbus's return to Europe: Sebastian Brant's *Narrenschiff*, the *stultifera navis* or *Ship of Fools*.[16] The design of the book is to equate all manifestations of human folly with the natural element that is as fickle and treacherous as any man without reason; the mad ship acts as "a floating body used to seclude lunatics, who were thus committed to the element that was in keeping with their unpredictable temperament."[17] The maritime metaphor capitalizes on the identification of the ship as an enclosed and self-contained microcosm that reproduces in miniature the social world from which the ship is detached: "our barge," Alexander Barclay translates Brant in 1509, "Lyke as a myrrour dothe represent agayne / the fourme and fygure of mannes countenaunce."[18] Perhaps only a cultural imagination that still encoded the sea as the morally transgressive and inherently repulsive realm of formless matter and unfinished creation was amenable to such a literary conceit.[19] Important here for my purposes is the form of the equation between land and sea that works by inversion, opposition, and definition *ex negativo*: a heterotopic vision that captured the self-image of society by turning the sea into its own negative countersite.

The ship of fools sails the ocean but has no destination: "We kepe the streme and touche nat the shore / In Cyte nor in Court we dare nat well auenter."[20] No greater conceptual difference from the spirit of Columbus's enterprise—and from the narrative drive of the journal—can perhaps be imagined than the lack of purpose and direction that defines Brant's mad voyage. Columbus was anything but uncertain or equivocal about his aims and motives, even if the eventual outcome of his Atlantic crossing was to be so different from what he had initially expected. "*23 October.* The best thing is to go where there is most business to be done, and I hold that it is not right to delay, but better to be on our way and keep moving until we find a profitable land."[21] The sea, to Columbus, was not the symbolic habitat of madness or a place of enforced exile, as for the yoyagers on Brant's textual vessel, but a mere obstacle on the way to somewhere else—a space to cross through speedily, a means of making land accessible, of putting it within reach. From this perspective, Columbus's journal and Brant's moral satire, though written at the same historical juncture and in response to the same worldly challenges (but composed, significantly, in proximity to different elements: respectively on water and on land), ostensibly define the opposite ends of a spectrum of symbolic possibility: the sea comes to signify either a modern space of economic potential and unlimited expansion, or a realm of moral transgression stretching beyond the ancient *limits* of the world.

Such a reading is familiar and certainly plausible, but what I want to argue here is that while these texts might be seen to occupy opposing conceptual ground with regard to the cultural meaning of the ocean voyage, they are also unified at their extremes: in both narratives, the image of the hybrid shipboard scenario suggests the transformational force of the maritime cultural encounter that might work against the grain of the contexts in which we are wont to place them. That is to say, when viewed from aboard ship rather than from the (historical or literary) shore, the *Santa María* can turn on its head the idea of an ethnically cleansed Spain that prepares itself for the conquest of the New World, and the ship of fools implies less the exclusion of socially marginalized "lunatics" than the heterotopic freedom of the ocean later given social and material shape by communities of pirates, freebooters, and buccaneers.[22] The reality of the ship, a tight internal power structure,[23] that was often viewed from outside as a source of infection, disease, and epidemics, whose very presence in the harbor "threatened the health of the city,"[24] complicates such contrapuntal readings but does not dispute, in my view, that real and metaphorical seas might indeed enable cultural definitions of the seafarer or voyager that are at odds with the wider historical and contextual circumstances of any particular maritime crossing.

To substantiate this claim—which I expect to be controversial—I want to take the image of the heterotopic shipboard community forward in time and examine its political implications during Britain's rise to the dominant sea power of the modern era—that is, the period from the early seventeenth to the late eighteenth century. I will concentrate on just four literary shipboard encounters, in each of which the ship can be read, in the terms suggested above, as an alternative cultural space that contradicts and even inverts the power structures of which it is nominally a part, thus offering an imaginative—and in at least one case, very real—escape from patterns of inequality and victimization. My examples are all taken from canonical texts: starting with one of Shakespeare's Roman plays (*Antony and Cleopatra*), moving on to novels by Aphra Behn (*Oroonoko*) and Daniel Defoe (*Robinson Crusoe*), and ending with the autobiography of Olaudah Equiano (*The Interesting Narrative*, also discussed in this volume by Gesa Mackenthun), I will pursue textual associations between sea voyaging, the heterotopia of the ship, and transnational confrontations and exchanges. The cultural definitions enabled by the shipboard encounters recorded in these texts, I will argue, emerge as strikingly different in substance and character, yet together they are representative of the diverging trajectories of two interlocked historical narratives: the growing technological and conceptual mastery of the ocean by European seafarers, and the parallel "loss" of control over the definition of ethnic and national identity that such maritime explorations intially set out to maintain.

II

Carl Schmitt locates the emergence of a (Eurocentric) global order based on the conceptual division between sea and land squarely in the sixteenth century. "For the first time in the history of mankind the contrast between *land* and *sea* serves as the world-embracing foundation of a global law of nations."[25] Only now—after circumnavigation had furnished material evidence that all the seas of the world were really just one vast navigable ocean—were land and sea fully conceived of as different *kinds* of spaces, fundamentally at odds with each other: while the land can be divided up into zones of occupation, into legally defined spheres owned by specific states, the sea is exterritorial, belongs to no one, and transcends all earth-related property laws. It lies beyond the realm, territory, and power of any single state.[26] England, Schmitt claims (meaning Britain), by being the first and only nation to seize the maritime energies of the new spatial world order—essentially, now, an oceanic rather than a terrestrial culture—emerged as the most powerful global player (in modern parlance) until the end of the nineteenth century,[27] a transition from an army of sheepshearers and landlocked farmers to a navy of pirates, sea dogs, and admirals that was still unthinkable at the start of the sixteenth century but that had, in Elizabethan times, long begun to exert its powerful influence on the cultural imagination.

Living in London, the greatest seaport in the country, where an official visitor from Venice claimed in 1596, "one sees nothing but ships and seamen" along the forty- or fifty-mile stretch down the Thames to the sea,[28] Shakespeare was an articulate witness to this incipient maritime consciousness. Especially significant here are the later plays such as *Pericles* or *The Tempest*, where the sea represents a cultural and often legally delicate sphere of political action. In *Pericles*, for instance—a tale of shipwreck, storm, dispersal, capture by pirates, loss of life, miraculous recovery, and eventual reunion—the sea serves to propel Pericles, the seafarer, in a centrifugal[29] and essentially imperial move away from his generic "home" toward new shores, and thus underwrites his imaginative existence so prominently that a recent critic has dubbed it "the play's second protagonist, facilitator of and actor in Pericles' imperial story."[30] The crucial use of the sea in *The Tempest* hardly requires much comment here, as the tropes of storm, shipwreck, and the island castaway, as well as the imaginative fusion of Atlantic and Mediterranean geographies in a plot that rehearses the political set piece of the coup d'état along with the power structures of colonial oppression, have been extensively discussed in recent criticism.[31] The play equates island, ship, and theater as symbolically and socially analogous sites, shaping Prospero's multiple roles as political sovereign, "captain of the ship of state," and master of ceremonies. At the end of the play, Prospero departs the island in a "bravely rigged" ship (5.1.227),[32] bearing fully reconstituted passengers that have all suffered the profound "sea change" of moral transformation.

While other Shakespearean plays engage the sea in terms equally responsive to the contemporary maritime experience—I'm thinking here for instance of the sea and its "merchant-marring rocks" (3.2.270)[33] in *The Merchant of Venice*, or of the shipwreck that separates the twins in *Twelfth Night*—none makes the categorial distinction between land and sea more central to its purpose than *Antony and Cleopatra*. Not only is the land-sea divide that Schmitt sees as the defining moment of political modernity constitutive of the dramatic action in this play—which Shakespeare based largely on his reading of Plutarch's *Life of Marcus Antonius*[34]—it is also, I want to argue here, the enabling condition and metaphorical correlate of Antony's "rioting in Alexandria" (2.2.76)[35] and all the associated cultural meanings of his hedonism so reviled by Caesar, as well as the origin of the political and erotic tension that eventually results in the nemesis of both protagonists.

Despite the classical setting, the play rehearses many issues of contemporary political concern,[36] including a debate over the status of the sea as either a theater of multi-ethnic, multi-cultural encounters or as simply a spatial extension of land-based forms of imperial rule. This conflict comes to a head in what is perhaps the most successful, certainly the most dramatically evocative, maritime scene in the play: the meeting of the "three world-sharers" (2.7.67) Antony, Octavius Caesar, and Lepidus on Pompey's galley in Act 2 where they celebrate their (temporary) success in averting a major political crisis. The symbolic force of this shipboard encounter derives from the juxtaposition of the unstable, murderous world of politics with the unpredictable and dangerous sea; the slippery planks of the boat made even more slippery by the blurred vision resulting from the considerable intake of wine. Their respective alcoholic consumption anticipates the fate of each of the three leaders: Caesar, the eventual victor and sole ruler of the Roman Empire, remains sober and complains about the "wild disguise"—that is, the oceanic drinking session—that "hath almost / Anticked us all" (2.7.119–20); Antony revels in drink-induced pleasure and proposes a toast to Lethe, the river of oblivion; while Lepidus loses control and is carried off board halfway through the scene. He will be the first to fall. Of the unequal trio, only Antony prefers ship to shore, a desire entirely in keeping with his "overflowing" character (compare 1.1.2) that champions dionysiac delights over the exigencies of public office. "The sea," John Gillies claims, "is Antony's symbolic element."[37] This speculative but accurate equation transfers onto the dramatic character the principal metaphoric associations of Fortune's traditional domain: amorphous essence, uncertainty, risk, hazard, dissolution, forgetting, ecstacy, swoon.

The sea is more than a purely symbolic entity when we consider the wider political and cultural contexts of the encounter aboard Pompey's galley. Even though the ostensible threat posed by Pompey's piracy to the rule of the triumvirs is quickly averted, the real drama enacted on board is the growing irreconcilability of Antony's desire for the "soft beds" of the East (compare 2.6.50) with Caesar's insistence on the "true" values of Roman masculinity. The point here is that Antony's Egyptian revels are no mere personal pleasure hunt but a political threat. Historically, Antony modeled his political career on Alexander, promoted a "cosmopolitan" concept of empire without surrounding vassal states, favored the East over the West, and fashioned his erotic liaison with Cleopatra in open defiance of the Roman preference for ethnic segregation.[38] The sea, to Antony, is the enabling condition of such a dream of union across the waters that separate (or, in his view, link) East and West, and he is the only character in this play of many travelers and vast spaces who ever voyages across the Mediterranean without an explicitly military agenda. Indeed, Antony alone, whose cultural crossings suggest tentative equality among different cultures rather than the automatic dominance of the West, manages to withstand the Roman impulse to conquer and subdue the sensual otherness of Egypt.[39] On board Pompey's galley, the opposing conceptions of the sea as a space of contact and hedonistic pleasure (Antony), of piracy and power politics (Pompey), or of masculine military aggression (Caesar) define the subliminal conflict in the dialogue among the world leaders.

That the world is heterotopically reflected in the ship is obvious to Mena, Pompey's sidekick, who suggests his master could be "lord of all the world" (2.7.58) if he cut loose the vessel to disconnect the triumvirs from the shore: "And when we are put off, fall to their throats. All there is thine" (2.7.69–70). The suggestion is intriguing for the implicit notion that only contact with the land sustains the triumvirs' power, but owing to Pompey's curiously misplaced sense of personal honor, the plan comes to nothing. Piracy, in other words, is not an option. On board it is Antony rather than the host who dominates proceedings, raising his glass and leading the revels to the disgust of Caesar, who fears that their "graver business / Frowns at this levity" (2.7.115–6). Antony's famous refusal to give an adequate description of the crocodile reflects the symbolic onboard triumph of his version of empire. "*Lepidus*: What manner o' thing is your crocodile? *Antony*: It is shaped, sir, like itself, and it is as broad as it hath breadth. It is just so high as it is, and moves with its own organs. It lives by that which nourisheth it, and the elements once out of it, it transmigrates" (2.7.38–42). What Antony is denying here in tautological circularity is the transfer of exotic or indigenous meaning into the semantic code of the conqueror,[40] a refusal of ethnic pigeonholing that did not carry the day at Actium.

For in the second and final shipboard encounter of the play, acted out across Antony and Cleopatra's combined fleet at the Battle of Actium, the symbolic triumph of Antony's seaborne conception of self and empire gives way to defeat and annihilation. The doomed couple decide to fight

Caesar by sea, for no better reason than "that he dares [them] to't" (3.7.29). The deeper reason for this foolish move is that for the two lovers, there is indeed no other possible stage than the open sea to live their alternative project of empire. At Actium their shipboard liaison proves catastrophic, as Cleopatra confirms every Roman stereotype of her character when, stung "like a cow in June," she "Hoists sails and flies" (3.11.14–5). The battle is lost twice, militarily by both lovers and symbolically by Antony alone, who, in a moment of recognition that makes him pronounce the maritime keyword of the play, feels his authority "melting" from him (compare 3.13.90).[41] He literally melts into ocean after Actium, consigning to the waves the dream of oceanic hedonism so powerfully evoked on Pompey's galley.

If we discover in Antony's maritime exploits (as I suggest we should) an oblique historical comment on the form of Britain's empire that was beginning to take political shape in Shakespeare's time,[42] the idea of cultural union across ethnic difference may seem rather anachronistic by contrast with, for instance, the voyage narratives collected in Richard Hakluyt's *Principal Navigations* (1589/1600). Generally, Hakluyt records voyages that resemble Columbus's expedition in spirit (and often in destination), motivated as they are by the desire for imperial expansion and economic profit. By comparison, if Antony's barge does not fully morph into a ship of fools, it certainly makes his enterprise look like a historical delusion in the context of the Atlantic colonizing projects of the early seventeenth century, when the play was written. Still, my claim here is that in his transgressive travels, Antony embraces a concept of the sea as a zone of freedom and open encounter rather than of colonial submission (admittedly a notion to which he is also frequently susceptible).

In the centuries that followed, cross-cultural maritime wanderings of the kind that Antony prefigured in Shakespeare's play were all too often instances of enforced rather than voluntary travel. In the final section, I want to discuss three such involuntary seafarers of the "long" eighteenth century, Oroonoko, Friday, and Olaudah Equiano, for all of whom the cultural crossings effected on board ship resulted in a sea change or profound transformation. My reasons for claiming these figures as protagonists of an alternative maritime narrative is that between them they chart a history of increasing individual agency on the part of the indigenous people Europeans encountered and frequently enslaved in those parts of the world the mental geography of the West would continue to define as "remote" or "peripheral."[43]

III

From a mercantile perspective, there was nothing at all peripheral about the North Atlantic trading network that the old seaports of Britain began

to control in the seventeenth century, and which included most prominently the coastal factories in West Africa, the colonial settlements in the
Caribbean, and the rapidly growing ports along the North American coast.
Each region was vital to the economic success of the new colonial system
that "helped to triple English shipping tonnage in the last half of the seventeenth century,"[44] and each was connected to the others by an ever-increasing flow of goods and people along English trade routes, "arteries of the
imperial body between 1650 and 1750." Enabling transnational links and
cross-cultural contacts, these trade routes "unified distant parts of the
globe, different markets, and distinct modes of production,"[45] and the
brokers of this global maritime circuit were a motley crew of seamen who
operated the engine of progress central to the rapid process of modernization in the eighteenth century: the sailing ship, "an extraordinary forcing-
house of internationalism."[46]

Images of the mixing and fusing of different cultures aboard ship con-
jure up the world of romantic sea adventures but quickly lose much of their
appeal when we recall that the cargo in the ship's hold included millions of
Africans transported by force across the Atlantic. Oroonoko and Olaudah
Equiano both fall victim to the slave economy that developed within this
North Atlantic scenario, and like Friday they suffer the violent displacement
that makes all three biographies—two fictional, one factual—resonate with
the inherent contradictions of an emerging global trading network that
rested so thoroughly on the denial of the rights of man.

Aphra Behn's Restoration novella *Oroonoko* (1688) opens in Coramantien (in modern-day Ghana), a slave factory on the Gold Coast but
described by Behn like an oriental kingdom, where a conflict between
Prince Oroonoko and his uncle, the king, over the love of Imoinda ends
with her being sold into slavery and transported across the Atlantic to
Suriname (historically still an English colony at the time the novella is
set). The transition to the second part of the tale begins, in appropriately
maritime fashion, "when there arrived in the port an English ship" (32–3).[47]
The melancholic prince is lured into a friendship with the English captain, a slave trader, who betrays Oroonoko and forces him and several
of his followers into a transatlantic passage. Arriving weeks later in the
Caribbean, Oroonoko is sold as a slave, meets Imoinda again, and eventually stages an abortive rising against his European captors. The novella
ends when Oroonoko is almost ritually dismembered as punishment for
leading the revolt of the Suriname slaves.

Oroonoko is a tale of two continents, and the sea is the great connector
between the two parts of the story. Reflecting the operational range of
the triangular trade system, the spatial framework is Atlantic rather than
Mediterranean, as it still was for Antony, or for Oroonoko's ethnic precur-

sor on the Elizabethan stage, Othello.[48] The linchpin of the action is the ocean voyage, which focalizes the terms of the cultural encounter at the center of the narrative. The keywords that describe the attitude of Oroonoko and his followers on board ship are *dignity* and *honor*: to preserve the former, they go on a hunger strike; after an appeal to the latter, they call off their onboard protest. The mediator between the captain and his human cargo is Oroonoko, whose main concern, in his negotiations with the captain, is that he would "give credit to his words" (36). The use of the word *credit* here is important, because for Oroonoko this expression is still owed to ancient forms of affective, precapitalist economies, based on one meaning of the word *credit*: "credence, faith, trust." The crucial point is that Oroonoko entirely fails to see that it is the modern, financial sense of *credit* that motivates the actions of his opponent, who is worried only that "the loss [through starvation] of so many brave slaves, so tall and goodly to behold, would have been very considerable" (34). Oroonoko is in fact made a willing tool of the slave-trading circuit when he believes the captain's false promise of freedom and in return orders his men to end their hunger strike, thus ensuring a safe Middle Passage.

That the opposing values of honor and business should be brought into such sharp contrast on board the transatlantic slaver epitomizes the inherently ambiguous function of the sailing ship as a catalyst of economic change. In terms of the story Behn tells, the ship, while sailing all along under the flag of an economically sanctioned racism, deceives her protagonist into mistaking it for a place where his old-fashioned code of honor still prevails. The social structure of the onboard debate—with Oroonoko and the captain each at the head of a hierarchically ordered body of followers—confirms the misconception so completely that Oroonoko fails to recognize the new in the guise of the old: this is neither a military nor a feudal hierarchy—social structures he is familiar with—but a purely mercenary shipboard alliance in the interest of maximizing financial profit. Upon arrival in the Caribbean, the ship releases Oroonoko into the hybrid, diasporic, and degrading existence of slavery that negates his own royal character so completely that he is eventually driven to the extreme of murdering Imoinda, in a desperate attempt to save his last vestige of self-respect and avoid their mutual child being born a slave.

The human cost of the slave economy Behn so suggestively evokes is all but occluded by Friday's willing acceptance of the master-slave relationship in Defoe's castaway tale *Robinson Crusoe* (1719). Oroonoko is "an African slave who was once a king,"[49] a proud, haughty figure who refuses to fit the image of the docile servant cut out for him by his oppressors. Friday, by contrast, is presented entirely as the creature of his master, Crusoe, who sees nothing in him but his "stark naked" (209)[50] appearance and his natural disposition to "subjection, servitude, and submission" (209). Crusoe proceeds to clothe him, feed him, convert him to Christianity, and teach him how to use firearms, until he can finally claim that "my man Friday was a Protestant" (241). All this is a colonial fantasy of white cultural supremacy and a direct reversal of the actual turn a historical castaway experience would have taken, which usually meant that displaced Europeans had to adapt to indigenous manners and customs, rather than vice versa.[51]

The one area where Crusoe has little to teach Friday is—importantly in this context—boatbuilding and navigation.[52] "I asked Friday a thousand questions about the country, the inhabitants, the sea, the coast, and what nations were near; he told me all he knew with the greatest openness imaginable" (217). Obviously, he knew quite a bit about island politics and local waterways. Crusoe also finds Friday "a most dextrous fellow at managing" his "little frigate" (226), and when they select a tree from which to build a canoe, "I found he knew much better than I what kind of wood was fittest for it" (228). Although Crusoe claims Friday "knew nothing what belonged to a sail or a rudder" and that when exposed to the technology of sail, "he stood like one astonished and amazed" (229), he might have seen a Spanish deep-sea vessel before (compare 224) and certainly did not take long to learn how to operate a sailing boat. Crusoe's claim that Friday "became an expert *sailor*" (229, my italics) only under his tuition is thus misleading when taken to mean that Friday's ability to handle a boat was entirely subject to his master's teaching. It is hardly surprising, then, that Crusoe feels attracted to his "new companion" (213), since with his maritime expertise, "this poor savage might be a means to help me [make my escape from this place]" (218).

Friday's evident seafaring skills square neither with Crusoe's description of him as a man of little or no learning, who had to be taught "every thing that was proper to make him useful, handy and helpful" (213), nor do they make it plausible why he would have simply accepted the terms of his servitude to Crusoe without ever contemplating a return journey to his own island. The geographical knowledge he willingly imparts to Crusoe certainly implies that the "poor honest creature" (225) is no inexperienced traveler. Crusoe, of course, can hardly be trusted as a narrator, and there is no reason to believe his implicit claims that Friday simply had no agenda of his own. Although we hear no details about the voyage that takes Crusoe and Friday to England, I find it suggestive to speculate that Friday did not respond to the new circumstances of his life in quite so futile a manner as Oroonoko. With his maritime skills and enough hunting experience to single-handedly kill a lion and a bear in the Pyrenees (compare 286–91)—neither of which animal is native to the Caribbean[53]—he would hardly have lacked the flexibility and understanding to adapt quickly to different living conditions. The paradigmatic shipboard encounter between him and Crusoe as they traveled to England aboard the ship recovered from the mutineers might thus not have been the lopsided master-servant relationship that the teller of the tale implies, but rather the meeting of two voyagers of unequal social power but comparable temperament. To assume that Friday took so badly to living in Europe as J. M. Coetzee thought in his 1986 rewriting of the Robinson tale, in which a melancholic and speechless Friday turns into a fat and passive alcoholic,[54] means to underestimate or even deny the personal resources that allowed indigenous people of the Caribbean or elsewhere to respond to the changes and challenges that washed up on their shore. It is, after all, Crusoe, not Friday, to whom "the island was certainly a prison" (111).

Friday's ship of exile, then, unlike Oroonoko's, no longer masks its identity and purpose to the involuntary indigenous voyager. A later black seafarer, spiritual heir to Oroonoko and Friday, who knows his ships and seas as well as any of his white shipmates, is Olaudah Equiano. Maybe Equiano shares nothing with Oroonoko and Friday, for apart from having actually lived, differences between him and his fictional precursors abound. Where the aristocratic Oroonoko grew up in an essentially feudal world of chivalry and warfare, and Friday emerged from alleged prehistoric savagery as the brainchild of the archetypal European colonizer, Equiano was plucked as an eleven-year-old from an African community he remembers, in his 1789 autobiography *The Interesting Narrative*, as taking pride in its traditions and customs, as full of dance, song, and poetry.[55] Actually, the account of his African origins in the opening chapter of this book is now believed to be written not from memory but largely copied from contemporary travelogues and other sources,[56] so there is a convergence of sorts in the fictional prehistory of all three characters.[57] Where the three come together historically, in the narrative sequence suggested here, is in the gradual progress toward the achievement of self-determination in the midst of a disenfranchised existence—still unthinkable for Oroonoko, only hinted at for Friday, but largely realized for Equiano. And each time, the moment that symbolically pits the idea of personal freedom against a context defined in terms of oppression unfolds as a heterotopic shipboard scenario.

Olaudah Equiano experienced many forms of slavery in his life, from being owned as a child by fellow Africans, to serving as the personal slave of several white masters, to what he reviled as the worst type of slavery of all, being forced to work in labor gangs on the West Indian sugar plantations. Despite adverse circumstances, Equiano carved out an identity for himself as a self-styled merchant in the Caribbean, starting modestly with "a glass tumbler" he purchased for three pence on one island, and sold for "a bit, or sixpence" on another (116). He eventually managed to buy his freedom after going through a process of primitive accumulation every bit as exemplary as Crusoe's tale of economic recovery from scratch—except that Equiano did not benefit from the entirely artificial setup devised by Defoe, because where Crusoe was an isolated individual living in a non-competitive world, with no one to threathen his possessions or lay claim to scarce commodities, Equiano had to prove his mercantile credentials in a complex social scenario that was as disadvantageous and hostile to him as was possible in the period.

The enabling condition of Equiano's rise to relative economic autonomy and freedom from slavery was his identity as a seaman.[58] Not only did the many ships that Equiano traveled on during his life offer him the material opportunity to reinvent himself first as a small trader and later as an able seaman, they also provided him with the independence of mind and body to redefine his cultural identity in response to an internationalism that he increasingly came to control, rather than being controlled by it. Vincent Carretta writes that "[t]he demands of seafaring life [permitted] him to transcend the barriers imposed by race, forcing even Whites to acknowledge him as having the responsibilities and capabilities, if not the rank itself, of the captain of a ship."[59] The implicit reference here is to an event recounted by Equiano as happening shortly after his manumission, when the untimely death of his captain midpassage forced him to assume the command of a ship he then safely steered into harbor. "Many were surprised," Equiano reports, "when they heard of my conducting the ship into port, and I now obtained a new appellation and was called captain. This elated me not a little, and it was quite flattering to my vanity to be thus styled by as high a title as any sable freeman in this place possessed" (144).

The sea here clearly serves, like in the opening scene of *The Tempest*, as a great social leveler. Knowledge and authority count high among seamen, whose lives depend on the navigational skills of their officers and who do not need to be told how to distinguish between an assumed authority—the power of birth or office—and an authority that rests on true ability and skills honed by experience.[60] That Equiano, the black seaman who was once a slave, should have commanded enough respect among his shipmates to turn around the social power structures he was exposed to on land testifies as much to his extraordinary personal resources as to his outstanding seafaring skills, and confirms the ship as a social space where such cultural inversions were not only imaginable but very real. Ships became Equiano's home—literally in the sense of providing his living space for much of his life; symbolically by making the national and ethnic parameters that defined his cultural existence as fluid as the sea itself.

Eventually settled in London, where he always longed to return after a major voyage, and embracing a cultural notion of "Britishness" as the defining mark of selfhood, he was juggling his identity between an "oppressed Ethiopian" (232)—as he styled himself in a petition to the queen in 1788—and the author of a celebrated narrative that was, as he proudly announced on the title page, "written by himself." Indeed that narrative, in which an eloquent English voice addressed a British reading public, and which carried as a frontispiece the portrait of an African writer in Western clothing, defines Equiano's cultural identity as a spectrum of possibilities rather than an ethnic or national essentialism. Perhaps the portrait could be taken as evidence of complete colonial assimiliation under the pressure of an imperialism that shaped mentalities as well as countries, but this would be to accord little or no personal agency to a writer who exudes confidence in his life on every page. I would rather choose to read this text as the testimony of an individual who has mastered exceptionably well the degrading existential circumstances of his life—which included slavery—instead of being mastered by them. And by producing a contemporary best-seller that is, in form and mind-set, "profoundly British,"[61] he exploded in turn any narrowly ethnic meaning this term might transport, writing himself into its semantic confines to the extent of assuming the voice and habit of a man of letters with a life story worth reporting: a spiritual autobiography that relies as much on the confirmation that "the Christian universe knows no outside"[62]—hence includes even this "African," as Equiano identifies himself on the book's cover—and on the intimate, deeply bodied knowledge that colonialism is always a two-way traffic.[63]

The progress toward personal agency I have claimed to find in the three maritime tales discussed in this section is perhaps most evident in the sequence of onboard meetings between the indigenous seafarer and his antagonist: Oroonoko and the English captain during the Middle Passage, Friday and Crusoe on their voyage to England, "Captain" Equiano and his generic white shipmate on their travels across the Atlantic. As the relations of dominance are slowly reversed in these pairings, the shipboard experience in all three narratives reflects, even enables (for Equiano), the possibility of a cultural expression beyond the terms dictated by transatlantic slavery. Antony knew how to use the sea as a means of escaping narrowly defined conceptions of the self, and in this sense Equiano's maritime identity converges with that of the Roman-Jacobean seafarer who blurred the ethnic boundaries within his Mediterranean world as passionately as Equiano blurred those of the Atlantic.

To be sure, any confidence we might invest in Equiano's benign version of Britishness is compromised by the realization that he used his freedom not only to campaign for abolitionism but also to imitate his former oppressors in thought and habit, to the extent of acting at one point as a slave trader himself (when he purchased slaves in Jamaica for a plantation project in central America [205]). Such contradictions should remind us first of all that none of the figures dealt with in this essay are in any sense our contemporaries but historical agents who, like Hamlet, had to deal with the forms and pressures of their day. Equiano's tale of the injustices of slavery was a major publishing success, but that racism did not stop being a shipboard reality will be all too apparent from one of the next essays in this volume, Alasdair Pettinger's analysis of the conditions of black voyaging on the nineteenth-century transatlantic steamer. Despite these strictures, the sea was clearly beneficial—even providential—to Equiano, allowing him to "stay afloat" in a sea of changes. No wonder that during his final years as a landlubber, he often thought, in an affectionate language that bespeaks a life shaped by exposure to the sea, "of visiting old ocean again" (223).

Notes

1. Christopher Columbus, *Journal of the First Voyage (Diario del primer viaje)*, parallel Spanish and English text, ed. and trans. B. W. Ife (Warminster: Aris & Phillips Ltd., 1990), 131.
2. We have, of course, not the original logbook, only Las Casas' transcript of what may or may not have been a copy of the original. For comments see Ife, "Introduction," Columbus, *Journal of the First Voyage*, v–xxv: vi; and Peter Hulme, *Colonial Encounters: Europe and the Native Caribbean, 1492–1797* [1986] (London: Routledge, 1992), 17.
3. Which he glosses as "the discovery of continuous sea passages from ocean to ocean." J. H. Parry, *The Discovery of the Sea: An Illustrated History of Men, Ships and the Sea in the Fifteenth and Sixteenth Centuries* (New York: Dial Press; London: Weidenfeld and Nicolson, 1974), viii.
4. *Ibid.*, xi.
5. See also his *Double Ghosts: Oceanian Voyagers on Euroamerican Ships* (Armonk, NY: M. E. Sharpe, 1997).
6. For a brief overview of the long-standing historical debate on whether the *Santa María* was a *nao* (as most naval historians now believe) or, like the *Niña* and the *Pinta*, a caravel, see Xavier Pastor, *The Ships of Christopher Columbus* (London: Conway Maritime Press, 1992).
7. Ife, "Introduction," Columbus, *Journal of the First Voyage*, xxiii; and Roger C. Smith, *Vanguard of Empire: Ships of Exploration in the Age of Columbus* (New York and Oxford: Oxford University Press, 1993), 141.
8. Smith, *Vanguard of Empire*, 135.
9. See *ibid.*, 134–5.
10. By one of those fatal ironies of history, the Jews were expelled from Spain just as the final negotiations between Columbus and the Spanish Crown were under way. See Peter Pierson, *The History of Spain* (Westport, CT: Greenwood, 1999), 52. Luís de Torres, the Marrano interpreter, had officially converted to Christianity only on August 2, 1492, the day before Columbus sailed, apparently to be eligible for the expedition.
11. Michel Foucault, "Of Other Spaces" [1967], trans. Jay Miskowiec, *Diacritics* 16, no. 1 (1986), 22–7: 24.
12. *Ibid.*
13. *Ibid.*, 27.
14. *Ibid.*
15. W. H. Auden, *The Enchafèd Flood, or The Romantic Iconography of the Sea* (London: Faber, 1951), 15.
16. Sebastian Brant, *Das Narrenschiff* (Nuremberg: Peter Wagner, 1494).

17. Alain Corbin, *The Lure of the Sea: The Discovery of the Seaside in the Western World, 1750–1840* [French original 1988], trans. Jocelyn Phelps (Cambridge: Polity Press, 1994), 8.

18. Sebastian Brant, *The Ship of Fools*, trans. Alexander Barclay (London: Rychard Pynson, 1509), fol. 11r.

19. For a brief account of repulsive images of the sea and its coasts in religious cosmogony, geology, literature, and popular symbolism in the West, see Corbin, "The Roots of Fear and Repulsion," *The Lure of the Sea*, 1–18.

20. Brant, *The Ship of Fools,* trans. Barclay, fol. 11r.

21. Columbus, *Journal of the First Voyage*, ed. Ife, 53.

22. On the self-organization of pirate communities, see Marcus Rediker, *Between the Devil and the Deep Blue Sea: Merchant Seamen, Pirates, and the Anglo-American Maritime World, 1700–1750* (Cambridge: Cambridge University Press, 1987), chapter 6; on the wider Atlantic canvas of the pirates' activities, see Rediker and Peter Linebaugh, *The Many-Headed Hydra: Sailors, Slaves, Commoners, and the Hidden History of the Revolutionary Atlantic* (Boston: Beacon Press, 2000), chapter 5.

23. See Greg Dening, *Mr Bligh's Bad Language: Passion, Power and Theatre on the Bounty* (Cambridge: Cambridge University Press, 1992), 19–33.

24. Corbin, *Lure of the Sea*, 16.

25. Carl Schmitt, *Der Nomos der Erde im Völkerrecht des Jus Publicum Europaeum* (Cologne: Greven Verlag, 1950), 144 (Schmitt's italics; my translation).

26. These principles, however, were far from being universally accepted in early modern times. For the seventeenth-century debate over the right of access to the oceans, which pitted the believers in a *mare liberum* (Hugo Grotius) against the defenders of a *mare clausum* (John Selden), see David Armitage, "The Empire of the Seas," *The Ideological Origins of the British Empire* (Cambridge: Cambridge University Press, 2000), 100–24; and James Muldoon, "Who Owns the Sea?," Bernhard Klein (ed.), *Fictions of the Sea: Critical Perspectives on the Ocean in British Literature and Culture* (Aldershot et al.: Ashgate, 2002), 13–27.

27. See his long essay *Land and Sea* [German original 1944], trans. Simona Draghici (Washington, D.C.: Plutarch Press, 1997).

28. Quoted in Alexander Frederick Falconer, *Shakespeare and the Sea* (London: Constable, 1964), xii.

29. Sara Hanna accords the sea "an eccentric, even centrifugal tendency" in Shakespeare's Greek plays. See her "Shakespeare's Greek World: The Temptation of the Sea," John Gillies and Virginia Mason Vaughan (eds.), *Playing the Globe: Genre and Geography in English Renaissance Drama* (Madison: Fairleigh Dickinson University Press, 1998), 107–28: 113.

30. Bradin Cormack, "Marginal Waters: *Pericles* and the Idea of Jurisdiction," Andrew Gordon and Bernhard Klein (eds.), *Literature, Mapping, and the Politics of Space in Early Modern Britain* (Cambridge: Cambridge University Press, 2001), 155–80: 157. See also Constance C. Relihan, "Liminal Geography: *Pericles* and the Politics of Place," *Philological Quarterly* 71, no. 3 (1992), 281–99.

31. For the latest exploration of *The Tempest*'s many meanings, including the maritime, see Peter Hulme and William H. Sherman (eds.), *The "Tempest" and Its Travels* (London: Reaktion, 2000); see also Peter Hulme's essay in this volume.

32. *The Tempest*. Quotation to *The Norton Shakespeare*, ed. Stephen Greenblatt et al. (New York and London: W. W. Norton, 1997).

33. *The Merchant of Venice*. Quotation to *The Norton Shakespeare*.

34. Available in a 1579 English translation by Thomas North.

35. All *Antony and Cleopatra* quotations are taken from *The Norton Shakespeare*.

36. For a recent overview, see Kenneth Parker, "'New Heaven, New Earth': Rome and Egypt and Shaping the English Nation," Pierre Iselin (ed.), *William Shakespeare: Antony and Cleopatra* (Paris: Didier érudition, 2000), 89–123.

37. John Gillies, *Shakespeare and the Geography of Difference* (Cambridge: Cambridge University Press, 1994), 116.

38. Compare *ibid.*, 113.

39. I develop these ideas at more length in "Die unendliche Vielfalt der Welt: *Antony and Cleopatra*," William Shakespeare, *Antonius und Kleopatra/Antony and Cleopatra*, parallel English and German text, trans. Frank Günther (Cadolzburg: ars vivendi, 2000), 352–75.

40. John Gillies even argues for a symbolic link between the exotic beast that Antony refuses to explain and Cleopatra's reptilian self-characterization as "wrinkled deep in time" (1.5.29), which would suggest that the passage is evidence of his refusal to participate in the discursive appropriation of Cleopatra's imaginative existence. See Gillies, *Shakespeare and the Geography of Difference*, 121–2.

41. The word *melt* occurs six times in the play, at least once in each act, and the varying contexts of its usage mirror Antony's transformations in the play. See my "Die unendliche Vielfalt der Welt: *Antony and Cleopatra*," 372.

42. The intellectual origins of imperial thought in the study of geography have recently been traced by Lesley Cormack in *Charting an Empire: Geography at the English Universities, 1580–1620* (Chicago: University of Chicago Press, 1997).

43. I am not the first to make an explicit connection between these texts. The triad has recently been suggested as a useful teaching package by Bill Overton in "Countering *Crusoe*: Two Colonial Narratives," *Critical Survey* 4, no. 3 (1992), 302–10.

44. Marcus Rediker, *Between the Devil and the Deep Blue Sea*, 20. See chapter 1 of Rediker's book for a detailed "Tour of the North Atlantic, c. 1740" (10–76).

45. *Ibid.*, 21.

46. Peter Linebaugh, "All the Atlantic Mountains Shook," *Labour/Le Travailleur* 10 (1982), 87–121: 112.

47. All *Oroonoko* quotations taken from Aphra Behn, *Oroonoko and Other Writings*, ed. Paul Salzmann, World's Classics (Oxford: Oxford University Press, 1994).

48. For a comparative reading of Othello and Oroonoko in terms of their spatial characteristics and the cartographic representation of Africa, see my "Randfiguren: Othello, Oroonoko und die kartographische Repräsentation Afrikas," Ina Schabert and Michaela Boenke (eds.), *Imaginationen des Anderen im 16. und 17. Jahrhundert* (Wiesbaden: Harrassowitz Verlag, 2002), 185–216.

49. Anne Fogarty, "Looks That Kill: Violence and Representation in Aphra Behn's *Oroonoko*," Carl Plasa and Betty J. Ring (eds.), *The Discourse of Slavery: Aphra Behn to Toni Morrison* (London: Routledge, 1994), 1–17: 1.

50. All *Robinson Crusoe* quotations are taken from Daniel Defoe, *Robinson Crusoe*, ed. Angus Ross (Harmondsworth: Penguin, 1965).

51. See Peter Hulme's essay in this volume.

52. Peter Hulme thinks differently when he calls navigation another "essential feature in Friday's education" received at the hands of Crusoe. See his excellent chapter on "Robinson Crusoe and Friday" in *Colonial Encounters*, 175–222: 210.

53. But in Defoe's garbled sense of Caribbean wildlife, bears do have a place, so this episode is consistent within the terms of the fictional world of the novel.

54. See J. M. Coetzee, *Foe* (Harmondsworth: Penguin, 1987). For other rewritings of *Robinson Crusoe*, see especially Michel Tournier, *Vendredi, ou les limbes du Pacifique* (1967), and Sam Selvon, *Moses Ascending* (1975). Both novels tell the Crusoe tale partly from Friday's perspective. For comments on all three rewritings, see Richard Phillips, "Unmapping Defoe's Island: Denaturalising Crusoe's World," *Mapping Men and Empire: A Geography of Adventure* (London: Routledge, 1997), 152–60.

55. All Equiano quotations are taken from Olaudah Equiano, *The Interesting Narrative and Other Writings*, ed. Vincent Carretta (Harmondsworth: Penguin, 1995).

56. See S. E. Ogude, "Facts into Fictions: Equiano's *Narrative* Reconsidered," *Research in African Literatures* 13 (1982), 30–43: 32; and Vincent Carretta, "Introduction," Equiano, *The Interesting Narrative*, ed. Carretta, ix–xxviii: xxiv–v. For a discussion of *The Interesting Narrative* in the context of eighteenth-century travel writing, see Geraldine Murphy, "Olaudah Equiano, Accidental Tourist," *Eighteenth-Century Studies* 27, no. 4 (1994), 551–68.

57. There is now a wider debate over Equiano's origins, specifically on the question of whether he was really born in Africa (in what is now Nigeria), or in South Carolina, as Vincent Carretta argues in a recent article may have been the case: "Olaudah Equiano or Gustavus Vassa? New Light on an Eighteenth-Century Question of Identity," *Slavery and Abolition* 20, no. 3 (1999), 96–105. Carretta's careful research suggests that irrespective of his precise place of birth, there is no doubt that Equiano—or Gustavus Vassa, the slave name under which he was more widely known—was ethnically African.

58. For the wider context of Black Atlantic seafaring, see W. Jeffrey Bolster, *Black Jacks: African American Seamen in the Age of Sail* (Cambridge, MA: Harvard University Press, 1997).

59. Carretta, "Introduction," xxii.

60. See Dening, *Mr Bligh's Bad Language*, 80–1; and his essay in the present volume.

61. Tanya Caldwell, "'Talking Too Much English': Languages of Economy and Politics in Equiano's *The Interesting Narrative*," *Early American Literature* 34, no. 4 (1999), 263–82: 280.

62. Adam Potkay, "History, Oratory, and God in Equiano's *Interesting Narrative*," *Eighteenth-Century Studies* 34, no. 4 (2001), 601–14: 606. Potkay takes issue with the recent tendency of reading Equiano outside the context of eighteenth-century oratorical and religious traditions, calling *The Interesting Narrative* "a rhetorical performance of considerable skill" (604). See also the responses by Srinivas Aravamudan and Roxann Wheeler in the same issue.

63. For a broad theoretical exploration of such notions, see Paul Gilroy, *The Black Atlantic: Modernity and Double Consciousness* (Cambridge, MA: Harvard University Press, 1993); and more recently (for the eighteenth century) Srinivas Aravamudan, *Tropicopolitans: Colonialism and Agency, 1688–1804* (Durham, NC: Duke University Press, 1999).

CHAPTER 6

The Red Atlantic; or, "a terrible blast swept over the heaving sea"

MARCUS REDIKER

I take my title from William Blake, the visionary poet and painter who in 1793 wrote *America, a Prophecy*, an account of the American Revolution and its place in the Atlantic's Age of Revolution. I use the poem to reflect upon some of the themes of *The Many-Headed Hydra: Sailors, Slaves, Commoners, and the Hidden History of the Revolutionary Atlantic*, a study of the development of capitalism in the anglophone North Atlantic, and the challenges from below to this world-transforming process. The book begins with English colonization in the early seventeenth century and ends with industrialization in the early nineteenth, exploring the deployment and discipline of labor on a global scale. Merchants, manufacturers, planters, and royal officials built trade routes, colonies, and a new economy, connecting the four corners of the Atlantic (northwestern Europe, West Africa, the Caribbean, and North America) by organizing the labor of servants, slaves, sailors, soldiers, urban and rural laborers, and factory workers. In undertaking such grand labors, these classically educated rulers cast themselves as Hercules, the mythical hero of antiquity, and employed the many-headed hydra as a symbol of disorder and resistance, a monstrous obstruction to the building of state, empire, and capitalism. The heads of the rebellious monster were dispossessed commoners, transported felons, religious radicals, insurgent servants and slaves, riotous urban laborers, and mutinous soldiers and sailors. To their horror, the rulers discovered that as they chopped off one head, two new ones grew in its place—such was the motive power of resistance. The heads, originally brought into productive combination by Hercules, soon developed among themselves new forms of cooperation against him—from mutinies and strikes to riots and insurrections and revolution. The setting of the clash was the "Red Atlantic," a historic space of violence and bloody oppression, but also of resistance, revolution, and emancipation.[1]

America, a Prophecy begins with Blake's symbol of revolution, red Orc, pinioned to the ground, his arms and legs bound by "tenfold chains" (Plate 1, line 12).[2] He breaks free of his manacles (figure 6.1).

> Solemn heave the Atlantic waves between
> the gloomy nations,
> Swelling, belching from its deeps red clouds & raging Fires!
> Albion is sick! America faints! enrag'd the Zenith grew.
> As human blood shooting its veins all round
> the orbed heaven
> Red rose the clouds from the Atlantic in vast wheels of blood
> And in the red clouds rose a Wonder o'er the Atlantic sea;
> Intense! naked! a Human fire fierce glowing, as the wedge
> Of iron heated in the furnace; his terrible limbs were fire
> With myriads of cloudy terrors banners dark & towers
> Surrounded; heat but not light went thro'
> the murky atmosphere
> The King of England looking westward trembles at the
> vision[.]
> (Plate 4, lines 2–12)

Red Orc, red clouds, red blood, red-hot iron: there can be no doubt about the color of revolution. Blake uses the word *red* seventeen times in the poem and evokes it in countless other ways.

Orc then offers his own paraphrase of the Declaration of Independence, which proves to be rather different from what Thomas Jefferson and the other Founding Fathers had in mind.[3]

> Let the slave grinding at the mill, run out into the field:
> Let him look up into the heavens & laugh in the bright air;
> Let the inchained soul shut up in darkness and in sighing,
> Whose face has never seen a smile in thirty weary years;
> Rise and look out, his chains are loose, his dungeon
> doors are open.
> And let his wife and children return from the opressors scourge;

Fig. 6.1 William Blake, "Orc," from *America, a Prophecy* (1793)

They look behind at every step & believe it is a dream.
Singing. The Sun has left his blackness, & has found
a fresher morning
And the fair Moon rejoices in the clear & cloudless night;
For Empire is no more, and now the Lion & Wolf shall cease.
(Plate 6, lines 6–15)

The king of England is not happy. He sends his angels of war to ask:

. . . Art thou not Orc, who serpent-form'd
Stands at the gate of Enitharmon to devour her children;
Blasphemous Demon, Antichrist, hater of Dignities;
Lover of wild rebellion, and transgresser of Gods Law;
Why dost thou come to Angels eyes in this terrific form?

The terror answer'd: I am Orc, . . .
The times are ended; . . .
That stony law I stamp to dust: and scatter religion abroad
To the four winds as a torn book, & none shall
gather the leaves . . .
(Plate 7, lines 3–7; Plate 8, lines 1–6)

Orc promises revolutionary renewal, which will not destroy humanity but
rather purify it.

For every thing that lives is holy, life delights in life;
Because the soul of sweet delight can never be defil'd.
Fires inwrap the earthly globe, yet man is not consumd;
Amidst the lustful fires he walks: his feet become like brass,
His knees and thighs like silver, & his breast and head like gold.
(Plate 8, lines 13–7)

In response, the king sends his punishing demons to spread pestilence
against the rebellious Americans.

Sound! sound! my loud war-trumpets & alarm
my Thirteen Angels!
Loud howls the eternal Wolf! the eternal Lion lashes his tail!
America is darkned; and my punishing Demons terrified,
Crouch howling before their caverns deep like skins
dry'd in the wind.

. . .

Fury! rage! madness! in a wind swept through America . . .
(Plate 9, lines 1–4; Plate 14, line 10)

Amid "the red flames of Orc . . . roaring . . . around / The angry shores" (Plate 14, lines 11–2), the Americans declare their rebellion: "no more I follow, no more obedience pay" (Plate 11, line 15). They unite in solidarity, what Blake calls "the fierce rushing of th'inhabitants together" (Plate 14, line 12). Sailors take direct action against property, tomahawking casks of tea and dumping it into Boston harbor; Tom Paine "casts his pen upon the earth" (Plate 14, line 15) and writes *Common Sense*.

> . . . all rush together in the night in wrath and raging fire
> The red fires rag'd! the plagues recoil'd! then rolld
> they back with fury [.]
> (Plate 14, lines 19–20)

The American revolutionaries repulse the plagues, which return to London, causing its people to rise in the century's greatest municipal insurrection, the Gordon Riots of 1780:

> The millions sent up a howl of anguish and threw off
> their hammerd mail,
> And cast their swords & spears to earth, & stood
> a naked multitude.
> (Plate 15, lines 4–5)

Blake knew whereof he spoke, for he had been in "the front rank" of the crowd that opened the doors of Newgate and liberated the prisoners during the June days of 1780. The American blast reverberated to the metropolis.[4]
The war would end in resistance from below when

> The British soldiers thro' the thirteen states sent up a howl
> Of anguish: threw their swords & muskets to the earth & ran
> From their encampments and dark castles seeking
> where to hide
> From the grim flames; and from the visions of Orc . . .
> (Plate 13, lines 6–9)

But the revolution of the red Atlantic would not end, for soon "France reciev'd the Demons light" (Plate 16, line 15):

> Stiff shudderings shook the heav'nly thrones!
> France Spain & Italy,
> In terror view'd the bands of Albion, and the ancient Guardians
> Fainting upon the elements, smitten with their own plagues
> They slow advance to shut the five gates of their law-built heaven
> Filled with blasting fancies and with mildews of despair
> With fierce disease and lust, unable to stem the fires of Orc;

> But the five gates were consum'd, & their bolts and hinges melted
> And the fierce flames burnt round the heavens, & round
> the abodes of men
> . . .
> And so the Princes fade from earth, scarce seen by
> souls of men . . .
> (Plate 16, lines 16–23; Plate d [fragment], line 5)

As the "lustful fires" (Plate 8, line 16) raced through the institutions of monarchy, a more hopeful future, republican and revolutionary, emerged from the conflagration. Of America, Blake concluded, "But tho' obscur'd, this is the form of the Angelic land" (Plate d [fragment], line 6). This was Blake's history, his prophecy. This was Atlantic revolution, the "terrible blast [that] swept over the heaving sea" (Plate 3, line 13).

What can Blake tell us more than two centuries later? What can the visionary help us to see? I would emphasize three points. *First*: Blake suggests that the fundamental processes of historical change in the Age of Revolution were Atlantic, not English, not American, not French, not confined to the "gloomy nations." It follows that these processes cannot therefore be apprehended by nationalist histories. Indeed, nationalist histories are often organized *against* the truths Blake presents, and hence they have obscured or even falsified the past, especially the transnational search for "a fresher morning," or, more grandly, the "Angelic land." Even the greatest of the histories from below, Edward Thompson's *The Making of the English Working Class* (1963), aimed to winnow out the English experience of the 1790s from the French and, more broadly, the Atlantic revolutionary moment. This has had blinding effects. The conservative nationalist historiography of the American Revolution and the radical nationalist historiography of the French Revolution have, of course, been even worse.[5]

Second: by linking the American Revolution to the Gordon Riots and the French Revolution, Blake shows that the experience of resistance ("the demon's light") circulated around the Atlantic. The workers of the Atlantic produced commodities that moved with the planetary currents around the world, but so, too, did their experience, which often flowed from American slave huts, Irish cottages, and the rolling decks of deep-sea vessels, across the Atlantic, back to the metropoles of Europe. Blake was not alone in understanding this: the United Irishmen saw a new world dawning in the west, as did Tom Paine, who hoped to see "the New World regenerate the Old." James Aitken, alias "John the Painter," came to America during the 1760s as an indentured servant, but, unable to bear his bondage, escaped his master, journeyed to Boston, and took part in the Boston Tea Party. Radicalized, he returned to London to wage revolutionary arson against the ships and shipyards of the Crown in order to damage imperialist naval efforts. Against the Eurocentric logic of Blake's contemporaries and against subsequent historians who have always emphasized causal movement from east to west, from Europe to America, we must consider the historic importance of motion from west to east, from America to Europe, especially in the history of movements from below.[6]

Third: in order to understand the Age of Revolution, Blake looks from below, considering the actions of sailors, slaves, soldiers, prisoners, women and children, black and white, the whole human race. These actors shrunk the world—the "Earth conglob'd, in narrow room" (Plate b, line 7)—as they expanded the human capacity to transform it. They voyaged over the waves of the Atlantic, carrying wherever they went a little piece of the "Human fire fierce glowing" (Plate 4, line 8). Sailors and soldiers carried the flames over the waters in all directions. Thousands did indeed throw their swords and muskets to the earth, and desert to the American side. They contributed to mutinies and urban mobs, linking the American Revolution to radical movements in England, Ireland, France, and St. Domingue. Thousands of slaves and free blacks flocked to the British army during the revolution and subsequently carried the news and experience of revolution to Nova Scotia, Bermuda, East Florida, the Bahamas, Jamaica, Belize, the Mosquito Shore, Dublin, London, and Sierra Leone.[7]

These "citizens of the world" moved more than themselves. They inspired the abolitionist movement of England, stirring Granville Sharp and Thomas Clarkson to publicize and fight the evils of slavery and the slave trade. They captured the attention of the major Romantic thinkers, Wordsworth, Southey, and Coleridge, advancing their discourse of the human spirit in the 1790s and directing it against bondage. Even a conservative such as Edmund Burke would recall transatlantic struggles for freedom as he tried to describe (and discredit) the revolutionaries of Paris in 1790: they reminded him of a "gang of Maroon slaves, suddenly broke loose from the house of bondage."[8] Yet another person duly influenced by the Atlantic motley crew was William Blake, who always considered himself to be a "Son of Liberty" and who knew the writings and likely the persons of slaves and former slaves such as Phyllis Wheatley, James Albert Ukawsaw Gronniosaw, Ottobah Cugoano, and Olaudah Equiano. What General Thomas Gage called "the flames of sedition" of the 1760s and 1770s fueled a new Atlantic cycle of rebellion in the 1790s.[9]

Blake thus saw global movements in the Age of Revolution—a connection to earlier struggles from below and a circulation of subversive experience. He showed that many of the most radical ideas of the Age of Revolution came from the Americas, but the circumvolutions were even older and more profound than he knew. Increasing opposition to private property in Europe, for example, owed much to the circulation of reports about native America. The communism of stateless, kingless, masterless, egalitarian tribes was carried in sailors' yarns and written accounts back to Europe, where it inflamed the imaginations of European thinkers from Sir Thomas More, to Michel de Montaigne, to William Shakespeare, generating in time an explosion of utopian thought and ultimately movements toward both humanism and enlightenment.[10] In the 1730s, Christian Gottlieb Priber sailed from Saxony to Charleston, South Carolina, divested himself of his worldly goods, and trekked into Indian country to build his City of Refuge, a communist society for runaway African slaves, European indentured servants, and Native Americans. He lived among the Cherokee as a wise and beloved member until seized and imprisoned by the English army, in whose captivity he died in 1743.[11] Another important figure in the transoceanic generalization of Native American ideas was "the great revolutionary of a revolutionary age," Jean-Jacques Rousseau, who was bewitched by the New World and its example of a new kind of liberty.[12]

Another source of Atlantic radicalism in Blake's day and after was the oppositional experience of African Americans, one expression of which was Jubilee, the biblical idea and practice (Leviticus 25) that freed slaves and servants, returned land to those who had lost it, canceled debt, and promised a year of no work.[13] The notion appeared in the King James translation of the Bible in 1611, found subversive use in the English Revolution of the 1640s, and had, by the 1770s, become part of the struggle against slavery in the Americas. In England, Thomas Spence made Jubilee a revolutionary theme for the working class, and a biblical support of the deeply held conviction that the greedy enclosure of land as private property was wrong, sinful, and criminal. The agitation eventually led to the Grand National Jubilee—the idea of the "general strike" as developed by James Benbow in 1822—and ultimately became a central idea in the struggle against slavery in the Americas, as churches from South Carolina to Massachusetts rocked to the Jubilee hymns following West Indian emancipation, preparing directly for the mighty struggle and epic Jubilee of the North American Civil War.[14]

A third source of Atlantic American radicalism was maritime, wherein the rough egalitarian, often democratic traditions of seafaring contributed revolutionary ideas, practices, and leaders. The sailor Crispus Attucks, a runaway slave of African American and Native American descent, lived in the small free black community in the port of Providence in the Bahama Islands but led Boston's multi-ethnic mob into battle against Captain Preston's "bloodyback" soldiers on the "fatal fifth of March," 1770, in the Boston Massacre. A second veteran of maritime experience was Thomas Paine, who, it is rarely remembered, had been part of a mutinous, multi-national crew aboard a privateering vessel during the Seven Years' War. A third was Thomas Spence, who grew up on the waterfront of Newcastle during the 1760s and 1770s, within the flux and reflux of Atlantic currents of revolution. A fourth was Olaudah Equiano, an African-slave-turned-sailor who helped to "make" the working class in England by connecting radical London artisans such as Thomas Hardy to the industrial proletarians of Sheffield, thereby making possible the world's first independent political working-class organization, the London Corresponding Society.[15]

All these sources of radicalism—and their transit to metropolitan Europe—can be illustrated in the story of Colonel Edward Marcus Despard, who was hanged in 1803 in London for his efforts to organize a revolutionary army to assassinate King George III, overthrow the state, and declare a republic. Despard, who had spent most of his life in the West Indies, brought to London a potent combination of experiences: he had marauded against New Spain, in which he had acquired the leadership style and some of the egalitarian customs of the buccaneers; he had been influenced by both the communism of the multi-racial Moskito Indians of Native America and the African American diaspora that followed the slave revolt within the American Revolution; and he had practiced a form of Jubilee when, as superintendent of British Honduras, he redistributed land to free blacks, much to the displeasure of the local oligarchs, who in the end got him removed from his position because of "his wild schemes of leveling equality." He returned to London with his African American wife Catherine to organize and lead soldiers, sailors, and other parts of the Atlantic proletariat in an insurrectionary attempt to seize the world's greatest capitalist city.[16]

If Blake's "Red Atlantic" was a place where revolutionary news, ideas, and practices formed and circulated, it was simultaneously a place of violence, oppression, and fatality.

> The bones of death, the cov'ring clay, the sinews shrunk & dry'd.
> Reviving shake, inspiring move, breathing! awakening!
> Spring like redeemed captives when their bonds &
>   bars are burst . . .
>   (Plate 6, lines 3–5)

Emancipation brought the dead back to the land of the living, but the cemeteries were deep with corpses. Blake's red Atlantic thus reflected not only the fires of revolution and a rubicund future, but a haunting bloodiness of the past. The Atlantic was, to Blake, a place of "human blood shooting its veins all round the orbed heaven," a place where "Red rose the clouds from the Atlantic in vast wheels of blood" (Plate 4, line 5–6). America was "the coast glowing with blood from Albions fiery Prince" (Plate 3, line 5). Albion's angel "glowd his horrid length staining the temple long / With beams of blood" (Plate 5, lines 6–7). With deep personal empathy, Blake summarized the violent history of America and, ever the prophet, predicted that it would not be remembered:

> A bended bow is lifted in heaven, & a heavy iron chain
> Descends link by link from Albions cliffs across the sea to bind
> Brothers & sons of America, till our faces pale and yellow;
> Heads deprest, voices weak, eyes downcast, hands work-bruis'd,
> Feet bleeding on the sultry sands, and the furrows of the whip
> Descend to generations that in future times forget.
> (Plate 3, lines 7–12)

One of the main purposes of *The Many-Headed Hydra* was to take up Blake's challenge to recall the violence and terror that were essential to the origin and development of Atlantic capitalism, and to stitch back together the body parts of proletarian victims as a necessary step in remembering their common histories. Most historians have refused to face the bloody side of the red Atlantic.[17]

One of the theses of *The Many-Headed Hydra* was that the Atlantic proletariat was "*terrorized, subject to coercion.* Its hide was calloused by indentured labor, galley slavery, plantation slavery, convict transportation, the workhouse, the house of correction. Its origins were often traumatic: enclosure, capture, and imprisonment left lasting marks."[18] It is widely known that the European colonial powers, England in particular, engaged in a genocidal land grab against America's indigenous peoples, and that they employed gruesome violence to set Africans to work on these new lands. Yet even these important truths understate the degree, variety, and breadth of violence and terror involved in the making of the Atlantic system. It is rarely remarked that *all* of the main transatlantic institutions of labor were built upon violence: the army, the navy, the merchant shipping industry, indentured servitude, plantation slavery, and ultimately the entire project of transatlantic settlement, production, and trade—in a word, colonization as a whole. Nor is it usually noted that some of the major figures of Anglo-Atlantic history not only practiced violence but raised it to the level of proud principle. Rulers identified deeply with the murderous Hercules, killer of not only monsters, but men, women, even his own children. The maritime hero, explorer, and slave trader Sir John Hawkins placed the image of a tortured African on his coat of arms. Sir Francis Bacon not only helped to formulate a science of terror and a theory of genocide but was himself a torturer of rebels, including Bartholomew Steere, a poor man who in the hope of "a merrier world" had rioted against enclosure in Oxfordshire in 1596. Others, from William III to George I, from Cotton Mather to John Adams, identified with Hercules. The violence of the Atlantic was planned at the highest levels and was in no way marginal or incidental.[19]

To the contrary, the violence was fundamental to and formative of the social and economic processes of Atlantic capitalism, and took four corresponding forms whose typology we may now explore. The originary form was the violence of expropriation. Second came the violence of the Middle Passage. Third was the violence of exploitation, and fourth was the violence of repression. Although there is a logic and an order to these types of violence (many thousands of people experienced them in just this order), it should be emphasized that they overlapped and coexisted in time. The violence of expropriation, for example, spanned the entire seventeenth, eighteenth, and early nineteenth centuries, and the violence of repression was, as we shall see, closely linked to it (and to the other two types) at every historic step. The four forms of violence had clear, interrelated purposes: they were instrumental to the formation, shipment, use, and control of labor power.

The violence of expropriation, which took numerous forms, was intended to separate people from the land, often ancestral holdings; it was meant, in short, to create proletarians—people who had no productive property, and hence nothing to sell but their labor. In England, whose history on this score moved Karl Marx to write about "primitive accumulation," expropriation was carried out by a combination of physical force and legal maneuver, sometimes combined as martial law. People were dispossessed by the dissolution of feudal retinues, by the closing of monasteries, by debt and foreclosure. Of special importance, especially in the seventeenth century and again in the late eighteenth, was the enclosure movement, in which arable farmland was transformed into pasturage, resulting in the eviction and displacement of hundreds of thousands of peasants, some of whom resisted and were jailed or imprisoned. The "strongest point" of the law, to the lord of the manor, lay, as one critic of enclosure remarked, in the phrase "*Take him Jaylor.*"[20]

Similar projects took place overseas, with different methods but the same result. In Ireland, expropriation often took a military form, as when Oliver Cromwell and his forces invaded in 1649, killed every tenth man in Drogheda, and vanquished the rest to labor on West Indian plantations. In native America, a combination of trade, disease, and war killed hundreds of thousands and dispossessed many more in a genocidal sweep through new lands. In Africa, the main form was military enslavement, as the indigenous clients of the slave traders sent armed troops on raids and into war to capture would-be plantation workers. In each of these cases, the integument of rural culture was gashed as the peoples of four continents were "freed" for labor in other places. A contemporary of Blake, the Afro-Jamaican revolutionary Robert Wedderburn, described the violence of expropriation in 1817: "He that first thrust his brother from his right [to the land] was a tyrant, a robber, and a murderer; a tyrant because he invades the rights of his brother, a robber, because he seized upon that which was not his own, a murderer, because he deprives his brother of the means of subsistence. The weak must then solicit to become the villain's slave." As Wedderburn explained, two results of expropriation were the crowding of the prisons and the gallows, both primary instruments of terror. Dispossession thus coincided with—and fueled—colonization.[21]

A second kind of violence, and a necessary sequel, was that of the Middle Passage, broadly understood to mean the temporal and spatial interlude between expropriation from the land and the exploitation of labor in a new setting. Vital to this violence was the array of prisons that made possible the labor systems of the Atlantic: the ship's hold, the tender boat, the prison hulk, the crimp house, the press room, the cookhouse, the storehouse, the barracoon, the factory, the trading post, the fort, the trunk, the cage, the city or county jail, the bridewell, the house of correction, and finally (in the later eighteenth century) the modern prison itself.[22] It follows from these material facts that there were many Middle Passages and hence many slaveries, involving those Wedderburn called "stolen people"— African slaves, obviously, in their millions, but also spirited indentured servants, kidnapped children, transported convicts, trepanned maidens, "barbadosed" laborers, banished "breeders," deported vagrants, press-ganged sailors, and exiled rebels. Equiano immediately saw when taken aboard a slaver at the age of ten that both sailors and slaves were subject to terror on the Middle Passage. Blake knew that Londoners had been "carried away in thousands . . . in ships closd up: / Chaind hand & foot."[23] The violence of the Middle Passage coincided with—and fueled—diaspora and exile.

The third form of violence was the actual use of the labor power— exploitation, the source of Blake's "work-bruis'd hands." The Atlantic economy depended on a variety of closely studied forms of physical discipline. The *dramatis personae* of the terror included the slave overseer with his whip; the boatswain with his rattan cane; the factory overlooker with his cane; the ship captain with his cat-o'-nine-tails; the schoolmaster with his birch; the regimental staff sergeant with his triangle and lash; the naval lieutenant followed by his club-wielding press gang of bullies; the hangman with his various instruments of torture—the "heavy iron chains," the muzzles and thumbscrews, the handcuffs, manacles, and irons, in short, the hardware of bondage. These figures organized theatrical public floggings and maimings, such as the one inflicted on the religious radical James Nayler, who suffered 310 lashes, a branding of his forehead, and a boring of his tongue for blasphemy in London in 1656. Mutinous sailors were "flogged round the fleet." Vagrants had a *V* seared onto the skin of their faces; runaways from the plantations were marked with an *R*. The bodies of sailors, slaves, and servants were routinely burdened with weights and chains. Mutilations were another raw assertion of power, especially in plantation regions: slave masters and their minions cut off the ears, noses, fingers, and legs of those who dared to rebel. Virginia's legislature ordered all counties to erect public whipping posts in 1662, primarily for the flogging of servants who had run away, and the masters who sat in the House of Burgesses granted their own kind the legal—as opposed to the "customary"—right to beat their servants in the same year. Jaspar Danckaerts, a member of the Labadists, a radical religious sect similar to the Quakers, wrote of a Maryland master who forced "a sick and languishing" servant to "dig his own grave, in which he was laid a few days afterward." Throughout the Revolutionary War, George Washington continually begged Congress to increase the number of lashes for mutinous soldiers from one hundred to five hundred. The long-term trend, beginning in the middle of the seventeenth century, was to racialize this violence of exploitation, targeting people of African descent. Blake, as heir to the religious radicalism of Nayler and others of the seventeenth century, knew that the "furrows of the whip" marked the bodies and the history of the Atlantic.[24]

The fourth and final type of violence, repression, depended on the sentence of death and execution, the ultimate power in the regime of terror. Authorities staged spectacular public killings, most commonly by hanging; then, as now, capital punishment was reserved largely for the poor. On those rare occasions when a person of higher station incurred the wrath of state, the honor of a more civilized death might be offered, by firing squad. Both methods were used by the leaders of the Virginia Company after they shipwrecked in Bermuda in 1609 and discovered that many of the "colonists" wanted to stay on the island, refusing to answer the authority of the gentlemen adventurers who wanted to get on with the moneymaking venture of colonization. Capital punishment stood at the very beginning of English overseas colonization.[25]

Rulers and their minions used considerable imagination in killing people, all to maximize the intended terror. They charged poor women with witchcraft and made them into grisly human fireworks as they burned them at the stake. They drowned gypsies. They flogged mutinous sailors to death, hanged them at the yardarm of their vessel, or tied them up, weighted them down, and threw them over the side so their skulls would be smashed against the side of the ship. They tied pirates at low water to Execution Dock in Wapping, the sailors' district in London, drowning them as the tide of the River Thames inched slowly above their gasping heads. Those who stole food (often to survive) they pinned to the earth and starved to death; others they hanged (but did not mortally strangle) and killed slowly. The rulers shattered the bones and ripped to pieces the bodies of those who challenged the most basic arrangements of social power. Some rebels they punished into the afterlife, hanging their bodies in chains to decompose beneath the action of the elements and the pecking of the carrion crow and vultures. For certain "crimes" they enacted an entire medley of capital punishments. When Governor Thomas Dale arrived in Virginia in 1611 to discover that many of the English settlers had deserted the young colony to live among the Powhatan Indians, he organized a military expedition, recaptured the renegades, and brought them back to Jamestown for an orgy of disciplinary violence. According to an eyewitness, "Some he apointed to be hanged Some burned Some to be broken upon wheles, others to be staked and some to be shott to deathe." He used these "extreme and crewell tortures" in order "to terrefy the rest for Attempteinge the Lyke."[26]

Repressive violence was often reactive, employed against the self-activity of the Atlantic proletariat and intended to maintain control over the various regimes of accumulation that were built by the force of the other three forms. Repressive violence could take military form, as in the slaughter of thirty thousand by the British army in the aftermath of the Irish rebellion of 1798, or it could take a legal one, as in the endless executions of the motley rebels who rose up against the social order of Atlantic capitalism during the cycles of rebellion that exploded in the 1640s, the 1730s, the 1760s, and Blake's own 1790s: the execution of the Leveller soldier and mutineer Robert Lockyer in 1649; the execution of the experienced rebel Will, who participated in slave conspiracies or revolts in Danish St. John's (1733), Antigua (1735–36), and New York (1741); the execution of the Akan-speaking Tacky, who led Jamaica's slaves into revolt in 1760; the execution of the Irish transatlantic revolutionary Edward Marcus Despard in 1803. This was violence meant to restore the social order.[27]

Another especially important aspect of the violence of repression was its use against the expropriated and exploited at those moments when they sought out alternative, anticapitalist ways of organizing themselves, especially when this involved a reappropriation of material life. This occurred when the commoners sought to seat themselves in edenic

Bermuda in 1610; when the Diggers retook and planted the commons at George's Hill and a dozen other places in England in 1649; when pirates seized the merchant ships in the 1710s and 1720s and made them into democratic and egalitarian workplaces; when the maroons fled the plantations in the 1730s and established autonomous communities in Jamaica, Suriname, and other places. The violence of repression sought consistently to destroy the commoning option or indeed any independent way of organizing social life. There would be no "Angelic land" if the rulers of the day could help it.

The two sides of the red Atlantic, the violence from above and the resistance from below, appeared not only in Blake's poetry in the 1790s, but in his graphic art as well. Blake was hired in 1791 by a radical London publisher, Joseph Johnson, to illustrate a book by Captain John Gabriel Stedman, a mercenary soldier who had spent four years in Suriname fighting the rebellious maroons who had escaped the plantations of the Dutch sugar colony. Blake engraved eighteen plates for Stedman's book, two of which speak to the themes of this essay: "The Execution of Breaking on the Rack" and "A Negro hung alive by the Ribs to a Gallows." They show how the knowledge of both violence and resistance circulated around the red Atlantic—how African rebels in America influenced Blake, who in turn represented their struggle to a metropolitan public.

Stedman wrote about two particularly memorable public executions. He had heard, in 1773, the story of a nameless slave who was executed for an unreported "crime" (figure 6.2). The eyewitness, who had lived in Suriname longer than Stedman, recalled:

> I saw a black man hang'd alive by the ribs, between which with a knife was first made an insision, and then clinch'd an Iron hook with a Chain—in this manner he kept living three days hanging with his head and feet downwards and catching with his tongue the drops of water / it being the rainy season / that were flowing down his bloated breast while the vultures were picking in the putred wound, notwithstanding all this he never complained. . . .

The dangling victim even took time to shame a fellow slave who was crying out while being flogged beneath the gallows. He called out to him: "'*you man? da boy fasi*'—'*are you a Man you behave like a boy.*'" The hooked man died after a "Comiserating Sentry" smashed in his head with the butt of his rifle. Blake used the story to engrave a haunting image of physical violence and spiritual resistance.[28]

The second execution occurred in 1776, when the rulers of Suriname put to death a man named Neptune, a free carpenter who dared to raise his hand against the authority of race and plantation: he had killed a white man, an

A Negro hung alive by the Ribs to a Gallows.

Blake Sculp.

Fig. 6.2 William Blake, "A Negro hung alive by the Ribs to a Gallows" (1790)

overseer of the Altona Estate, Para Creek, in a dispute (figure 6.3). Neptune's African executioner tied him to a rack on the ground, chopped off his left hand, then with an iron bar "broke to Shivers every Bone in his Body till the Splinters Blood and Marrow Flew about the Field, but the Prisoner never uttered a Groan, or a Sigh." Neptune bore his torture defiantly, singing songs "With a Clear Voice," conversing, joking, laughing, and palavering with those watching the ordeal. Blake depicted Neptune as a serene, Christ-like martyr.[29]

To understand these events and Blake's depiction of them, we must realize that they were in no way unusual. Many poor people in Europe and the Americas managed during the seventeenth and eighteenth centuries to turn the gallows into a dramatic set by defying the authorities at the very moment when they were supposed to be penitently teaching lessons about the social order to those assembled. In the western Atlantic many an enslaved African gave what Stedman called "a hearty laugh of Contempt at the Magistrates who attended the Execution"; many "manfully went without heaving a sigh or complaining." Stedman wondered, "Now How in the name of heaven Human nature Can go through so much Torture, With So much Fortitude is truly Astonishing." He and many others who witnessed such violence marveled at "the intrepidity with which the Negroes bore their punishment."[30]

It was in fact a commonplace for enslaved "Coromantees"—meaning Akan speakers from the Gold Coast—to behave in this stoic, courageous way at the gallows. Aphra Behn, who herself lived in Suriname, was one of the first to write about such resistance, when in her novella of 1688 the heroic Oroonoko, described as a "*Coramantien*, a Country of *Blacks* so called," sat smoking a pipe as the executioner chopped off his fingers, nose, ears, and arms. He "gave up the Ghost, without a Groan, or a Reproach." Writing more than a century later, the West Indian planter-historian Bryan Edwards said the same thing of the Coromantee, who, he explained, "meet death, in its most horrible shape, with fortitude or indifference." One man being burned to death "uttered not a groan, and saw his legs reduced to ashes with the utmost firmness and composure." Two others being hanged "never uttered the least complaint." Another planter-historian, Edward Long, gave the point made by Behn and Edwards a characteristically vicious twist: Coromantees "despise death (more through stupidity than fortitude), and can smile in agony."[31]

It is not clear that Blake understood either the origins or the full Atlantic circuit of what he engraved. The cultural form of the gallows resistance began in the martial ways of Akan-speaking peoples on the Gold Coast of Africa, crossed the Atlantic in slave ships of howling misery, reappeared in the plantations of Suriname, where it was observed by a mercenary soldier, who in turn carried it back across the Atlantic to a radical publisher and eventually Blake, the artist. But it is clear that Blake used the tortured rebels to express his own hopes of freedom. Moved by Stedman's stories,

Fig. 6.3 William Blake, "The Execution of Breaking on the Rack" (1790)

Blake not only engraved Neptune and the nameless man hooked by the rib in sympathetic ways, but he soon, in writing *America, a Prophecy*, made Neptune the basis of his image of red Orc, who was likewise pinioned to the ground, and called "the image of God who dwells in darkness of Africa" (Plate 2, line 8). It is also clear that Blake contributed to the anti-slavery movement, which advanced as it made the violence and the resistance of colonial slavery real to readers throughout metropolitan Europe.[32] Blake's "Red Atlantic" was thus a place where history was made, where torture met dignity, and where violence met the promise of hopeful things to come:

> On those vast shady hills between America & Albions shore;
> Now barr'd out by the Atlantic sea: call'd Atlantean hills:
> Because from their bright summits you may pass to
> the Golden world
> An ancient palace, archetype of mighty Emperies,
> Rears its immortal pinnacles, built in the forest of God . . .
> (Plate 10, lines 5–9)

Notes

1. This essay draws on the ideas and evidence presented in Peter Linebaugh and Marcus Rediker, *The Many-Headed Hydra: Sailors, Slaves, Commoners, and the Hidden History of the Revolutionary Atlantic* (Boston: Beacon Press, 2000).
2. All *America* quotations taken from William Blake, *America, a Prophecy* [1793], *The Poetry and Prose of William Blake*, ed. David V. Erdman (New York: Doubleday, 1965), 50–8.
3. David V. Erdman, *Blake, Prophet against Empire: A Poet's Interpretation of the History of His Own Time* [1954] (New York: Dover, 3rd ed., 1991), 24–5; and Linebaugh and Rediker, *The Many-Headed Hydra*, 347–8.
4. Erdman, *Blake*, 9; and Peter Linebaugh, *The London Hanged: Crime and Civil Society in the Eighteenth Century* (London: Allen Lane, 1991), 368–70.
5. E. P. Thompson, *The Making of the English Working Class* (London: Gollancz, 1963).
6. Thomas Paine, *The Rights of Man, Part I* [1791], *Thomas Paine: Political Writings*, ed. Bruce Kuklik (Cambridge: Cambridge University Press, 1989), 50. For Aitken, who was captured, convicted, and hanged, see *The Trial at Large of James Hill . . . , Commonly known by the Name of John the Painter* (London: G. Kearsly and Martha Gurney, 2nd ed., 1777); and M. J. Sydenham, "Firing His Majesty's Dockyard: Jack the Painter and the American Mission to France, 1776–1777," *History Today* 16 (1966), 324–31.
7. Julius Sherrard Scott III, "The Common Wind: Circuits of Afro-American Communication in the Era of the Haitian Revolution," Ph.D. dissertation, Duke University, 1986; and Linebaugh and Rediker, *The Many-Headed Hydra*, 241–7.
8. Edmund Burke, *Reflections on the Revolution in France* [1790], ed. J. C. D. Clark (Stanford, CA: Stanford University Press, 2001), 188.
9. Helen Thomas, *Romanticism and Slave Narratives* (Cambridge: Cambridge University Press, 2000); Joan Baum, *Mind-Forg'd Manacles: Slavery and the English Romantic Poets* (North Haven, CT: Archon Books, 1994); Lauren Henry, "'Sunshine and Shady Groves': What Blake's 'Little Black Boy' Learned from African Writers," Tim Fulford and Peter J. Kitson (eds.), *Romanticism and Colonialism: Writing and Empire, 1780–1830* (Cambridge: Cambridge University Press, 1998), 83–5; and Gage to Dartmouth, September 7, 1774, *The Correspondence of General Thomas Gage, 1762–1775*, ed. Clarence E. Carter (New Haven, CT: Yale University Press, 1931), vol. 1, 370. See also Linebaugh and Rediker, *The Many-Headed Hydra*, 246–7.
10. William Brandon, *New Worlds for Old: Reports from the New World and Their Effect on the Development of Social Thought in Europe, 1500–1800* (Athens: Ohio University Press, 1986).

11. Knox Mellon Jr., "Christian Priber and the Jesuit Myth," *South Carolina Historical Magazine* 61 (1960), 75–81; and "Christian Priber's Cherokee 'Kingdom of Paradise,'" *Georgia Historical Quarterly* 57 (1973), 310–31.

12. R. R. Palmer, *The Age of the Democratic Revolution: A Political History of Europe and America, 1760–1800*, 2 vols. (Princeton, NJ: Princeton University Press, 1959/1964), vol. 1 [1959], 114.

13. Recent work on romanticism, race, and colonialism includes Alan Richardson, "Romantic Voodoo: Obeah and British Culture, 1797–1807," *Studies in Romanticism* 32 (1993), 3–28; D. C. Macdonald, "Pre-Romantic and Romantic Abolitionism: Cowper and Blake," *European Romantic Review* 4 (1994), 163–82; and Alan Richardson, "Colonialism, Race, and Blake's 'The Little Black Boy,'" *Papers on Language and Literature* 26 (1996), 233–48. I would like to thank Ralph Dumain of the C. L. R. James Institute for bibliographic help.

14. Linebaugh and Rediker, *The Many-Headed Hydra*, 290–300.

15. Alyce Barry, "Thomas Paine, Privateersman," *Pennsylvania Magazine of History and Biography* 101 (1977), 459–61; and Linebaugh and Rediker, *The Many-Headed Hydra*, 239–40, 293–4, 334–41.

16. Linebaugh and Rediker, *The Many-Headed Hydra*, chapter 8.

17. Peter H. Wood, "Slave Labor Camps in Early America: Overcoming Denial and Discovering the Gulag," Carla Gardina Pestana and Sharon V. Salinger (eds.), *Inequality in Early America* (Hanover, NH, and London: University Press of New England, 1999), 222.

18. Linebaugh and Rediker, *The Many-Headed Hydra*, 332.

19. *Ibid.*; and Marcus Wood, *Blind Memory: Visual Representations of Slavery in England and America, 1780–1865* (Manchester: Manchester University Press, 2000), 222–3.

20. Linebaugh and Rediker, *The Many-Headed Hydra*, 118.

21. Wedderburn, quoted in Linebaugh and Rediker, *The Many-Headed Hydra*, 314.

22. Scott Christianson, *With Liberty for Some: 500 Years of Imprisonment in America* (Boston: Northeastern University Press, 1998), 16, 18; and Linebaugh and Rediker, *The Many-Headed Hydra*, 17, 58.

23. William Blake, *Jerusalem: The Emanation of The Giant Albion* [1804], *The Poetry and Prose of William Blake*, ed. Erdman, 214.

24. Jaspar Danckaerts and Peter Sluyter, *Journal of a Voyage to New York and a Tour of Several of the American Colonies in 1679–80* [1867], trans. and ed. Henry C. Murphy (Ann Arbor, MI: University Microfilms, Inc., 1966), 217; Ray Raphael, *A People's History of the American Revolution* (New York: New Press, 2001), 312; and E. P. Thompson, *Witness against the Beast: William Blake and the Moral Law* (New York: New Press, 1993).

25. Linebaugh and Rediker, *The Many-Headed Hydra*, 29–35.

26. George Percy, "A Trewe Relacyon of the Procedeinges and Ocurrentes of Momente wch have hapned in Virginia," *Tyler's Quarterly Historical and Genealogical Magazine* 3 (1921–2), 259–82: 280.

27. Linebaugh and Rediker, *The Many-Headed Hydra*, 119, 201–3, 221–4, 248–54.

28. John Gabriel Stedman, *Narrative of a Five Years Expedition against the Revolted Negroes of Surinam—Transcribed for the First Time from the Original 1790 Manuscript*, ed. Richard Price and Sally Price (Baltimore: Johns Hopkins University Press, 1988), 103–5.

29. *Ibid.*, 546–7. Blake also drew upon Stedman as he composed *The Songs of Experience* in 1793. Stedman had written about the wild cats of Suriname, with their flashing, sparkling eyes, which moved Blake to write: "Tyger! Tyger! burning bright / In the forest of the night, / What immortal hand or eye / Could frame thy fearful symmetry?" See Linebaugh and Rediker, *The Many-Headed Hydra*, 348–9.

30. Peter Linebaugh, "The Tyburn Riots against the Surgeons," Douglas Hay, Peter Linebaugh, and E. P. Thompson (eds.), *Albion's Fatal Tree: Crime and Society in the Eighteenth Century* (New York: Pantheon, 1975), 65–117.

31. Aphra Behn, *Oroonoko; or, The Royal Slave* [1688], ed. Lore Metzger (New York: W. W. Norton, 1973), 5, 77; Bryan Edwards, *The History, Civil and Commercial, of the British West Indies* [1793], facs. reprint of 1819 ed. (New York: AMS Press, 1966), vol. 2, 74, 79, 80, 82; and Edward Long, *The History of Jamaica, or General Survey of the Antient and Modern State of that Island; Reflections on its Situation, Settlements, Inhabitants, Climate, Products, Commerce, Laws, and Government*, 3 vols. (London: T. Lowndes, 1774), vol. 2, 474.

32. David V. Erdman, "Blake's Vision of Slavery," *Journal of the Warburg and Courtauld Institutes* 15 (1952), 242–52; and Linebaugh and Rediker, *The Many-Headed Hydra*, 344–51.

CHAPTER 7

Chartless Voyages and Protean Geographies
Nineteenth-Century American Fictions of the Black Atlantic

GESA MACKENTHUN

Chartless Voyages

In his South Sea romance *Mardi* (1850), Herman Melville sends his multi-cultural crew of Oceanic warriors and philosophers on an allegorical journey through the colonial world in search of the white maiden Yillah, who has been abducted by hostile natives. During their "chartless voyage," they circle the earth from east to west, thus imitating the imperial master narrative of the westward course of empire. Exclaiming that the journey will take them "West, West! West, West!," the protagonist Taji indicates his explorer's passion: west, the direction to which "prophet-fingers" point; west, to which, "at sun-set, kneel all worshipers of fire," to which "in mid-ocean, the great whales turn to die" and to which "face all the Moslem dead in Persia":

> West, West! Whitherward mankind and empires—flocks, caravans, armies, navies; worlds, suns, and stars all wend!—West, West!—Oh boundless boundary! Eternal goal! Whitherward rush, in thousand worlds, ten thousand thousand [sic] keels! Beacon, by which the universe is steered![1]

In search of their ever-evasive goal, eternal knowledge, which endows their romantic quest for the maiden Yillah with a universal framework, the protagonist Taji and his companions travel through an imaginary Pacific archipelago, but their sojourn is at the same time an allegorical circumnavigation of the British Empire and its postcolonial offshoot in America. Their Swiftean flight takes them from Dominora (England) and other symbolic European countries to Vivenza (the United States), Kolomba (South America), around Cape Horn, and on to China, India, and Africa (called Hamora, after the race of Ham). The journey, which gives them occasion to observe and philosophize on the multiple instances of social inequality in the capitalist world, ends abruptly when a sudden storm blows their ship off its western course before the coast of West Africa and chases them back into the Mediterranean. Having reached the end of that ancient sea, their ship spins around its own keel, "and from that inland sea emerged" into space (with "[the] universe . . . before us")—only to find itself back in the Pacific archipelago where their journey began.[2] But before taking off, the travelers have occasion to admire the "great pointed masses" of the Egyptian pyramids; "Granite continents" that, they think, were "not built with human hands."[3]

Interestingly, it is off the coast of Africa where Taji and his Laputian friends are stopped in their tracks and transported back to Egypt. Their forced return to the site of antiquity, frequently regarded as the origin of the *translatio imperii et studi* that they claim to enact, is preceded by their eloquent condemnation of the African slave trade, which, they complain, tears "Hamora's" children from its soil "to till a stranger's." "Oh, tribe of Hamo!," Yoomy exclaims, "thy cup of woe so brims, that soon it must overflow upon the land which holds ye thralls." And the philosopher Babbalanja, "bowing to the blast" of the storm that has arisen, cries: "Thus, oh Vivenza! retribution works! Though long delayed, it comes at last—Judgment, with all her bolts."[4]

While *Mardi*'s "chartless voyage"[5] exposes many of the ills of colonialism and slavery, its mythical plot reiterates some of the most powerful ideological narratives of imperialism, such as the already noted metaphor of the westward course of empire or the plot of captivity and heroic quest for the white maiden who has been abducted by swarthy natives. In keeping with his real-life predecessors Christopher Columbus, Hernán Cortés, and James Cook, Taji readily identifies himself—or lets himself be identified—as a demi-god.[6] The novel only partly reveals the prehistory of Yillah's abduction, which the traumatized Yillah herself cannot remember. What surfaces from her jumbled account is the familiar story of an island tribe that finds a group of European discoverers on its shore, at first sight takes them for gods, learns better when the newcomers respond with violence to some petty offense, and ends up killing them in revenge and self-protection.[7] The child Yillah, who is the only survivor of the massacre, is adopted into the tribe and, like many Euroamerican children adopted into Indian tribes, subsequently forgets her European origin.

Mardi begins with a reference to the voyage of the *Bounty*, whose purpose was to transport breadfruit from the Pacific to the Caribbean, where smart colonial entrepreneurs hoped to turn it into a cheap staple diet for African slaves.[8] Aware of this actual link that connects the Atlantic and Pacific Oceans, the novel uses the means of extended allegory in order to fuse their political and symbolic histories. Both the voyage of the *Bounty* and Melville's experimental circumnavigation in *Mardi* suggest that, as much as the two oceans were geographically separated by the natural barrier of Cape Horn, they were economically linked by a colonial apparatus of plantation slavery and the increasingly important economy of whaling.

The chivalric quest plot of Melville's romance is overwritten with the Gothic plot of Taji's pursuit by the three spectral sons of the priest Aleema, whom he killed in order to rescue the maiden—only to lose her again. This primal scene of colonial violence, which effectually presents itself as the response to the anterior violence of the natives themselves and thereby inverts the usual encounter situation on tropical beaches, taints Taji's romantic quest in a similar way as the quest for colonial riches is tainted by the blood of African slaves.[9]

On several narrative levels, I want to argue, *Mardi* collapses the geographical and metaphorical differences between the Atlantic and Pacific Oceans, integrating them into a larger imaginary geography of the colonial world—a geography ruled by metaphorical processes of conversion and inversion. In the following pages, I will explore similar metaphorical transactions between different oceanic spaces in other nineteenth-century American novels. In order to introduce one of the theoretical figures I am going to use in describing these literary processes of condensation, displacement, and overdetermination, let us briefly return to the geographical site that forms the terminal point of Taji's colonial journey. Because his ship is caught by the cosmic whirlwind at roughly the same place—the mouth of the River Nile—that is said to have been inhabited by one of Greek mythology's wise old men of the sea, the sea god Proteus, son of Oceanos and the nymph Tethys. Each day Proteus arises from the waves of the Mediterranean in order to guard Poseidon's seal flock on the island of Pharos, which would later become the seat of the famous lighthouse of Alexandria. Proteus is a prophet and a shape shifter. In *The Odyssey*, Homer relates how Menelaus tries to catch him in order to learn about his future and to find his way home. But Proteus evades him by assuming the shapes of fire, water, a lion, a dragon, and a wild boar. Holding on tight, Menelaus is able to press Proteus into revealing his knowledge, but the information is rather distressing. The old man tells Menelaus that he would have to return to the waters of the Aegyptos (the Nile) and give sacrifice to the gods if he ever wants to find his way home.[10]

The mythical figure of the sea prophet Proteus is useful for distinguishing the multi-cultural world of ships and sailors from the dualism that inspired the ideological framework of the emerging world of nation-states with its increasingly racialist ascriptions of identity. One such Protean sailor, who was kidnapped into the world of the Black Atlantic only to turn out one of its most articulate and widely published critics, is Olaudah Equiano. In the year 1768, two years after his manumission, Equiano puts it into his head to sail for Smyrna in Turkey. He greatly enjoys the hospitality of the people there and the abundance of excellent food and wine. In particular, he notices, the Turks are less reserved about entertaining a black man than they are about Christians.[11] Equiano maintains his interest in Turkey even after his return to London and after having seen the major ports of the Mediterranean. But his "roving disposition" prevents him from returning to Smyrna for a number of years. In the meantime, he joins various ventures to the Caribbean and his most quixotic journey, John Phipps's expedition to the North Pole in 1773. Having reached farther north than any previous expedition and barely surviving the beginnings of the Arctic winter that threatens to crush their ship, Equiano returns to England with two intentions: he is determined to become a "first-rate Christian," and he wants to return to Smyrna, "there to end my days."[12] These two goals prove incompatible: Equiano becomes a Christian and never returns to the Islamic splendor of Smyrna. His intended trip to Turkey is prevented first by his participation in the rescue of the African slave John Annis, and then by his being called back from the outbound ship by his late captain Mr. Hughes. Equiano reads these events as providential ("what was appointed for me I must submit to"), but at the same time he undergoes a spiritual crisis, "blaspheming" against God and experiencing "awful 'visions of the night.'"[13] His subsequent conversion experience can easily make us forget that Equiano the "Ethiopian" had almost become a convert to Islam. It is a set of coincidences like this that drives him from one port, and one temporary cultural identity, to the next—much like a ship tossed between the waves.

In both narratives, Melville's *Mardi* and Equiano's autobiography, the Eastern Mediterranean functions as a site of fascination and otherness: a place whose ancient attractions are recognized but ultimately spurned in favor of the intellectual and material promises of the colonial Atlantic and the imperial Pacific. These promises, which lie at the core of early national political rhetoric, were often defined in opposition to oriental culture. The nationalist poets of the early republic—like Philip Freneau, Joel Barlow, and Timothy Dwight—celebrated the founding of the United States as the fulfillment of biblical and secular prophecies of an empire of knowlege, commerce, and peace, and, using the cultural trope of *ex oriente lux*, projected their imperial vision toward the regions beyond the vast expanse of the Pacific Ocean. The early novelists Royall Tyler and Susanna Rowson, by contrast, defined the political identity of the United States by setting it apart from oriental despotism.[14] Updike Underhill, the protagonist of Tyler's novel *The Algerine Captive* (1797), is captured by Barbary pirates while under way on a slaving venture to Africa. Although the fetters of his Algerian captivity are rather light and he is allowed to walk around freely and practice his profession as physician, Underhill persistently compares his own captivity with that of the Africans he had helped to enslave. Being himself a captive of Muslims, his experiences of the horrors of the slave ship, and his guilty awareness of his own complicity with the institution of slavery, recede, and Underhill's original plan to become an abolitionist gradually gives to his discovery of the true values of liberty and democracy. Although his beliefs in Christianity and republicanism are at times seriously shaken by his disputes with a well-informed Islamic religious leader, they are finally reinforced by his observation of Islamic "despotism," and he returns to America a prodigal son.

Halfway through his narrative, whose burlesque domestic part is separated from the oriental narrative by the voyage of the slave ship, Underhill hopes that the "wounds" he received "when a slave myself may expiate for the inhumanity" he was "necessitated" to impose on the Africans as a slave ship surgeon. And indeed, by the end of his tale he has all but forgotten about the continuing participation of his compatriots in the transatlantic slave trade. His own experience as a captive "in Africa" now allows him to become reconciled with the necessary compromise inherent in America's political system. He concludes his narrative by appealing to his countrymen to keep "union among ourselves. For to no nation besides the United States can that ancient saying be more emphatically applied; BY UNITING WE STAND, BY DIVIDING WE FALL."[15]

Tyler's emphasis on the need to surmount internal divisions between the advocates and the opponents of slavery and to define American civilization in strict opposition to oriental despotism anticipates the ideological debates of the antebellum period, which witnessed a massive increase in abolitionist activities and a growing fear about political friction over the issue of slavery; of slave revolts such as had been witnessed in various places in the Caribbean and southern states; and of the haunting recognition—unavoidable in face of an increasing number of racial "mongrels"—that official "scientific" theories about the biological incompatibility of the races were unfeasible. With the growing contribution of African American writers and orators to the discourse about slavery, there can be observed a return of the trope of African splendor, as it is evident in the passage from *Mardi* I quoted at the beginning. These discussions, as I will show, left their traces in antebellum fictions of maritime America.

The Grandeur of Egypt

The notion of the grandeur of the non-Christian Mediterranean, more precisely the splendor of ancient Egypt, is a pervasive presence in American texts of the Black Atlantic; it provides a historical and cultural backdrop to the theme of slavery and emancipation. In the pages to follow, I will trace this presence in a series of fictional tales involving shape-shifting ships and hybrid geographies: Edgar Allan Poe's *Arthur Gordon Pym* (1837), Maxwell Philip's *Emmanuel Appadocca* (1854), and Herman Melville's novels *Moby-Dick* (1851) and *Benito Cereno* (1855). I will argue that, whether intentionally or not, these texts subvert official discourses of oceanic colonialism and imperialism—in their forms of Atlantic slavery and Pacific exploration—whose amnesiac and idealist rhetoric they counter with "motley" (though hardly more realistic) representations of the colonial world.

As Bernhard Klein shows, Egypt occupies the discursive site of a Protean and hedonistic counterpart of Caesarian imperialism in Shakespeare's *Antony and Cleopatra*.[16] It is interesting to see how the ideologeme of Egypt as the antithesis of Western colonial discourse reappears in antebellum American fictions of the Black Atlantic. The discourse of African splendor reproduces a contemporary debate about the African origin of ancient civilization and counteracts the dominant racialism of white supremacists such as Samuel G. Morton or Josiah C. Nott with a "subterranean network of allusions to the age of African grandeur."[17] The idealized image of Africa was popularized by the travel writings of Mungo Park and John Ledyard, as well as philosophical treatises of European intellectuals that celebrated Africa as the origin of civilization. Many intellectuals throughout Europe and America argued, like John Stuart Mill, that "it was from Negroes [the original Egyptians] . . . that the Greeks learnt their first lesson in civilization; and to the records and traditions of these Negroes did the Greek philosophers . . . resort as a treasury of mysterious wisdom."[18] African American abolitionist orators like Frederick Douglass and Martin Delany referred to the African origins, via the culture of ancient Egypt, of occidental humanism as it is encapsulated in freemasonry. Delany writes that "to Africa is the world indebted for its knowledge of the mysteries of Ancient Freemasonry," and he asks: "Was it not Africa that gave birth to Euclid, the master geometrician of the world? And was it not in consequence of a twenty-five years' residence in Africa that the great Pythagoras was enabled to discover that key problem in geometry—the forty-seventh problem of Euclid—without which Masonry would be incomplete?"[19] Delany regarded Moses—a "fugitive slave" from Egypt and initiate to the masonic knowledge imported from Ethiopia—as the major transmitter of the secrets of architecture.[20] Douglass followed suit when he wrote in 1854 that

> [we] traced the entangled threads of history and of civilization back to their sources in Africa. We called attention to the somewhat disagreeable fact— agreeable to us, but not so to our Teutonic brethren—that the arts and appliances and blessings of our civilization flourished in the very heart of Ethiopia, at a time when all Europe floundered in the depths of ignorance and barbarism. We dwelt on the magnificence and stupendous dimensions of Egyptian architecture, and held up the fact . . . that the race was master of mechanical forces of which the present generations of men are ignorant.[21]

The trope of African splendor makes a rather unexpected appearance in Edgar Allan Poe's novel *The Narrative of Arthur Gordon Pym of Nantucket* (1837). As probably no other writer at his time, Poe articulates the fear ravaging the American South after the black rebellions of Haiti and Nat Turner, as well as the anxiety, among pro-slavery and anti-slavery circles alike, about the growing racial hybridization that the peculiar institution produced. He chooses the high seas and exotic beaches as settings for expressing these fears.

Taking its materials from real and imaginary narratives of exploration, the plot of *Pym* involves mutiny, shipwreck, cannibalism, a last-minute rescue, and a series of weird discoveries on board the rescue ship. The action culminates with the most extraordinary discovery of all—that of the Antarctian island Tsalal, whose inhabitants are as black as pitch (down to their teeth) and whose phobia of everything white mirrors, and ridicules, scientific racism's obsession with the cultural meanings of the shades of skin color and the shapes of cranial bumps. The plot ends with treachery, live entombment, and a hairbreadth escape in a native boat that takes the two survivors, Arthur Gordon Pym and his "mongrel" companion Peters, toward the abyss of the South Pole. As they rush, Ulysses-like, into the cataract, a chasm throws itself open to receive them: "But there arose in our pathway a shrouded human figure, very far larger in its proportions than any dweller among men. And the hue of the skin of the figure was of the perfect whiteness of the snow."[22] Here Pym's narrative ends, but the novel as such closes with a "Note" by the "editor"—Mr. Poe himself—informing the reader that Pym suddenly and distressingly died before being able to complete his narrative and that Peters has vanished in Illinois.[23]

Pym translates the dualistic concepts of antebellum racial theories into semantic hyperbole and geographical fantasy. The cultural apartheid on Tsalal even extends to the chemical composition of the water, which consists of differently colored strands that never mingle. But Poe's narrative at the same time constantly shatters these binaries, either by inverting them or by overwriting them with a narrative of cultural hybridization. The latter is most evident in the increasing importance that the ethnic "hybrid" Peters receives in the second part of the novel. The former is enacted, for example, when Pym symbolically slips into the skin of an African slave and falls asleep in his coffinlike hiding place in the hold of the first ship. Awakening, he realizes that he must have slept for an excessively long period of time.[24] Suffering from thirst and hunger, from the "close atmosphere of the hold" as well as a "multitude of gloomy feelings," he is "overpowered . . . with a desire to sleep, yet trembled at the thought of indulging it, lest there might exist some pernicious influence, like that of burning charcoal, in the confined air of the hold." The roll of the brig tells him that the ship must have reached the "main ocean" and that "no ordinary gale was blowing" outside. Pym finally falls into a kind of "stupor" in which he has "dreams . . . of the most terrific description," of being "smothered to death between huge pillows, by demons of the most ghastly and ferocious aspect," and of being held in the embrace of "immense serpents." He dreams of finding himself in limitless and awe-inspiring deserts and black and silent morasses covered with "immensely tall trunks of trees, gray and leafless," which were "swaying to and fro their skeleton arms" and "crying to the silent waters for mercy, in the shrill and piercing accents of the most acute agony and despair."[25] The soul-landscape of Pym's slave ship fantasy undergoes a change of scene, "and I stood, naked and alone, amid the burning sand plains of Zahara. At my feet lay crouched a fierce lion of the tropics," which inevitably attacks him—only to turn out, upon awakening, to be Tiger, Pym's Newfoundland dog.[26] Arthur languishes on in the hold until his faithful dog turns aggressive and attacks him. Having managed to defeat man's best friend, Pym hears Augustus calling out for him but realizes that he is unable to utter a syllable. Only at the very last moment is he able to extract himself from his paralysis and be saved from live entombment.[27]

As Wilson Harris realizes in his reading of Poe's "schizophrenic sea," Pym's imprisonment in the hold of the *Grampus* resembles the "drowning at sea within the black hold of a slave ship."[28] Like a slave during the Middle Passage, the Nantucket boy is locked into the hold, suffers from thirst and hunger, and is haunted by dreams of Africa. This act of fictional displacement is contrasted by a hyperbolical deployment of contemporary racial theories in the description of the island Tsalal as a place of primeval and "treacherous" savagery. But surprisingly, this characterization of Tsalal is called into question by the possible signs of advanced civilization that Pym and Peters encounter during their trip through the wilderness. Searching for an exit from the system of caves into which they were thrown during a native ambush, they are intrigued by the shape of the caves, as well as certain inscriptions on their walls. While Peters favors the view that the hieroglyphics were indeed human-made, Pym determines that they were "the work of nature."[29] Yet the surroundings remind him "of those dreary regions marking the site of degraded Babylon." They behold what seem at first sight the remnants of ancient buildings, "huge tumuli, apparently the wreck of some gigantic structures of art." But at a second glance Pym decides that "no semblance of art could be detected."[30]

The evocation of Babylon can be joined to other instances in which Tsalal is described as a place of racial apartheid. But the presence of human writing would also turn Tsalal into a place of civilization—a kind of artificial Africa where, it was believed, the present rule of savagery had likewise been preceded by an ancient civilization. While the tumuli are reminiscent of the Egyptian pyramids, the reference to the possibility of ancient writing recalls the Africanists' thesis that writing itself originated in Africa.[31] The nature of the stone structures and the inscriptions remains ambivalent within Pym's narrative. But in the appendix, "Poe" (the editor) implicitly contradicts the rash conclusion of his protagonist in stating that after extensive philological examination the inscriptions must be identified as human products, consisting of the Ethiopian verbal root "To be shady," the Arabic verbal root "To be white," and the Egyptian word meaning "The region of the south."

As Dana Nelson remarks, the editor's acceptance of the inscriptions and stone formations as the work of human beings destabilizes Pym's colonial self-image.[32] In this conflict between his two narrators, Poe reveals the arbitrariness of racial theory's color symbolism. The editor's deciphering of the cave inscriptions suggests the (former) existence of a civilized "black" culture in the novel's geographically displaced Africa and turns Pym's womblike cave into the cradle of human civilization—an Egyptian tomb decorated with prophetic murals. But far from celebrating the Ethiopian origins of classic civilization, as some of his enlightened contemporaries did, Poe's text neutralizes their historical theories in a phantasmagoric play on geography and cultural difference.[33]

Seventeen years after the publication of *Arthur Gordon Pym*, the Trinidadian writer Maxwell Philip published his pirate novel *Emmanuel Appadocca, or, Blighted Life: A Tale of the Boucaneers* (1854)—a text that likewise transfers the discourse of African splendor to Western waters, but in a vastly different way. The tragic hero of Philip's novel, an illegitimate son of a British plantation owner and a Trinidadian mulatto woman, takes revenge on his father for having abused his mother and abandoned him. A self-declared avenger of all victims of European colonial exploitation and parental disavowal, Appadocca plies the Caribbean in a highly technologized ship like an oceanic version of Robin Hood and redistributes the goods from the captured merchant ships to the poor inhabitants of the islands. Like Cooper's famous pirate, the Red Rover, Appadocca and his crew live at sea; indeed their power would dissolve if they went on land and exposed themselves to the superior military force of Britain. Of course, a lonely guerrilla battle like this cannot be victorious; as the Red Rover before him, Appadocca is defeated in the end—not by the clumsy British warship that tries to persecute him, nor by a storm at sea that his ship masters with ease, but by the power of history—a self-declared destiny that orders him to commit suicide after having accomplished his personal revenge.

Although a sea novel apparently unconcerned with the issue of slavery, *Emmanuel Appadocca* was written in response to the passing of the Fugitive Slave Law in the United States (1850), which required American citizens to return escaped slaves to their southern owners. As Philip declares in his preface, his book was inspired by the practice of southern plantation owners to keep slave women as mistresses and to beget children on them for the sole purpose of exploiting their workforce.[34] His story of Appadocca's "blighted life" is meant to condemn the enormous crime inflicted upon people of African descent throughout the Americas. Apart from the significant reference to slavery in the preface, however, the figure of Appadocca remains ethnically ambivalent. His complexion is said to be of a light olive color that "showed a mixture of blood, and proclaimed that the man was connected with some dark race, and in the infinity of grades in the population of Spanish America, he may have been said to be of that which is commonly designated Quadroon."[35] Yet at other times, his skin color is uniformly described as pale or very light—at least in part the result of his habit of spending most of his time in his cabin.[36]

Appadocca's African roots become evident through his intellectual identification with the pan-Atlantic struggle against exploitation and slavery, and through his esoteric knowledge of astronomy and mathematics. Having studied mathematics and astronomy at Paris, he acquired a knowledge of cosmic and technological processes that would greatly assist him in his later career as a pirate. His ship, for example, is a complex machine— anticipating Captain Nemo's *Nautilus* in Verne's novel. A set of mirrors on the top masts allows the seamen to see beyond the horizon, thus proving them technologically superior to their enemies. Appadocca proves his masonic skill when he is taken prisoner on board the English warship and scribbles a series of mathematical formulae on the cabin wall that, as he explains, help him predict the hurricane that will eventually destroy the enemy ship and seal the fate of his own life.

The observation of celestial constellations occupies a central place in the novel, and it readily blends with the theme of human rights. It is during a starlit night on the River Thames in London, surrounded by the beauty and the despair of England's capital (he saves the life of a girl who wants to commit suicide with her illegitimate child), that Appadocca determines to take revenge on his father. Touched by the parallel between the girl's fate and his mother's, he exclaims that he will "'vindicate the law of nature which has been violated in me, and in your child.'"[37] Appropriating the law of nature that guides the planets above to become the moral basis of his "right" to strike out against the "false systems" of humankind, he justifies his intention with the argument that his father has violated "the natural contract between parent and child."

Appadocca's identification with the "wretched of the earth" becomes most obvious during his conversations with his friend Charles—who is also the son of the British commander who persecutes him. Charles is quite stupefied when Appadocca confronts him with an extended critique of capitalist exploitation, including the enslavement of Africans. He weakly responds that after all "commerce, and the voyages" were "the proper stimulants to civilization and human cultivation." This elicits the following rejoinder from Appadocca:

> The human mind does not require to be pioneered by Gog and Magog in order to improve. It is not in the busy mart, not at the tinkling of gold, that it grows and becomes strong; nor is it on the shaft of the steam-engine which propels your huge fabrics to rich though savage shores that it increases. No: there it degenerates and falls into the mere thing whose beginning is knack, whose end is knack. The mind can thrive only in the silence that courts contemplation. It was in such silence that among a race, which is now despised and oppressed, speculation took wing, and the mind burst forth, and, scorning things of earth, scaled the heavens, read the stars, and elaborated systems of philosophy, religion, and government: while the other parts of the world were either enveloped in darkness, or following in eager and uncontemplative haste the luring genii of riches. Commerce makes steam engines and money—it assists not the philosophical progress of the mind.[38]

Appadocca rhetorically constructs Africa as the birthplace of Western civilization, which has subsequently been desecrated by being turned into the human warehouse of the colonial economy. Appadocca's own expertise in the science of astronomy acquires another meaning in this context, as it is a manifestation of the secret knowledge he shares with the ancient magi of Egypt and Ethiopa. In evoking the trope of Ethiopian splendor, the text clearly marks Appadocca as a person of African descent; yet he is a spokesman for *all* victims of an inhuman and exploitative system, and his tragic end marks Philip's bleak outlook on the future of race and class relations in America.[39]

Both Arthur Gordon Pym and Emmanuel Appadocca experience ship-board memories of Africa: Pym by enduring nightmares and fits of suffo-cation in the hold; Appadocca while predicting his own future by way of astronomical calculations. Both Pym and Appadocca possess the Protean gift of prophecy: Pym's nightmare in the ship's womb prefigures his near suffocation on the black island; Appadocca predicts the moment of his and his enemies' destruction. Both texts, moreover, employ the image of Egyptian grandeur—but while the Africanist rhetoric provides Appadocca with a raison d'être and a justification for his revenge, it remains a largely unrecognized sign of cultural confusion and anxiety in Poe's novel.

Hybrid Geographies

The transfer of ancient Egypt to the New World rips the ideological seams of discourses that defend slavery and racism in America. It must be seen as part of a larger metaphorical transaction in which the Atlantic world is in-fused with historical reminiscences dating back to the Mediterranean past. Other fictional texts of the Black Atlantic would carry this process of se-mantic hybridization into the Pacific. This is most obviously the case in Herman Melville's novella *Benito Cereno* (1855) and—less obviously—his novel *Moby-Dick* (1851).

In *Benito Cereno*, a text based on an actual slave ship revolt on a Spanish ship off the coast of Chile in 1817, Melville metaphorically blends the real event with allusions to the history of Atlantic slavery, from its introduction to the Caribbean by Columbus and the first successful postcolonial revolu-tion in St. Domingue (1791) all the way to the *Amistad* slave ship revolt in 1839.[40] *Benito Cereno*'s evocation of the beginnings of the transatlantic slave trade, semantically fused with references to two successful black re-bellions in the New World, betrays, as Eric Sundquist argues, Melville's

> recognition that slavery was hemispheric and that its fullest literary represen-tation as well as its fullest political critique required a view that embraced sev-eral cultures, several nations, much as DuBois was later to recognize that the attack on American racial injustice and the reconstruction of African Ameri-can cultural history had to be pursued in a diasporic Pan-African framework.[41]

In addition to that, Melville generates an ambivalent narrative voice in which the personal, limited, and benevolently racist point of view of the American captain Amasa Delano is constantly relativized by an unidenti-fied narrative voice-over that compares the blacks, whom Delano regards as primitive savages, with the Sphinx, Nubian sculptors, and the sculptures guarding Egyptian tombs.[42] Carolyn Karcher, who points out this second-level discourse of African splendor, adds that a "close analysis of Melville's narrative technique uncovers countless examples of the ways he challenges readers to resist Delano's dangerous distortions and to reexamine Africans in the light of their native culture, as described in contemporary travel accounts and abolitionist tracts."[43] *Benito Cereno* thus develops a "subterranean network of allusions to the age of African grandeur" with which it counteracts the racialism that Delano shares with his supremacist contemporaries.[44] Delano regards blacks as valuable "natural" servants and hairdressers but deems them altogether incapable of political action: of carrying out a rebellion and then covering up the deed by enacting an instant and intricate shipboard masque. Ironically, his blindness toward the mental faculties of Africans both blocks his perception and saves his life.

Though set in the Pacific, then, Melville's novella can be seen to document the "rhizomorphic, fractal structure of the transcultural, international formation" of the Black Atlantic.[45] With its very particular juxtaposition of different times and geographical spaces, a juxtaposition that violates and subverts the normal order of history and narrative, Melville's method is reminiscent of what Michel Foucault has called heterotopia: a radical disruption of conventional orders of time and space as it is found, for example, in modernist and postmodernist fictional texts.[46] Read in terms of Foucault's concept of heterotopia, *Benito Cereno* constructs a discursive "zone" that "desiccate[s] speech, stop[s] words in their tracks, contest[s] the very possibility of grammar at its source." Melville's ambivalent narrative strategy leads to the dissolution of straight-cut beliefs—the supremacists' belief in the mental inferiority of Africans as well as the abolitionists' claim of their "natural" meekness and timidity.

Benito Cereno's rhetorical project to disclose the interconnectedness of different geographies and histories is already anticipated in Melville's novel *Moby-Dick*, published four years earlier. Here is Ishmael's account of the *Pequod*'s rounding, *Flying Dutchman*–like, of the Cape of Good Hope on her way to the whaling grounds in the Pacific Ocean:

> But, at last, when turning to the eastward, the Cape winds began howling around us, and we rose and fell upon the long, troubled seas that are there; when the ivory-tusked Pequod sharply bowed to the blast, and gored the dark waves in her madness, till, like showers of silver chips, the foam-flakes flew over her bulwarks; then all this desolate vacuity of life went away, but gave place to sights more dismal than before.
>
> Close to our bows, strange forms in the water darted hither and thither before us; while thick in our rear flew the inscrutable sea-ravens. And every morning, perched on our stays, rows of these birds were seen; and spite of our hootings, for a long time obstinately clung to the hemp, as though they deemed our ship some drifting, uninhabited craft; a thing appointed to desolation, and therefore fit roosting-place for their homeless selves. And heaved and heaved, still unrestingly heaved the black sea, as if its vast tides were a conscience; and the great mundane soul were in anguish and remorse for the long sin and suffering it had bred.[47]

As the *Pequod* approaches her doomed end, it becomes clear that the memory of the "anguish" and "suffering" of the black sea of conscience are clinging on to her like the log on the line. In the chapter "The Log and Line," the *Pequod*, which has just suffered the destruction of her compass and quadrant, loses her log. While Ahab deliriously cries out that he will replace all the lost instruments with the power of his magic, the black cabin boy Pip, who lost his mind after jumping from a whale boat and being cast away in the open sea, fantasizes that his own self was pulling on the line, and he cries for a hatchet to prevent his alter ego from coming on board. When Ahab asks Pip, "Who art thou, boy?," the boy replies in the style of a fugitive slave bill: "One hundred pounds of clay reward for Pip; five feet high—looks cowardly."[48] At other points in the novel, Pip is cast as the agent of Atlantic memory. For example, he addresses Queequeg, who prepares for his death, asking him whether he could do him a favor if "the currents carry ye to those sweet Antilles where the beaches are only beat with water-lilies" and "[seek] out one little Pip, who's now been missing long: I think he's in those far Antilles."[49]

The *Pequod* has sailed straight for the Azores, from there to the Cape Verde Islands, the whaling grounds off the Patagonian coast, then straight to St. Helena and the Cape of Good Hope. On her zigzag course through the Atlantic, Ahab's ship never touches on the Antilles. Clearly, therefore, Pip's talk of having gone overboard in the Antilles must be understood metaphorically, or, as Starbuck suggests, in terms of forgotten childhood or collective memories.[50] Pip has not gone overboard in the Antilles, but— like the baby ghost in Toni Morrison's novel *Beloved*—he seems to remember the fates of the thousands of slaves who have. Pip's mental condition endows him with a power of vision that transcends time, place, and individual memory and conjures up the "black" Atlantic past even while the *Pequod* meets her doomed end in the Pacific—an end that allegorizes America's imperial future.

Just like *Benito Cereno*—if in a less accentuated way—*Moby-Dick* condenses various historical moments. It geographically displaces the memory of the "Black Atlantic" to the Pacific, thus suggesting a thematic link between America's past (and present) involvement in the transatlantic slave-based economy and its Western future. In condensing various historical moments and geographies, Melville's narratives suspend linear time and the artificial divisions of space, replacing them with a transnational spatiality, as well as a "modern" temporality in which the present is shot through with images from the past and, in *Moby-Dick*, prophetic images of the future. In aesthetically subverting the determinist teleology of Manifest Destiny with a complex temporality, Melville exchanges the chronotope (or time-space) of imperial history with a subaltern and heterotopic memory.[51]

Protean Ships

Ships are miniature geographies—social spaces in which the hierarchies of landed societies are acted out, often in extreme ways, and are therefore in constant danger of being subverted. Greg Dening has argued that the mutiny on the *Bounty* was not the result of too much shipboard violence but of the ambivalent cultural semantics acted out on board a ship that was turned into a swimming greenhouse, which resulted in the erosion of social order.[52] The Protean character of the *Bounty*, as well as the fatality of her voyage, is shared by most fictional ships in the texts I've discussed. Their hybridity, of which Poe's blundering discovery vessels are only the bluntest example, betrays the ambivalences and contradictions of American colonial societies. Emmanuel Appadocca's pirate ship, along with its captain, is a truly fantastic shape shifter—best anticipated in sea literature by James Fenimore Cooper's famous Red Rover and his power of masquerade.[53] Within hours, it is able to mutate from a schooner into a brig into a brigantine into a wreck, thereby bringing confusion and near destruction onto the persecuting British navy ship. It is to the Protean powers of his ship that Appadocca owes his independence and his success. And while the Spanish slaver *San Dominick* in *Benito Cereno* becomes a veritable stage for acting out the social drama of slavery and rebellion, it is of course the *Pequod* that most clearly symbolizes the Protean nature associated with ships ever since Sebastian Brant's *Ship of Fools*.

Named after the presumably extinct New England tribe, the *Pequod* is figured in Africanist terms. She "was apparelled like any barbaric Ethiopian emperor, his neck heavy with pendants of polished ivory. She was a thing of trophies. A cannibal of a craft, tricking herself forth in the chased bones of her enemies. All round, her unpannelled, open bulwarks were garnished like one continuous jaw, with the long sharp teeth of the sperm whale, inserted there for pins."[54] Her "long rows of teeth on the bulwarks glistened in the moonlight; and like the white ivory tusks of some huge elephant, vast curving icicles depended from the bows."[55] Moreover, the "Ethiopian" ship and her multicultural and "motley" crew—representing all races of humankind—seem to form a living organism:[56]

> They were one man, not thirty. For as the one ship that held them all; though it was put together of all contrasting things—oak, and maple, and pine wood; iron, and pitch, and hemp—yet all these ran into each other in the one concrete hull, which shot on its way, both balanced and directed by the long central keel; even so, all the individualities of the crew, this man's valor, that man's fear; guilt and guiltlessness, all varieties were welded into oneness, and were all directed to that fatal goal which Ahab their one lord and keel did point to.[57]

Representing the *e pluribus unum* of American democracy, the *Pequod* is an allegorical ship of state. But at the same time she is a ghost ship and a slaver. As the crew boils the meat of a whale in the tryworks in order to store the oil in casks under deck, Ishmael describes their faces at work, "all begrimed with smoke and sweat" and strangely reflecting the red heat of the fire:

> As they narrated to each other their unholy adventures, their tales of terror told in words of mirth; as their uncivilized laughter forked upwards out of them, like the flames from the furnace; as to and fro, in their front, the harpooneers wildly gesticulated with their huge pronged forks and dippers; as the wind howled on, and the sea leaped, and the ship groaned and dived, and yet steadfastly shot her red hell further and further into the blackness of the sea and the night, and scornfully champed the white bone in her mouth, and viciously spat round her on all sides; then the rushing Pequod, freighted with savages, and laden with fire, and burning a corpse, and plunging into that blackness of darkness, seemed the material counterpart of her monomaniac commander's soul.[58]

Laden with memories of the colonial Atlantic past, Ahab's specter ship rushes toward her prophesied and prophetic destruction. The *Pequod* goes down accompanied by the "archangelic shrieks" of a sky-hawk that she drags with her into the vortex because its wing had been accidentally nailed to the mast by Tashtego seeking to secure Ahab's red flag. The end of Melville's symbolic ship of state presents a bleak comment on the impending domestic crisis on the eve of Civil War, as well as the imperial project of American expansion into the Pacific.

The fictional ships of early American literature, this essay has tried to argue, function as repertories of colonial memories and as imaginary stages for enacting colonial conflicts. In imagining Protean ships, hybrid geographies, and oceanic contact zones, antebellum novels of the Black Atlantic frequently suspend and subvert the clean divisions of imperial discourse, and they disclose the complex interconnectedness between the seemingly dissociated histories of various maritime areas—the Mediterranean of antiquity, the Atlantic of the Middle Passage, and the Pacific of America's imperial future. Reading the seas—whether real or imaginary—can give us new insights into processes and relations that are often hidden on land under a cluster of discursive layers. Reading and rereading the seas may also direct us to charting new analytical courses through the marvelous histories of mariners and nations, oceans and voyagers.

Notes

1. Herman Melville, *Mardi, and a Voyage Thither*, ed. Nathalia Wright (Putney, VT: Hendricks House, 1990), 482.
2. *Ibid.*, 487, 404–86.
3. *Ibid.*, 486.
4. *Ibid.*, 485–6. *Mardi* includes a long description of southern slavery, including a parody of one of its major defenders, John Calhoun, whom Melville calls Nulli—an allusion to the

nullification crisis (466–9). Standing in front of the Statue of Liberty, the travelers read the inscription: "In—this—re—publi—can—land—all—men—are—born—free—and—equal. . . . Except—the—tribe—of—Hamo." The U.S. Senate is a huge banquet of overweight fellows filling themselves with exquisite food and drink with a "quaffing, guzzling, gobbling noise" (448, 450).

5.   Having returned to the Pacific islands, Taji sighs, "Oh, reader, list! I've chartless voyaged." Melville, *Mardi*, 487.

6.   *Ibid.*, 145.

7.   *Ibid.*, 269.

8.   *Ibid.*, 1.

9.   Michael Berthold has provided an excellent reading of the imperial implications of *Mardi*: "'born-free-and-equal': Benign Cliché and Narrative Imperialism in Melville's *Mardi*," *Studies in the Novel* 25 (1993), 16–27.

10.   Homer, *The Odyssey*, trans. E. V. Rieu (Harmondsworth: Penguin, 1946), 73–9 (Book 4: 355–570).

11.   Olaudah Equiano, *The Interesting Narrative and Other Writings*, ed. Vincent Carretta (Harmondsworth: Penguin, 1995), 166–7.

12.   *Ibid.*, 178–9.

13.   *Ibid.*, 181–2.

14.   Like Tyler's *Algerine Captive*, Susanna Rowson's play *Slaves in Algiers; Or, A Struggle for Freedom* (1794) was published in the context of the diplomatic wrangling between the United States and the Barbary States over access to Mediterranean markets that would finally lead to the Tripolitan War in the first decade of the nineteenth century. See Joseph Schöpp, "Liberty's Sons and Daughters: Susanna Haswell Rowson's and Royall Tyler's Algerine Captives," Klaus H. Schmidt and Fritz Fleischmann (eds.), *Early America Re-Explored: New Readings in Colonial, Early National, and Antebellum Cuture* (New York et al.: Peter Lang, 2000), 291–307.

15.   Royall Tyler, *The Algerine Captive* [1797], ed. Don L. Cook (New Haven, CT: College & University Press, 1970), 224.

16.   See his essay in this volume (chapter 5).

17.   Gloria Horsley-Meacham, "Bull of the Nile: Symbol, History, and Racial Myth in 'Benito Cereno,'" *New England Quarterly* 64, no. 4 (1991), 225–42. On the same topic, see Martin Bernal, *Black Athena: The Afroasiatic Roots of Classical Civilization* (London: Vintage, 1987), and Wilson Jeremiah Moses, *Afrotopia: The Roots of African American Popular History* (Cambridge: Cambridge University Press, 1998).

18.   Quoted in Horsley-Meacham, "Bull of the Nile," 235.

19.   Martin Delany, *The Origin and Objects of Ancient Freemasonry* (1853), quoted after Robert S. Levine, *Martin Delany, Frederick Douglass, and the Politics of Representative Identity* (Chapel Hill: University of North Carolina Press, 1997), 8.

20.   Levine, *Martin Delany*, 9.

21.   Frederick Douglass, quoted in Levine, *Martin Delany*, 9.

22.   Edgar Allan Poe, *The Narrative of Arthur Gordon Pym of Nantucket*, ed. Harold Beaver (Harmondsworth: Penguin, 1983), 239.

23.   *Ibid.*, 240.

24.   *Ibid.*, 63–4.

25.   *Ibid.*, 65–6.

26.   *Ibid.*, 66.

27.   *Ibid.*, 79.

28.   Wilson Harris, *The Womb of Space: The Cross-Cultural Imagination* (Westport, CT: Greenwood, 1983), 21.

29.   Poe, *Pym*, 225.

30.   *Ibid.*, 230.

31.   Horsley-Meacham, "Bull of the Nile," 234.

32.   Dana Nelson, *The Word in Black and White: Reading "Race" in American Literature, 1638–1867* (New York: Oxford University Press, 1992), 104.

33.   The Tsalal episode—besides its obvious references to Africa—is inscribed with the colonial encounters on Hawaii, in New Zealand, and at the American northwest coast.

34.   Maxwell Philip, *Emmanuel Appadocca, or Blighted Life: A Tale of the Boucaneers* [1854], ed. Selwyn Cudjoe (Amherst: University of Massachusetts Press, 1997), 6.

35.   *Ibid.*, 23–4.

36.   *Ibid.*, 91–2, 223.
37.   *Ibid.*, 101–6.
38.   *Ibid.*, 116.
39.   The universalist dimension of *Emmanuel Appadocca* distinguishes Philip's novel from those of other African American writers, like Frederick Douglass and Martin Delany. However, contrary to the slavery literature of most of their contemporaries, both Douglass and Delany transcend the boundaries of national and continental discourse in their fictional treatments of slave ship mutinies on the high seas and in their concern with the United States' involvement in the African slave trade. See Frederick Douglass, "The Heroic Slave" [1853], *The Narrative and Selected Writings*, ed. Michael Meyer (New York: Modern Library, 1984), 299–348; and Martin R. Delany, *Blake, or The Huts of America* [1861], ed. Floyd J. Miller (Boston: Beacon Press, 1970).
40.   For full readings of this complex metaphorical network, see Carolyn Karcher, "The Riddle of the Sphinx: Melville's 'Benito Cereno' and the *Amistad* Case," Robert F. Burkholder (ed.), *Critical Essays on Herman Melville's "Benito Cereno"* (New York: G. K. Hall, 1992), 196–229; H. Bruce Franklin, "Past, Present, and Future Seemed One," Burkholder (ed.), *Critical Essays on Herman Melville's "Benito Cereno,"* 230–46; and Eric Sundquist, *To Wake the Nations: Race in the Making of American Literature* (Cambridge, MA: Belknap Press, 1993), chapter 2.
41.   Sundquist, *To Wake the Nations*, 136.
42.   Herman Melville, "Benito Cereno," *Billy Budd, Sailor and Other Stories*, ed. Harold Beaver (Harmondsworth: Penguin, 1970), 215–307: 222, 269, 274.
43.   Karcher, "Riddle of the Sphinx," 199.
44.   Horsley-Meacham, "Bull of the Nile," 242 *passim*.
45.   Paul Gilroy, *The Black Atlantic: Modernity and Double Consciousness* (Cambridge, MA: Harvard University Press, 1993), 4.
46.   See Michel Foucault, *The Order of Things: An Archaeology of the Human Sciences* (New York: Vintage, 1973), xviii. Foucault's famous example is the "disorderly" fiction of Jorge Luis Borges. For a further application of the concept to postmodernist fiction see Brian McHale, *Postmodernist Fiction* (London: Routledge, 1987), 44–5. McHale suggests the term *zone* for the disorderly time-space produced by heterotopian fiction—a term that is quite appropriate to *Benito Cereno*, as it adds a political or "conflictual" quality to the more neutral geographical terms *space, area,* or *world.*
47.   Herman Melville, *Moby-Dick*, ed. Harrison Hayford and Hershel Parker (New York: W. W. Norton, 1967), 201.
48.   *Ibid.*, 427.
49.   *Ibid.*, 397–8.
50.   Starbuck, who listens to Pip's talk, feels reminded of incidents when, "'in violent fevers, men, all ignorance, have talked in ancient tongues; and that when the mystery is probed, it turns out always that in their wholly forgotten childhood those ancient tongues had been really spoken in their hearing.'" *Ibid.*, 398.
51.   I take the concept and terminology from Walter Benjamin's theses on history. See his "Über den Begriff der Geschichte," *Illuminationen* (Frankfurt: Suhrkamp, 1977), 251–61: 253. Eric Sundquist suggests the use of Bakhtin's concept of chronotope—an aesthetic site where time and space "thicken" and "take on flesh"—to describe the temporality of *Benito Cereno*. See Sundquist, *To Wake the Nations*, 162; and Mikhail Bakhtin, *The Dialogic Imagination*, ed. Michael Holquist (Austin: University of Texas Press, 1981), 84.
52.   Greg Dening, *Mr Bligh's Bad Language: Passion, Power and Theatre on the Bounty* (Cambridge: Cambridge University Press, 1992), 19–33, *passim*.
53.   The Rover's ship masquerades as a slaver in order to escape the authorities. For a full discussion, see Gesa Mackenthun, *Fictions of the Black Atlantic in American Foundational Literature*, chapter 3 (forthcoming from Routledge in 2004).
54.   Melville, *Moby-Dick*, 67.
55.   *Ibid.*, 95.
56.   I owe the term *motley crew*, as well as a fair amount of inspiration, to Peter Linebaugh and Marcus Rediker, *The Many-Headed Hydra: Sailors, Slaves, Commoners, and the Hidden History of the Revolutionary Atlantic* (Boston: Beacon Press, 2000).
57.   *Ibid.*, 454–5.
58.   *Ibid.*, 353–4.

CHAPTER 8

"At Sea—
Coloured Passenger"

ALASDAIR PETTINGER

I

Abolitionist writings of the mid–nineteenth century made much of the ironies evident in the contrast between Britain and the United States. Britain, a monarchy, had abolished slavery in its colonies in 1833, while in the United States, a republic, the "peculiar institution" continued to thrive in the South. But even in the North the free black population faced the kinds of systematic discrimination and prejudice that were virtually unheard of in Europe. This is evident especially in the accounts of African American travelers who crossed the Atlantic in the 1840s and '50s.

Here is William Wells Brown, writing from Liverpool in 1849:

> No person of my complexion can visit this country without being struck with the marked difference between the English and the Americans. The prejudice which I have experienced on all and every occasion in the United States, and to some extent on board the *Canada*, vanished as soon as I set foot on the soil of Britain. In America I had been bought and sold as a slave, in the Southern States. In the so-called free States, I had been treated as one born to occupy an inferior position,—in steamers, compelled to take my fare on the deck; in hotels, to take my meals in the kitchen; in coaches, to ride on the outside; in railways, to ride in the "negro car;" and in churches, to sit in the "negro pew." But no sooner was I on British soil, than I was recognised as a man, and an equal. The very dogs in the streets appeared conscious of my manhood. Such is

the difference, and such is the change that is brought about by a trip of nine days in an Atlantic steamer.[1]

Interestingly, the rhetoric of "travel" operates in more ways than one in Brown's narrative. If the journey is figured as a journey from oppression to freedom, oppression and freedom themselves are defined in terms of the ability (or not) to move freely, and cross the frontiers of race, sex and class.

For Brown, oppression in America is most readily symbolized not by the threat of kidnappers, or the laws preventing him from voting or holding public office, or the difficulty of getting a job or furthering his education, but by the restrictions on movement in public places. And writing of his return to Philadelphia, the single scene he chooses to encapsulate what he has come home to involves his first attempt to board an omnibus alongside two white men who had disembarked from the same steamer: "'We don't allow niggers to ride in here,'" he is told.[2]

Conversely, his freedom in Europe is signified by his ability to go where he likes. He felt, he says, "at home wherever I went,"[3] moving effortlessly from place to place, welcome everywhere, barred from nowhere. His narrative often pauses at those (many) points where he describes the democracy of public spaces, as if to emphasize the pleasure of the difference. He revels in the crowding and jostling on the streets of Dublin.[4] At a sidewalk café, he drinks "in sight of hundreds who were passing up and down" as "all Paris appeared to be on the Boulevards."[5] In the British Library, he observes "old men with grey hairs, young men with mustaches—some in cloth, others in fustian, indicating that men of different rank can meet here."[6] In Edinburgh, he sees "a gentleman with a coloured lady on each arm"—something unthinkable, he notes, in New York or Philadelphia.[7] The walls of Shakespeare's birthplace he finds "covered with names, inscriptions and hieroglyphics, in every language, by people of all nations, ranks and conditions, from the highest to the lowest, who have made their pilgrimage there."[8]

He finds "a great deal of freedom" at the Great Exhibition, which he celebrates in a passage worth quoting at length:

> The servant who walks behind his mistress through the Park feels that he can crowd against her in the Exhibition. The Queen and the day labourer, the Prince and the merchant, the peer and the pauper, the Celt and the Saxon, the Greek and the Frank, the Hebrew and the Russ, all meet here upon terms of perfect equality. This amalgamation of rank, this kindly blending of interests, and forgetfulness of the cold formalities of ranks and grades, cannot but be attended with the very best results. I was pleased to see such a goodly sprinkling of my own countrymen in the Exhibition—I mean coloured men and women—well-dressed, and moving about with their fairer brethren. This, some of our pro-slavery Americans did not seem to relish very well. There was no help for

it. As I walked through the American part of the Crystal Palace, some of our Virginian neighbours eyed me closely and with jealous looks, especially as an English lady was leaning on my arm. But their sneering looks did not disturb me in the least. I remained the longer in their department, and criticised the bad appearance of their goods the more.[9]

But these transatlantic slave narratives also have interesting things to say about the voyage itself, and in particular shed light on the practices of segregation and discrimination on the ships of the British and North American Royal Mail Steam Packet Company (later known as the Cunard Steam Ship Company Limited), which began passenger services in 1840.[10]

Brown himself makes passing reference to some unpleasantness on his outward voyage, elaborated later when in Paris, at the close of the first session of the Peace Congress:

> [J]ust as I was leaving Victor Hugo, to whom I had been introduced by an M.P., I observed near me a gentleman with his hat in hand, whom I recognized as one of the passengers who had crossed the Atlantic with me in the *Canada*, and who appeared to be the most horrified at having a negro for a fellow passenger. This gentleman, as I left M. Hugo, stepped up to me and said, "How do you do, Mr. Brown?" "You have the advantage of me," said I. "Oh, don't you know me; I was a fellow passenger with you from America; I wish you would give me an introduction to Victor Hugo and Mr. Cobden." I need not inform you that I declined introducing this pro-slavery American to these distinguished men.[11]

Four years earlier, another fugitive slave, Frederick Douglass, had faced humiliating discrimination on his journey to Britain. In his second autobiography, *My Bondage and My Freedom* (1855), he tells how, on applying for a passage to England, he discovered he was prohibited from occupying the first cabin and had to make do with the "rude forecastle deck." This did not prevent first-cabin passengers visiting him, however, and he soon found "all color distinctions were flung to the winds, and I found myself treated with every mark of respect." But when he was invited to deliver a lecture on slavery, some Southern passengers were determined to prevent him from speaking.

> They went so far as to threaten to throw me overboard, and but for the firmness of Captain Judkins, probably would have (under the inspiration of *slavery* and *brandy*) attempted to put their threats into execution. I have no space to describe this scene, although its tragic and comic peculiarities are well worth describing. An end was put to the *melée*, by the captain's calling the ship's company to put the salt water mobocrats in irons. At this determined order, the gentlemen of the lash scampered, and for the rest of the voyage conducted themselves very decorously.[12]

I will return to "this scene" later. But the story did not end there. On his return—by the same steamer—a year and half later, Douglass again found that despite paying his first-cabin fare, "the Liverpool agent had ordered my berth to be given to another, and had forbidden my entering the saloon!"[13] Douglass detailed the conversations he had with company officials—including one with the Liverpool agent, Charles MacIver, who claimed that "the London agent, in selling me the ticket, had acted without authority"—in a letter to *The Times*—"sincerely believing that the British public will pronounce a just verdict on such proceedings. I have travelled in this country 19 months, and have always enjoyed equal rights and privileges with other passengers, and it was not until I turned my face towards America that I met anything like proscription on account of my colour."[14]

An editorial published in the newspaper two days later shared his outrage, condemning the company for allowing its agents to succumb "to a miserable and unmeaning assumption of skin-deep superiority by the American portion of their passengers."[15] The following week appeared a letter from MacIver, complaining that Douglass had suppressed an earlier conversation in which it had been explained to him that the reason for the precaution was the incident on the outward voyage in which Douglass "was the cause, whether intentionally or unintentionally on his part, of producing, by the observations he made use of, serious disturbance on board, which required the authority of the captain to quell, in order to restore peace and safety."[16]

On the same day, *The Times* printed a letter from Charles M. Burrop, "of Asgill, Virginia, United States, Head Manager of the Cunard Company of Liners," defending the action of the company, claiming it could not afford to ignore the "absolute and invincible disgust on the part of the great majority of white men, and particularly of white women, not less in England than in America, to come into close contact with blackamores" if it meant profits would be affected by travelers canceling tickets when they discovered that blacks had booked a passage on the same vessel.[17] To which correspondent Samuel Cunard himself was moved to reply, pointing out that "no such person, or any other individual in the United States, holds any share or interest in the steam ships alluded to, and that the statements set forth in that letter are entirely untrue." And he continued: "No one can regret more than I do the unpleasant circumstances respecting Mr Douglass' passage; but I can assure you that nothing of the kind will again take place in the steam-ships with which I am connected."[18]

Douglass later claimed that this promise was kept: "and the like, we believe, has never since occurred on board the steamships of the Cunard Line."[19] In fact, this was a bit of wishful thinking, for cases of racial discrimination on Cunard's ships were recorded at least up to the Civil War. In 1850, Henry Highland Garnet was "caged up in the steward's room of one of Cunard's vessels, and although a first class passenger, I was not allowed to go into the saloon, or to eat at the table with white humanity."[20] That same year, William and Ellen Craft faced difficulty in obtaining tickets in Halifax, where "they baffled us shamefully at the Cunard office. They at first said that they did not book till the steamer came; which was not the fact. When I called again, they said they knew the steamer would come full from Boston, and therefore we had 'better try to get to Liverpool by other means.' Other mean Yankee excuses were made, to whom Mr Francis Jackson, of Boston, kindly gave us a letter, went and rebuked them, that we were able to secure our tickets."[21]

In 1851, Clarissa and Josephine Brown were denied passage by a Cunard agent in Boston unless they were classified as servants of their white companion, the Reverend Charles Spear.[22] Two years later, Samuel Ringgold Ward was prevented from taking his meals with the rest of the passengers on the *Europa*, Edward Cunard—son of Samuel, who managed the business in Halifax, Boston, and New York—drawing his attention to the "'prevalent feelings in this country in respect to coloured people, and if you eat at the cabin table Americans will complain. We cannot allow our ship to be the arena of constant quarrels on this subject; we avoid the difficulty by making the rule that coloured passengers shall eat in their state rooms, or we can't take them.'"[23]

The following year, James Watkins arranged to be joined by his wife and children who, having initially planned to travel on "one of the Cunard line of steamers," found that the company "refused to bring them across, on account of their colour."[24] And in 1859, Caroline Putnam traveling on the *Europa* found that "the captain, with the concurrence of the owners, subjected [her] to the indignity of being refused places at the public table, merely on the ground that American passengers objected to associate with persons of colour. This unworthy submission to foreign prejudice was denounced by Lord Brougham in Parliament, and was the subject of indignant comment in many of our journals."[25]

I should perhaps add that this sad history did not come to an end with Emancipation. When Langston Hughes met Nancy Cunard—a great-granddaughter of the shipping magnate—in Paris in 1937, he told her, "I had come to France on a Cunard Line vessel, thinking it would please her, since I knew she was of that family. To my surprise, she had never set foot on a Cunard liner and never intended to do so, she said, because the line segregated Negroes. Instead she travelled on French boats."[26]

Not wanting to weaken the force of the rhetorical contrast between Britain and the United States, the authors of some of these accounts tended to present these episodes as simply signs of the intermediary character of the transatlantic voyage, a compound of (good) British and (bad) American ways of doing things, so that any unpleasantness might be seen as merely the residue of what has been left behind (if traveling east) or an anticipation of what is to come (if traveling west). Douglass, for instance, makes of his outward voyage a tale of prejudice overcome, as the initial allocation of cabin gives way to effective freedom of the whole ship, and the subsequent protests of certain southern passengers are—in a dramatic denouement—quelled by the "gallant" Captain Judkins. By contrast, he represents the discrimination he faced on his return as "something which painfully reminded me of the kind of life which awaited me in my native land."[27]

Samuel Ringgold Ward, reflecting on his treatment, bitterly denounces the way the Cunard company is run on purely "business" lines, placing the relative financial advantages of attracting one class of customers rather than another above considerations of moral principle. He describes Edward Cunard as

> an Englishman perverted, according to his own showing—like the Yankee, making the dollar come before right, law, or anything. He does not "share" Yankee feeling—he only accommodates, panders to it! That is all! . . . Worse, however, than Yankee arrogance, is the easy accommodating virtue of a Yankeefied Englishman.[28]

But this transitionality does not actually explain very much. Cunard in any case was a British company, which held the contract (issued by the Admiralty) for carrying the Royal Mail. In the early days, a steamer carrying the mails had to carry a naval officer on board—which often led to friction between him and the crew.[29] There were clear tensions between the public pronouncements of Samuel Cunard himself, the decisions made by the company's agents on shore, as well as the discretion exercised by the ships' captains themselves. As we shall see, the combination of these forces by no means resulted in a coherent pattern; the effects were rather unpredictable, giving the impression of improvisation and experiment. Certainly, the discrimination faced by passengers cannot be deduced from—as if they were simply a kind of average of—more settled policies in force on either side of the ocean.

II

For one thing, these policies were far from settled. In the United States, the racial segregation of public facilities was quite new. Cases of segregation on stagecoaches and passenger vessels were reported from the 1820s, and the practice was adopted by several railroads built in New England in the 1830s. But it was not until 1841 that the practice was established enough to be given a definite name: *Jim Crow*—a song-and-dance routine popularized by the blackface entertainer Thomas D. Rice—came to be adopted in Massachusetts for the car reserved for black travelers.[30]

It is worth emphasizing that segregation—often thought to have originated in the South in the 1890s—emerged first in the antebellum North following the abolition of slavery there in the early decades of the new republic. By 1830, only around thirty-five hundred slaves remained in the North, most of them in New Jersey.[31]

In the South, there were few public facilities to which a slave would have access. When slaves did make use of stagecoaches, riverboats, and railroads, it was usually in the company of their owners (and such slaves were excluded from segregation provisions in the North). Traveling unescorted, black men and women would be expected to carry a "pass" from their master (if a slave) or papers proving their status (if free) and could be challenged to produce them. Otherwise, social mingling was not normally a cause for concern: on the plantation, blacks and whites would coexist in close proximity within what was increasingly coming to be thought of as an extended "family," where roles were clearly and hierarchically defined, because everyone knew everyone else.

In the "free States," however, public facilities were in theory open to all who could afford them. Especially in cities, and the modes of transportation between them, former slaves could mix with former slaveholders on terms of formal equality. Racial antipathies toward black people, which in the South were enshrined in a social order sanctioned by law and custom, were in the North, by contrast, a source of anxiety, and drew forth calls for special measures to prevent black and white strangers sharing the same public spaces. With segregation, "race" for the first time becomes a practical problem, requiring the development of informal codes by which such individuals could be differentiated on the basis of their physical appearance, rather than on the documentation they were obliged to carry. Given that race in the United States was officially defined in matrilineal terms, the pertinent facts of a person's ancestry were not always evident on the basis of observation alone. This anomaly was frequently exploited by light-skinned fugitive slaves and others who "passed" for "white," and its ironic implications were often underlined by abolitionists. As Charles Lenox Remond pointed out, in an article condemning his treatment on the railroad between Boston and Salem:

> It happens to be my lot to have a sister a few shades lighter than myself; and who knows, if this state of things is encouraged, whether I may not on some future occasion be mobbed in Washington Street, on the supposition of walking with a white young lady![32]

Segregation had to rely on a rather ad hoc and changing "common sense" that identified what particular characteristics to look out for, which ones were likely to give away the presence of that single black great-grandmother. (For a while, it was thought that the half-moon on the thumbnail was one such sign.[33]) It thus did not just separate races, but partly *defined* them, singling out the features that were thought to form the proper basis on which to classify individuals in this way. Hence W. E. B. DuBois's classic formulation: "the black man is a person who must ride 'Jim Crow' in Georgia."[34] What race you were ultimately depended on the decisions of those authorized to assign you to one seat or entrance rather than another. And it is worth emphasizing that those decisions were legitimated by a complex ensemble of legal, administrative, and cultural norms ill suited to produce consistent results.

The anxieties to which segregation was a response were not, of course, uniquely "racial." The first half of the nineteenth century was preoccupied with the moral dilemmas posed by urbanization and the mingling of strangers in public spaces.[35] There was widespread concern for the character and conduct of those loosed from their moorings in a relatively fixed rural order, lacking a communal framework to help them deal with the challenges and temptations of anonymous city life. In response, voluntary reform movements developed a range of initiatives that targeted personal behavior, through the establishment of institutions (such as Sunday schools, asylums, boardinghouses, and savings banks) and practices (such as district visiting and charitable relief).[36]

These initiatives helped to create new ethical cultures that encouraged the formation of certain habits and skills (such as thrift, sobriety, industriousness, civility, prudence, and certain standards of diet and personal hygiene). But the aim was not so much to impose external conformity on their subjects as "to train them to control themselves"; not merely "to form an outward regularity, but to touch inward springs."[37] Recent scholarship on liberal governance has emphasized the importance of these emerging technologies of the self, creating the forms of self-mastery, self-regulation, and self-control necessary to govern a nation of free and "civilized" citizens.[38]

Insofar as vulnerable or dangerous segments of the population were targeted as individuals, there was some optimism regarding the reformatory enterprise. But when considered en masse—in much more open and loosely regulated public spaces—the specter of the mob, the rabble was evoked more menacingly, and more coercive measures were often called for to deal with the heterogeneous crowds on the streets, in public gatherings, or on boats and trains. For instance, in 1837 the board of aldermen refused a request to make Boston's Faneuil Hall available for a meeting to protest the recent murder of Elijah P. Lovejoy, editor of an abolitionist newspaper in Alton, Illinois. And the segregation of railroads in Massachusetts was not imposed by law but introduced by the railroad companies themselves, in (rather open-ended) regulations such as this one (dated 1841) of the New Bedford & Taunton branch railroad: "Passengers . . . will take such seats as may be assigned to them by the conductor."[39]

These restrictions on individual freedoms were made on the pretext of safeguarding public order. But they were challenged: and the arguments did not rest solely on the grounds of asserting "rights" (of assembly, of speech, of movement) but also involved claims that the threat of disorder was much exaggerated, suggesting that crowds were in fact more self-regulated than civic authorities and company officials were willing to acknowledge. In Boston, William Ellery Channing argued it was a "severest libel on this city" to suggest that its citizens cannot be "trusted to come together to express the great principles of liberty, for which their fathers died."[40] As a result of his and others' protests, the hall was subsequently made available for the meeting, which passed off without serious incident.

The abolitionists also challenged the policies of the railroad companies, claiming that there was no evidence of any "general public opinion demanding such regulation."[41] Frederick Douglass argued that the prejudice occasionally shown to him by white strangers with whom he shared cars on the Massachusetts railroads (as opposed to overzealous company officials, who were the usual cause of complaint) soon dissipated when someone of importance broke the taboo and sat next to him, causing others to eagerly abandon their earlier rudeness. This indicated, he suggested (though perhaps a little simplistically), that their feelings were more a sign of "pride and fashion" rather than arising from "a natural . . . inherent . . . invincible repugnance," and therefore clearly open to the moderating influence of moral suasion.[42] Although the campaigners failed to convince the courts that the practice was illegal and unconstitutional, segregation in Massachusetts (but not elsewhere) was abandoned by the railroad companies by 1843.[43]

The uneven and inconsistent way such restrictions on individual freedoms operated suggests not only significant variation in the depth and extent of racial antagonism among the public at large (or rather in the perception of such antagonism) but also the different considerations that needed to be taken into account when governing different kinds of public spaces. Let us return to the transatlantic steamer.

III

Passengers crossing the Atlantic in the middle of the nineteenth century frequently commented on the cramped and confined accommodations and the difficulties in passing the time for want of variety of incident. The early Cunard ships took cabin passengers only, with fares out of the range of most people.[44] Nevertheless, conditions were spartan compared to their competitors, and furthermore the company seemed to treat complaints rather dismissively: "'Going to sea was a hardship,'" wrote Charles MacIver Senior to a dissatisfied traveler; "'the Company did not undertake to make anything else out of it.'"[45]

The *Cambria*, which brought Douglass to Liverpool in 1845, carried ninety-five passengers, including: the bishops of Oregon and Massachusetts; the chief commissioner of the Canada Land Company; several officers in the British army; the Hutchinson Family singing group; slaveholders from Georgia, New Orleans, and Cuba; the English travel writers Sir James E. Alexander and George Warburton; General Welsh, "proprietor of menageries, director of circuses"; as well as Douglass and his white abolitionist companion James Buffum.[46] Even such a partial list of passengers, all of whom were affluent enough to afford the fare, suggests a far-from-homogeneous group. Douglass remarks that his fellow passengers "were made up of nearly all sorts of people, from different countries, of the most opposite modes of thinking on all subjects. We had nearly all sorts or parties in morals, religion, and politics, as well as trades and callings, and professions."[47] It is easy to imagine how such differences could have been a source of possible tension on a ship that was not much more than two hundred feet long on a voyage that took nearly two weeks.

That order was generally maintained on such vessels is—at least as far as the passengers are concerned—evidence of the success of liberal techniques of governance. To some extent, these relate to the organization of space and time on board. With only first-class ticket holders entitled to dine in the saloon—the others having to take their meals in their cabins—large public gatherings were discouraged, and with no steerage passengers, all were spared contact with emigrants of the lower classes. The often uneventful days—barring storms, or the sight of icebergs, whales, or other ships—were punctuated with regular mealtimes and the sound of the half-hour bells, to which routines were added the customary forms of amusement encouraged on board, such as card games, singing, reading, and conversation. Religious services were usually held on Sundays.

The success of these unobtrusive forms of management is indicated by the relative infrequency by which rules and regulations on board are referred to in travelers' accounts, for it is usually only when they seem arbitrary and imposing that they merit attention. When the showman Phineas T. Barnum sailed to New York in February 1847, he became involved in an argument with Captain Judkins for not allowing the "celebrated preacher," the Reverend Dr. Robert Baird, to preach to passengers in the forward cabin, as this was—Judkins declared flatly—"'against the rules of the ship.'" Barnum protested in no uncertain terms, until Judkins threatened him: "'If you repeat such language, I will put you in irons.'" Barnum suggested that if he arrived in New York in such a condition, it might stretch the credulity of those upholding "'Yankee ideas of religious intolerance.'" Baird himself, on being apprised of the situation, quietly conceded, saying, "'if the rules of this ship are so stringent I suppose we must submit.'" Afterward, Judkins apologized to Barnum for his manner, and the two "'washed down' their differences in a bottle of champagne, and were excellent friends from that moment."[48]

The arbitrary nature of the rules was also evident in the practices of the company relating to the treatment of black passengers. The year before Douglass's outward voyage, a church minister returning from the United States on the *Acadia* noted in his journal that

> [t]he only disagreeable circumstance that occurred in the home-ward voyage was the exclusion of a young gentleman, a passenger from Hayti, who had paid a cabin passage, and yet was not permitted to enter the saloon and dine at the common table. About one-third of the passengers joined in a request to the captain that he should be invited to join us in the saloon. The remonstrance was unheeded. The Captain at one moment saying that it was contrary to orders, and at another time declaring that he had no authority on the subject, but that the American passengers would not tolerate it. Finding no redress from Captain Judkins, we drew up a remonstrance to the owners at Glasgow and Liverpool, against this ungenerous outrage on the feelings of a coloured gentleman in a British vessel carrying her Majesty's mail. Most of the British and colonial passengers, and several of the New Englanders, signed the remonstrance; but the Southerns contemptuously refused, and one young Southern, from New Orleans, who spent most of the voyage at the card-table, got up a counter petition that the cow should be admitted to the saloon. The jest only showed the breeding of the slaveholder, and was not relished by the passengers.[49]

The remonstrance may have had some effect, for a year later Judkins appears to have taken a relaxed attitude to Douglass, who—despite the prohibition imposed on him at Boston—found that "one part of the ship was about as free to me as another. My fellow-passengers not only visited me, but invited me to visit them, on the saloon deck."[50] It would appear that the captain was permitted some discretion in deciding whether to enforce the discriminatory conditions set by the agents on shore, and was guided by an assessment of the consequences of allowing such racial mixing on board. In the earlier voyage, it seems that Judkins risked the anger of a substantial proportion of the passengers, but this anger found a relatively safe outlet in the form of the remonstrance, subsequently published in the *Glasgow Argus*.[51] In the later voyage, it is possible that Judkins's more relaxed attitude owed something to Douglass's own circumspection, for he admitted that his own visits to the saloon deck "were but seldom. I preferred to live within my privileges, and keep upon my own premises. I found this quite as much in accordance with good policy, as with my own feelings."[52]

It is clear that the decks of a transatlantic steamer were negotiated spaces, in which custom and routine made it relatively easy to impose racial segregation—but this was by no means inevitable. Every voyage would have been different, and the captain would have been required to read the characters and moods of the passengers, in order to weigh the risk of granting—or withholding—black travelers the right to associate with whites. Assailed by conflicting requests, he would have to be fairly certain that any decision he made would not lead to anything more serious than grumbles or—at worst—formal complaints.

More coercive measures were introduced only as a last resort—when disorder actually broke out. And even then, the passengers sometimes quietly (and good-humoredly) dealt with the problem among themselves:

> Today, the passengers formed themselves into a court of Criminal Sessions, to try one of their own number for disturbing the public peace. He was arraigned under the name of Jingle Jingle, Esq., and his offence was disturbing the company in the fore-cabin, by rising and making sundry noises at half-past five o'clock in the morning. The ex-Governor of the State of____was appointed judge; Mr A____clerk of court; Mr B____constable; Professor____attorney-general; and Messrs____and____defendant's counsel. A huge hand-spike served as the mace of the court. A jury was impanneled, and a most impartial trial was granted. The speeches of the learned gentlemen, who conducted the prosecution and defence, would have done honour to Westminster Hall. The jury found the pannel guilty, and the judge, in consideration of its being his first offence, sentenced him only to eat his soup with a fork, and to have no grog till he arrived at New York.[53]

On other occasions, however, the crew could be called on to deal with them more forcibly or at least restrain them until handed over to authorities on shore. This apparently happened rarely, and indeed the incident on the *Cambria* in 1845 is the only case I have come across.[54]

It is difficult to reconstruct the sequence of events from the available sources, which disagree considerably—not surprising given the controversial subject and the partisan views at stake. Douglass's various accounts of the episode are perhaps the least reliable, not so much because they are not entirely consistent with each other, but because they are pressed into the service of an overtly didactic rhetorical form (abolitionist speech, exemplary autobiography). But I think there is enough evidence to suggest that Judkins miscalculated on this occasion, despite his being lionized as the hero of the hour by Douglass and his friend John Hutchinson.[55]

Judkins must have judged there to have been little risk in allowing Douglass to move freely about the ship, and permitting his *Narrative* to be circulated among the passengers.[56] But on the last evening of the voyage, when—as George Warburton's account informs us—spirits customarily ran high, feelings of animosity he may not have bargained for made their appearance:

> It is usual to prolong the dinner hour beyond the ordinary time; a quantity of wine is put upon the table, and the gifted in song and eloquence edify the company by the exercise of their powers. The sea, by this time, has lost its horrors to even the most tender susceptibilities; every one is in high good-humour and excitement at the prospect of a speedy release from their confinement, and it is generally made the occasion of great rejoicing. Very flattering things are said of the qualities of the ship and the skill and virtues of the captain, of the vast advantages of such speedy communication between the two greatest nations in the world—which is always a highly popular observation. Then the captain "is quite at a loss for words to express the deep sense he entertains of the honour conferred on himself and his ship by the gentleman who has just now so eloquently spoken." As soon as these agreeable subjects are exhausted, the passengers find it agreeable to walk on the deck a little and cool their heads, heated with champagne and eloquence. At this unfortunate time, on the occasion I speak of, the negro abolition preacher made his appearance on the quarter-deck and commenced a lecture on the evils of slavery, and the stain fixed by it on the character of the United States, using no measured terms of condemnation of the free and enlightened community.[57]

Douglass claimed that he only agreed to give the lecture because personally invited to do so by the Captain, who urged the passengers not to interrupt his address.[58] Nevertheless, before long

> a New Orleans man, the master of a ship in the China trade and who had been, during the greater part of the voyage, and was more particularly on this occasion, very much intoxicated, poked himself into the circle, walked up to the speaker with his hands in his pockets and a "quid" of tobacco in his mouth, looked at him steadily for a minute, and then said, "I guess you're a liar."[59]

The confrontation drew in other members of the party, and voices and fists were raised. The ugly scene lasted "for at least an hour," according to Warburton, though "in the mean time, this demon of discord had vanished, and we saw or heard no more of him or his lectures."[60] Hutchinson puts it rather differently, describing how the speaker was "so disturbed . . . that he was forced to suspend, and with a sentence half-finished, he retreated under the awning and thence down the stairs to the steerage, his only hiding place, where he was sheltered from the wrath of those blood-thirsty Americans whose 'chivalry' was so much shocked."[61] It is only later that the captain emerged—disturbed from "a siesta after a luxurious banquet tendered him by his friends"[62]—and in a scene that may not have been witnessed by Douglass (despite his accounts giving the impression that it was) restored order, separating the disputants with the assistance of other members of the crew.[63] It seems that Warburton has a point when he claims that "but for the certainty of being immediately amenable to English law, it would have been the occasion of great violence, if not loss of life."[64]

If Judkins had gently dissuaded Douglass from giving his lecture, this would have been less an unprincipled stand, siding with one group of passengers against another, but rather the result of weighing up the consequences of angering one rather than the other. While he risked a petition through antagonizing the defenders of equal rights in 1844, he risked even more by allowing drunken slaveholders to feel offended in 1845. After all, the "mobs" associated with anti-slavery activity in the North were anti-abolitionists; their predominantly pacifist opponents could only be accused of inciting violence, not of actually perpetrating it (though this would change somewhat after the passage of the Fugitive Slave Act in 1850). That angry supporters of slavery were more of a liability than angry abolitionists would surely have been an important consideration for the captain of a ship responsible for maintaining the safety of his passengers and crew and the punctual delivery of cargo and mail.

It is easy to condemn Cunard captains for not making a more principled stand on the rights of speech and movement of black passengers. For instance, Samuel Ringgold Ward argued: "if any one made a disturbance on board . . . *that* was the person to be deprived of his rights, and not an innocent person."[65] But it may have been a luxury they could have ill afforded. On land, the threat of disorder in a public hall, or on a branch railroad—exaggerated or not—may have been something worth risking, given the greater resources available to contain it. The authorities could disperse crowds and bring in reinforcements from elsewhere. At sea, however, even with the hills of Ireland on the horizon, the danger of losing a passenger overboard was real indeed, as the barely disguised glee at the prospect of a "negro tossed to the sharks" voiced in some American newspapers chillingly reminds us.[66]

As we have seen, the episode was cited as excuse for the discrimination faced by Douglass on his return voyage, and despite the assurances of Cunard himself, those more immediately involved in the day-to-day governance of his ships continued to impose restrictions on black passengers. Not consistently, however, as accounts of trouble-free voyages exist, too.[67]

The recent attention to—indeed, creation of the category of—"air rage" reminds us that these issues are still with us today. Although it is often referred to in conjunction with its many cognate forms ("road rage," and so on) and sometimes treated as an instance of the growing problem of incivility in society at large, it is also generally acknowledged that the problem cannot be tackled without considering the passenger jet as a specific "contact zone," examining such matters as overcrowding, comfort, the availability of alcohol, the training of crew, and air quality. In like manner we should treat the steamships crossing the Atlantic 150 years ago. The decisions relating to the restrictions on black passengers must be understood in relation to the organization of the ship, and the character and conduct of the passengers, even their moods, as they change during the voyage.

William Wells Brown concludes his account of his meeting in Paris as follows:

> I only allude to this, to show what a change comes over the dreams of my white American brother, by crossing the ocean. The man who would not have been seen walking with me in the streets of New York, and who would not have shaken hands with me with a pair of tongs while on the passage from the United States, could come with hat in hand in Paris, and say, "I was your fellow passenger."[68]

This "change" is undeniable, but Brown can only make sense of the man's conduct during the crossing in reference to the fixed coordinates of New York and Paris, as if his hostility on board can be attributed purely to the fact that he was *not yet* in Europe, but rather *still* under the malign influence of the America he has left behind. However, rather than consider the ship as a means of traveling from one country to another, we might think of it—as does the narrator of Herman Melville's *Redburn* (1849)—as a strange country in itself, with its own language and customs.[69] Without attending to the particular ethical cultures of transatlantic steamers—the complex and changing conditions that encouraged some habits and customs and discouraged others—we will not be able to understand this neglected history of racial discrimination at sea.

Notes

1. William Wells Brown, *Three Years in Europe; or, Places I Have Seen and People I Have Met* (London: Charles Gilpin, 1852), 8–9.
2. William Wells Brown, *The American Fugitive in Europe: Sketches of Places and People Abroad* (Boston: John P. Jewett and Company, 1855), 312.
3. *Ibid.*, 303.
4. Brown, *Three Years in Europe*, 11–9.
5. *Ibid.*, 70–1.
6. *Ibid.*, 109.
7. *Ibid.*, 167.
8. Brown, *American Fugitive*, 223–4.
9. Brown, *Three Years in Europe*, 210–2.
10. For useful background on the early years of the Cunard line, see Francis Hyde, *Cunard and the North Atlantic, 1840–1973: A History of Shipping and Financial Management* (London: Macmillan, 1975). See also F. Lawrence Babcock, *Spanning the Atlantic* (New York: Knopf, 1931); Henry Fry, *The History of the North Atlantic Steam Navigation—with Some Account of Early Ships and Shipowners* [1896] (London: Cornmarket Press, 1969); Frank C. Bowen, *A Century of Atlantic Travel, 1830–1930* (London: Sampson Low, Marston and Co., 1932[?]); and H. Philip Spratt, *Transatlantic Paddle Steamers* (Glasgow: Brown, Son and Ferguson, 1961).

11. Brown, *Three Years in Europe*, 34–5.
12. Frederick Douglass, *My Bondage and My Freedom* [1855], fac. ed. (New York: Dover, 1969), 366–7.
13. *Ibid.*, 390.
14. *The Times*, April 6, 1847.
15. *The Times*, April 8, 1847.
16. *The Times*, April 13; 1847.
17. *Ibid.*
18. *Ibid.*
19. Douglass, *My Bondage*, 390–1. A claim he persisted in making right through to the revised edition of his third autobiography, *The Life and Times of Frederick Douglass . . . written by himself* [1892] (New York: Collier Books, 1962), 258.
20. Henry Highland Garnet to Julia Garnet (September 13, 1861). See C. Peter Ripley (ed.), *The Black Abolitionist Papers, Vol. 1: The British Isles, 1830–1865* (Chapel Hill: University of North Carolina Press, 1985), 497.
21. William Craft, *Running a Thousand Miles for Freedom* (London: William Tweedie, 1860), 108.
22. See William Edward Farrison, *William Wells Brown: Author and Reformer* (Chicago and London: University of Chicago Press, 1969), 192–3.
23. Samuel Ringgold Ward, *Autobiography of a Fugitive Negro* (London: John Snow, 1855), 228.
24. James Watkins, *Struggles for Freedom; or The Life of James Watkins, Formerly a Slave in Maryland, US* (Manchester: James Watkins, 19th ed., 1860), 41.
25. Matthew Davenport Hill (ed.), *Our Exemplars Poor and Rich; or, Biographical Sketches of Men and Women Who Have, By an Extraordinary Use of their Opportunities, Benefited their Fellow Creatures* (London: Cassell, Petter and Galpin, 1861), 286. See also Sarah P. Remond to Editor, *Scottish Press*, December 20, 1859, reprinted in Ripley, *Black Abolitionist Papers, Vol. 1*, 470.
26. Langston Hughes, *I Wonder as I Wander* [1956] (New York: Hill and Wang, 1993), 318.
27. Douglass, *My Bondage*, 390.
28. Ward, *Autobiography of a Fugitive Negro*, 229–30.
29. Bowen, *A Century of Atlantic Travel*, 35.
30. Louis Ruchames, "Jim Crow Railroads in Massachusetts," *American Quarterly* 8, no. 1 (1956), 62. On Rice, see W. T. Lhamon, *Raising Cain: Blackface Performance from Jim Crow to Hip Hop* (Cambridge, MA, and London: Harvard University Press, 1998).
31. Leon F. Litwack, *North of Slavery: The Negro in the Free States* (Chicago: University of Chicago Press, 1961), 14.
32. Charles Lenox Remond, "The Rights of Colored Citizens in Traveling," *The Liberator* (February 2, 1842), reprinted in Louis Ruchames (ed.), *The Abolitionists: A Collection of Their Writings* (New York: G. P. Putnam's Sons, 1963), 183.
33. See Werner Sollors, "The Bluish Tinge in the Halfmoon; or, Fingernails as a Racial Sign," *Neither Black nor White yet Both: Thematic Explorations of Interracial Literature* (New York and Oxford: Oxford University Press, 1997), 142–61.
34. W. E. B. DuBois, *The Dusk of Dawn* [1940], DuBois, *Writings*, ed. N. Huggins (New York: Library of America, 1986), 666.
35. For a succinct characterization, see Serge Moscovici, *The Age of the Crowd: A Historical Treatise on Mass Psychology* [1981], trans. J. C. Whitehouse (Cambridge: Cambridge University Press, 1985), esp. 4–5.
36. One of the best surveys of such reform movements in the United States is Paul Boyer, *Urban Masses and Moral Order in America, 1820–1920* (Cambridge, MA, and London: Harvard University Press, 1978).
37. William Ellery Channing, in an 1837 address to Boston Sunday school teachers, quoted in Boyer, *Urban Masses*, 51.
38. For a useful introduction to recent scholarship on liberal governance—which takes as its point of departure the (still largely unpublished) lectures given by Michel Foucault in his course titled "Sécurité, Territoire et Population" at the Collège de France (1977–8)—see Graham Burchell, Colin Gordon, and Peter Miller (eds.), *The Foucault Effect: Studies in Governmentality* (Hemel Hempstead: Harvester Wheatsheaf, 1991); Andrew Barry, Thomas Osborne, and Nikolas Rose (eds.), *Foucault and Political Reason: Liberalism, Neo-*

Liberalism and Rationalities of Government (London: UCL Press, 1996); and Nikolas Rose, *The Powers of Freedom: Reframing Political Thought* (Cambridge: Cambridge University Press, 1999).

39. Quoted in Ruchames, "Jim Crow," 63.

40. Quoted in Truman Nelson (ed.), *Documents of Upheaval: Selections from William Lloyd Garrison's* The Liberator, *1831–1865* (New York: Hill and Wang, 1966), 135.

41. Ruchames, "Jim Crow," 72.

42. Douglass, *My Bondage*, 402–5.

43. Ruchames, "Jim Crow," 74–5.

44. First- and second-cabin fares were set at $120 (£35) and $70 (£25) in 1850 (Hyde, *Cunard and the North Atlantic*, 40). The much cheaper option to travel steerage was available only on sailing ships at this time (Bowen, *A Century of Atlantic Travel*, 37).

45. Hyde, *Cunard and the North Atlantic*, 75.

46. My main sources of information about this voyage are: George Warburton, *Hochelaga, or England in the New World*, 2 vols. (London: Henry Colburn, 1847), vol. 2, 354–63; Douglass, *My Bondage*, 365–8; John W. Blassingame (ed.), *The Frederick Douglass Papers: Series One: Speeches, Debates and Interviews, Vol. 1: 1841–46* (New Haven, CT, and London: Yale University Press, 1979), 61–6, 82–4, 90–2, 139–43; *Liberator*, September 26, 1845; October 7, 1845; October 10, 1845; October 31, 1845; James E. Alexander, *L'Acadie; or, Seven Years' Exploration in British America*, 2 vols. (London: Henry Colburn, 1849), vol. 2, 258–62; and John Wallace Hutchinson, *Story of the Hutchinsons* [1896], 2 vols. (New York: Da Capo Press, 1977), vol. 1, 142–7.

47. *Liberator*, September 26, 1845.

48. Joel Benton, *A Unique Story of a Marvellous Career: Life of Hon. Phineas T Barnum*, chapter 14, http://encyclopediaindex.com/c/ptbnm10.htm (July 27, 2001).

49. George Lewis, *Impressions of America and the American Churches* (Edinburgh: W. P. Kennedy, 1845), 390–1. On the page on which this quotation appears, the running header reads, "At Sea—Coloured Passenger."

50. Douglass, *My Bondage*, 366.

51. *Glasgow Argus*, August 5, 1844. This letter is reproduced in Glasgow Emancipation Society, *Tenth Annual Report* (Glasgow: n.p., 1844), appendix 2, 40–1, and the incident discussed in appendix 1, 21–2.

52. Douglass, *My Bondage*, 366–7.

53. George Combe, *Notes on the United States of America, during a phrenological visit in 1838–9–40*, 3 vols. (Edinburgh: Maclachlan, Stewart & Co., 1841), vol. 1, 17.

54. Babcock asserts that it was "the last such disturbance to occur on a Cunard ship" (*Spanning the Atlantic*, 126) without referring to any previous disturbance.

55. Douglass, *My Bondage*, and 367; John Hutchinson, *Story of the Hutchinsons*, vol. 1, 146.

56. Hutchinson, *Story of the Hutchinsons*, vol. 1, 145.

57. Warburton, *Hochelaga*, vol. 2, 358–9.

58. *Liberator*, September 26, 1845; Blassingame, *The Frederick Douglass Papers*, vol. 1, 63, 82, 90, 140.

59. Warburton, *Hochelaga*, vol. 2, 359.

60. *Ibid.*, 360.

61. Hutchinson, *Story of the Hutchinsons*, vol. 1, 146.

62. *Ibid.*

63. Douglass makes much play on the threatened use of "irons" (mentioned also by Hutchinson), as it permits him to emphasize the "tragic and comic peculiarities" (*My Bondage*, 367) of slaveholders facing the prospect of a taste of their own medicine. Warburton and Alexander, however, do not specify how order is restored.

64. Warburton, *Hochelaga*, vol. 2, 361.

65. Ward, *Autobiography of a Fugitive Negro*, 232.

66. Quoted in the *Liberator*, October 3, 1845.

67. See, for instance, the experiences of Henry Highland Garnet: "My ticket was given me without a remark; an elegant state-room with *six berths* was placed at my disposal, and my seat at the table was between two young American gentlemen. . . . And I am happy to say that I did not receive a look, or hear a word during the whole voyage, that grated upon my very

sensitive feelings" (letter to his wife, Julia Ward Williams Garnet, September 13, 1861, printed in Ripley, *The Black Abolitionist Papers, Vol. 1*, 497). And of Caroline Putnam: "We are glad to record that on her return, in a mail-packet belonging to the Company by which she had been thus treated, Mrs Putnam was permitted to take her place at table without objection, although American slaveowners were among the passengers. An auspicious omen!" (Hill, *Our Exemplars Poor and Rich*, 286).

68. Brown, *Three Years in Europe*, 35.
69. See Herman Melville, *Redburn* [1849] (Harmondsworth: Penguin, 1976), 117.

CHAPTER 9

Slavery, Insurance, and Sacrifice in the Black Atlantic

TIM ARMSTRONG

In March 2000, the American insurance company Aetna apologized for participating, more than 150 years earlier, in the insurance of slaves. Later the same year in California, the Slavery Era Insurance Policies Bill was passed, requiring insurance companies working in the state to disclose any slave policies in their archives. Both these acts are part of the ongoing debate on "reparations" for slavery, a debate that itself participates, at the historiographic level, in a culture of catastrophe and compensation in which, ironically enough, insurance is itself central. In this essay, I will investigate that culture in relation to a specific issue, slavery and marine insurance, using the notorious case of the *Zong* and others. As we will see, the topic demands that in looking at forms of risk and subordination we also attend to a number of others issues, including, perhaps surprisingly, that of maritime cannibalism.

Most policies produced to support recent accusations relate to a trade that developed in the American South in the last two decades of slavery. Insurance was most commonly taken out on slaves hired out for manufacturing, construction, railroad work, or forestry—that is, on an investment to be safeguarded over a fixed term.[1] In many ways, this represented the inevitable logic of slavery, as a patriarchal, agricultural system came to be one increasingly penetrated by capitalist modes of production. At the same time, life insurance, and thus the situating of the individual within a logic of exchange, was becoming increasingly common in the nineteenth century.[2] But are these two equivalent? Were the slaves insured as property or as persons?[3] As we will see, the unstable status of the insured slave, given the mixture of personhood and property intrinsic to slavery, is an important issue in the development of life insurance.

In Transit: Insuring Slaves

The history of insurance begins with the sea. Three developments are central to the conceptual framework established by marine insurance: first, the "bottomry" agreement or "sea loan" in which money is loaned at a steep rate for a voyage, the risk falling to the lender. Second, the concept of "general average," the idea that losses undertaken to save a boat (jettisoning or cutting down masts in a storm, for instance) represent a risk shared among those investing in a voyage—usually seen as the oldest form of joint-stock enterprise. And third, in the notion of "Perils of the Sea"—the earliest form of the concept of insurable risk.[4] Life insurance is a late development, requiring among other things a statistical view of life expectancy. Throughout most of Europe in the early modern period, insurance on the lives of persons was banned—associated with blasphemy (death is God's prerogative), with conspiracy (killing the insured), and with gambling (bets on the lives of kings, and so on). The United Kingdom was the exception—partly, Geoffrey Clark suggests, because of the absence of a Roman law tradition and its dictum that the free person cannot be valued: *hominis liberi nulla estimatio.*[5] But even in England, constraints were placed on life insurance during the eighteenth century, reflecting a suspicion of the practice after the collapse of dubious schemes in the period of the South Sea Bubble. The legal concept of "insurable interest" was developed to overcome these problems, suggesting that one could insure the life of another only to the extent that one could demonstrate financial dependency.[6] This is part of the evolving conception of risk, compensation, and the commoditization of human relations implicit within modernity. What is less obvious is that the notion of insurable interest may have a relation to slavery.

In Europe, a loophole existed in the prohibition of life insurance: the ransom insurance that travelers could take out against capture by Barbary pirates or others. This is the *Ordonnance de la Marine*, source of much modern maritime law, drafted by Louis's minister Colbert in 1681:

Article 9
All seafarers, passengers and others, may take insurance upon the liberty of their persons, and in that case the policy shall set out the name, the nationality,

residence, age and quality of the person thus insuring himself; the name of the ship, that of the port of departure and that of her final destination, the sum to be paid in the event of capture to cover the ransom and the expenses of returning home, the person to whom the money is to be paid by the insurers, and the penalty for delay in the payment.

Article 10
Insurance upon the life of persons other than slaves is forbidden. [Défendons de faire assurance sur la vie des personnes.]

Article 11
Nonetheless, one may take insurance upon a person whom one ransoms from captivity [esclavage], for the amount of the ransom, which the insurers must pay if on the journey home the person is captured anew, killed, or drowned, or perishes by other cause, natural death excepted.[7]

Douglas Barlow, in the modern translation from which this is taken, adds the clause "other than slaves" to Article 10, arguing that "slave-cargo insurance escaped the prohibition in Article 10 [because] in law slaves were not persons"—that is, slaves were, by common usage, articles of trade. Yet this seems a retrospective construction of the collocation of these articles. As John Wesket noted as early as 1781, it is *by analogy with* ransom provisions that the French began to insure the lives of "black captives (slaves)" from Guinea to the colonies.[8] Clark spells out the reasoning:

> [T]he legal variance granted by the Sun King had had important practical consequences since French merchants involved in the slave trade wanted to insure their human cargoes on the Middle Passage and needed a legal basis to remove the insurance of slaves from the *Ordonnance*'s ban. Ransom insurance provided the loophole. Because a ransom could be seen as a price on freedom, the law could treat insurance against captivity as something different in kind from the money valuation of human life itself, payable whatever the circumstance of death. According to this legal fiction, then, slaves acquired on the Guinea coast could be regarded as held in ransom . . . thereby allowing slave traders to insure for the market price of their goods. (16)

In what seems akin to a legal version of Gödel's Principle, the enslaved European has a "market" price set from outside the system of humane law; his or her entry into the market in persons is prompted by an external hazard—though one that has an afterlife. As Article 11 states, the insurance of the person does not necessarily stop the moment they are ransomed, but instead lasts through the voyage home, until their return or the termination of the policy. So while ransom insurance nominally serves to protect "liberty" rather than a life, it is perforce the *life* that is valued on the return: "the insurers must pay if on the journey home the person is captured anew, killed, or drowned, or perishes by other cause, natural death excepted."

It is this liminal, in-transit condition that is assigned to the slave-at-sea: purchased off a captor, and thus having an assigned monetary value; en route to a form of redemption that is simply a realizing of value. Those who can insure a person against capture, the *Ordonnance* states, include family members who have a financial interest in the insured—an early version, surely, of "insurable interest." But at the same time, the doctrine of assignability meant that "insurable interest was required only at the inception of the policy, [which] meant that subsequent lack of interest could not annul the contract"[9]—a negotiability of the valued life that again parallels that of the slave.

Slavery thus occupies a middle position in the progress from insurance on goods to insurance on persons, providing a way of thinking about the value of a life. The ransom as an externally imposed "market" value serves as a historically contingent measure for what was to become a more general equation of the person and economic value.[10] In origin, then, when we insure our lives we are imagining the possibility of capture, or "buying ourselves back from death." But the life so imagined is anything other than for-ourselves; it is a life lived in a state of negation. Behind this equation lurks the thinking on slavery that descends from Aristotle to Hegel: the slave has given up his or her existence to others and accepted subordination rather than face death.

The more historically specific question of whether slaves are people or cargo is raised starkly in a series of legal cases relating to the insuring of slaves. Most took place under the administration of William Murray, Lord Mansfield—the Lord Chief Justice credited with establishing and regularizing the corpus of English commercial law needed by an expanding trade; his maritime law is codified in James Park's *A System of the Law of Marine Insurances* (1787). According to the legal thinking that evolved in this period, slave ships could be insured against shipwreck, piracy, arrest, and shipboard rebellion—unpredictable forces constituting "Perils of the Sea." The deaths of slaves owing to sickness or want of water and provision ("natural death") were not insurable; the same eventually applied to death where voyages were prolonged by poor winds (which could theoretically have been anticipated as a hazard) or by miscalculation.[11] What is the purpose of these distinctions? They cannot clearly be explained by the assumption that "natural death" was entirely predictable, since death rates on the Middle Passage could rise catastrophically for reasons beyond the master's control.[12] Rather, the implication is that it is not the human life of a slave that is insured, but rather his or her status as goods in transit; and as in insurance generally, what cannot be insured in goods is their own internal constitution, their inherent weaknesses.

The problems generated by considering humans as goods are also reflected in the law's treatment of slave insurrections. Slaves killed in a rebellion are treated as general average, destroyed in order to preserve the ship. As John Wesket explains in 1781: "The average arising from insurrection is understood to mean *general average*, and to be borne by the value of ship and cargo, &c. not by that of the slaves only, as a particular average thereon; because the loss or damage (whether to ship, or cargo, or both) which happens by means of an insurrection, and the endeavours used in quelling the same, arises from the *whole* interests, together with the lives of the crew, being in danger." But insurrection implies agency, making slaves something more than goods. Weskett notes that a clause is normally inserted in insurance contracts to specify that slave ships are "free from loss or average, by trading in boats; and also from *average* occasioned by *insurrection* of slaves, if under 10 *per cent*."[13] This seems to imply that insurrection up to a certain level is *expected*, both on the coast of Africa and on board ship; again, it attributes an agency to the slave. In another case involving a Bristol slaver in 1785, *Jones vs. Scholl*, there was a question of how losses of slaves following an attempted rebellion were to be decided. The policy had, as usual, indemnified such losses above "10. *per cent* to be computed on the first cost of the ship, outfit and cargo"—that is, they were part of general average. But what losses were to be allowed, given that the owners claimed for a range of damage from those killed to subsequent deaths, and even market losses caused by the reputation of rebelliousness? The jury, under Mansfield's direction, decided that those who were lost by wounding or bruising were covered; but not those who "swallowed salt water, and died in consequence thereof, or who leaped into the sea, and hung upon the sides of the ship, without being otherwise bruised, or who died of chagrin, were not to be paid for"; Mansfield himself ruled out market losses as "too distant." This is a strict general average interpretation: only immediate "sacrifices" of goods are allowed; the consequent damages, which relate to the status of the slaves as persons and personalities, are ignored, except insofar as they constituted an external peril threatening the ship.[14] The law was, again, struggling with the paradoxical status of slaves, as goods that might in a sense threaten themselves.

The uncertain status of slaves was drawn out in a remarkable set of cases brought in appeal in the Louisiana Supreme Court in 1842. They involved the slave transport *Creole* in 1841, traveling from Richmond to New Orleans; the legal issues included deviation (loaded at ports not specified in the policy), overcrowding and negligence that prompted a rebellion in which one of the owner's agents was killed, and "arrest" of foreign powers (the slaves sailed to the Bahamas, where the British released those not involved in the murder, causing a diplomatic incident). This case looms large in African-American memory—with fictional versions of the events written by Frederick Douglass ("The Heroic Slave"), William Wells Brown, Lydia Maria Child, and Pauline Hopkins—though the subsequent insurance cases have received little or no attention.[15] An incisive set of briefs was prepared by Slidell, Benjamin and Conrad for the Merchants' Insurance Company, which was contesting liability—written by the young Judah P. Benjamin, later Confederate attorney general and then in exile a famous barrister in England.[16]

Benjamin's successful argument covered a variety of issues, but one central plank was the assertion that slaves are inherently prone to rebellion. He invokes a distinction, "as old as the contract of insurance," between the "inherent vices of the subject insured" and "external accidents."[17] In a passage that surely invokes Shylock's plea in *The Merchant of Venice*, the Jewish lawyer asks: "Now, what in the present case was the 'vice propre de la chose'? What is a slave? He is a human being. He has feelings and passions and intellect. His heart, like the white man's, swells with love, burns with jealousy, aches with sorrow, pines under restraint and discomfort, boils with revenge, and ever cherishes the desire of liberty" (27). The slave feels the same feelings as others, and some things more passionately. He "is prone to revolt in the very nature of things. . . . Will any one deny that the bloody and disastrous insurrection of the Creole was the result of the inherent qualities of the slaves themselves, roused, not only by their condition of servitude, but stimulated by the removal from their friends and homes . . . and encouraged by the lax discipline of the vessel, the numerical weakness of the whites, and the proximity of a British province" (28). According to the French legal tradition Benjamin draws on, death from despair and from rebellion are equally part of the situation and state of soul of the captive: "*L'une et l'autre ont pour motif les même causes, qui prennent naissance dans le caractère de la chose.*"[18] Because "intrinsic" risks are not insured, slave rebellion is, Benjamin insists, only covered where it is specifically inserted as a risk in the policy (33–4). Adding that the 10 percent clause normally limits the risk to catastrophic rebellion, Benjamin draws out the logic of earlier cases under Mansfield: rebellion is intrinsic to slavery. Moreover, slavery is, he argues in a brief for one of the other cases, an institution that has since Justinian been described as *contra naturam*, and a result of local conditions rather than of universal application; the British thus had no obligation to return slaves. The more general implication is that the slave's situation is temporary and reversible.[19] The slave can never definitively be treated as an owned thing.

We can turn now to the most famous of all cases relating to slavery and insurance, *Gregson vs. Gilbert:* the case of the slave ship *Zong*. It was an action on the value of "certain slaves"—that is, 134 out of around 470 embarked—who were thrown overboard over a period of days from November 29, 1781, after the boat missed Jamaica, with sickness endemic and water supplies low. Captain Luke Collingwood thus brutally converted an uninsurable loss (general mortality) into general average loss, a sacrifice of parts of a cargo for the benefit of the whole. The owners were awarded damages in which the losses were allowed; but in an appeal hearing before Mansfield and two others this judgment was overturned, since the captain's mistake could not be called a "Peril of the Sea," and there were a number of factors suggesting that water supplies were not seriously depleted.[20] Murder was not the issue in law: despite commenting on the shocking nature of the case, Mansfield insisted repeatedly that in law it was as if horses had been jettisoned. But as the records of the arguments around the case made by the abolitionist Granville Sharp suggest, murder, and specifically murder at sea, was central to the way in which the case was in fact argued.[21]

We need to introduce another concept here. The traditional term for the loss of goods under duress at sea is *sacrifice.* As one authority explained in 1824, "a *sacrifice* made for the *preservation* of the ship and cargo is general average."[22] Sacrifice can thus be seen as one of the earliest concepts informing notions of collective enterprise and shared risk, well before the earliest example the *OED* gives of *sacrifice* used in the secularized sense of giving up of something for a larger good, in *Romeo and Juliet.* The slaves killed by Collingwood were claimed as general average sacrifice. The discourse of sacrifice permeates every aspect of the *Zong* case. The petition to the Court of Exchequer prepared for the insurers of the ship demanded an inquiry into "whether the said Luke Collingwood did not make a wanton of wicked sacrifice of the Lives of the Said Slaves so thrown into the sea."[23] During the trial Mr. Heywood, counsel for the insurers, applied the term to the case itself: "if your Lordship was to determine in favour of these owners I don't know but Millions of our fellow Creatures may herafter fall sacrifice to this very Decision" (41–2). We can see this as an attempt to draw out the ambiguous logic of commercial sacrifice in relation to a human cargo. But another topic also intrudes: the comparison between this case and those of maritime peril in which crew members are sacrificed by lot—a form of sacrifice that we might see as offering a parallel with general average.

Two issues were important here. The most telling legally was the nature of the emergency that caused the slaves to be jettisoned. General average sacrifice applies only to situations of immediate peril. The situation was not, counsel for the insurers suggested, catastrophic; no one was on short rations; water was available within sailing distance; more slaves were killed after the "providential shower" of December 1. The second issue was the nonrandom nature of the selection of slaves. Another counsel, Davenport argued that "[t]here never was a Moment of short Allowance for that is the only thing that I call actual necessity—then one easily sees why the slaves are to go first & why the sick ones are to go or those that would sell for the least Money are to go before the more Healthy and Valuable[,] one easily sees when this Captain had missed Jamaica" (8–9). It was awareness of that he had "lost his Market" that determined and structured Collingwood's actions.

Why is randomizing the selection of slaves so important to the argument? General average sacrifice is supposed to be enacted under pressure: one seizes the goods nearest to hand for jettison rather than (say) carefully sorting out the cheapest cargo. Random selection thus might be seen as way of mimicking a state of emergency, disguising human agency as Nature. But there is more to it than this, since slaves are of course human beings who exist as part of a collectivity on a ship. Mr. Pigot, also acting for the insurers, raised the issue of randomizing selection via a recent well-known precedent: the case of Captain J. N. Inglefield and the Royal Navy ship *Centaur*. The *Centaur* sailed from Jamaica in September 1782, and after a gale became leaky lost her mast and rudders; as she was sinking, Inglefield and some others got off in a pinnacle, which drifted for weeks without food and water.[24] For Pigot—ignoring Inglefield's self-selection for the boat and rumors of cannibalism—this provides a model of action in which collective suffering is morally superior, and the casting of lots a secondary expedient in cases of necessity: "Captain Inglefield distributed that Water as long it lasted equally—Did they even upon the footing of equality cast lots for their Lives? No, they trusted . . . [in Providence]" (29). The Court of Exchequer petition made a similar argument: "And your Orators [the formal term for a petitioner] charge that if there had been an absolute & immediate necessity that any lives should be lost in order to preserve the rest (which your Orators charge was not the case) Lot ought to have been first cast that it might have been known on whom the Lot fell to become sacrificed" (124). Here, the sacrificial logic of lots—of distributing risk randomly—serves as a possible amelioration of murder. In the absence of lots and catastrophe, a selective commercial logic is assumed to operate, and insurance nullified. On the *Zong*, commercial sacrifice becomes blood sacrifice, a targeting of victims who will bear the cost rather than a distribution of risk across the ship.

We will return to the issue of drawing lots. But to draw the argument thus far together, it is clear that the legal position of the slave is unstable: goods and yet not goods; an external threat, but also internal to the ship in terms of general average; an unpredictable risk whose resistance is predictable. The aim of abolitionist discourse is often to draw out these contradictions, and to insist on a confusion of goods and persons. Granville Sharp threatened an indictment for murder over the *Zong* case, and after much protest the recovery of such losses through insurance was legislated against in a series of statutes from 1788. Sharp's own protest to the Admiralty insisted on collapsing the distinction between life and property:

> The *property* of these poor injured Negroes *in their own lives*, notwithstanding their unhappy state of slavery, was infinitely superior, *and more to be favoured in law*, than the slave-holders' or slave-dealers' iniquitous claim of property in their *persons*: and therefore the casting them alive into the sea, though *insured* as property, and valued at thirty pounds per head, is not to be deemed the case of throwing over goods, &c.[25]

A note by Sharp in the record of the case, responding to the Solicitor General's claims that the slaves are "real Property," elaborates:

> But at the same time it is also the Case of throwing over living Men, and tho' in one sense they may be considered *as goods,* yet this does not alter their existence & actual Rights *as living Men;* so that the property in their Persons is only a limited property, *limited* I say by the necessary consideration of their *human Nature.* . . . (48)

Existence is a key term here, suggesting an actuality that has been destroyed. Indeed, a related distinction had been drawn by Mansfield in his famous judgment on James Somerset (the 1772 case declaring that slavery was such an evil that it could not be legally sustained on English soil in the absence of any "positive law" justifying it). Mansfield distinguished between the contract for sale, which remained a valid commercial document about an abstract person, and "the person of the slave himself," the body that is before the court and over which the owner is exerting "so high an act of dominion" in taking the slave against his or her will to the West Indies. In earlier cases, settled out of court, slaves were produced under a writ of habeas corpus, and Mansfield referred to this point of origin in his judgment.[26] For this reason producing the human body, refusing its liminal, contractual, and in-transit status, is central to abolitionist writings and iconography.

Maritime Cannibalism, or Why Eating People Is Wrong

What are we to make of the rather strange comparison between the *Zong* and instances of shipwreck and the drawing of lots? What ties them together is an understanding of the logic of sacrifice in which the pressures of maritime life produce particular sets of decisions. Shipwrecks have regularly produced boatloads of starving passengers and crew, or groups of castaways, who have resorted to cannibalism. Many of those eaten were, of course, already dead, but in numerous cases documented in the huge corpus of shipwreck narratives, it is the living who are killed and eaten, almost inevitably after the drawing of lots. This is the "Custom of the Sea," for centuries regarded as a tragic and horrific but unavoidable part of maritime life. It was only with the prosecution of the crew of the *Mignonette* in 1884, for killing and eating Richard Parker, the ship's boy, that the practice was judicially condemned.

The question of *why* this hitherto invisible "crime" becomes visible is a complex one. In his magisterial book on the *Mignonette* case, Brian Simpson argues that one reason the legal establishment tried the crew was in order to resist the harsher implications of Social Darwinism and the utilitarian calculus (a calculus of sacrifice that is, we have seen, part of the logic of insurance).[27] The sailors had selected Parker because he was closest to death, and he had no dependents. But the final judges, in a highly moralistic argument, demanded that the starving should resist eating others, even if it meant their own death. This is akin to Granville Sharp's argument against the jettisoning of slaves—evil cannot be justified by necessity. A case of human jettison, involving the male passengers in an overcrowded longboat being thrown into icy seas by the sailors manning it, had already been prosecuted in America.[28] But I want to avoid rushing to the conclusion that abolition and cannibalism simply intersect on a humanitarian trajectory in which both are increasingly unacceptable. Instead, we need to investigate the history and theory of eating people.

Simpson reports that popular legend had it that the *Mignonette* survivors were prosecuted because they failed to observe the Custom of the Sea, not drawing lots. Lots are an ancient practice, described as early as the story of Jonah—a precedent raised in defense of the crew by Sir George Baker.[29] Central to Jonah is the way in which the lots enact a providential and sacrificial logic. The mariners respond to the storm that the Lord sends by throwing "the wares that were in the ship into the sea, to lighten it of them" (sacrifice). They cast lots in order to ascertain which of them is being punished. When Jonah admits that he is the cause of the tempest, and suggests he be thrown overboard, the sailors at first refuse to do so—this delay is important in later narratives—before crying: "We beseech thee O Lord, we beseech thee, let us not perish for this man's life," adding—and again, this disavowal is significant—"and lay not upon us innocent blood: for thou, O Lord, has done as it pleased thee." Jonah is finally tossed overboard, the seas calm, and a religious sacrifice is offered.

This providential pattern is reflected in English sea narratives. *Mr James Janeway's Legacy to his Friends* (1674) includes a series of stories involving the possibilities of cannibalism. In one, after near starvation, "[t]he Motion is, that which the Marriners, in *Jonahs* Vessel, put in execution, *Come let us cast Lots*, &c. onely with this difference, they cast Lots to find out the delinquent; and these, which of them, should dye first, to be a Sacrifice for ravenous Hunger to feed upon: concluding, as he in that case, *It is expedient for us that one man should dye for the People, and that the whole Ships Company perish not.*" As the marginal reference notes, this echoes the words of the high priest Caiaphas in John 11:50, declaring that Jesus should die so that the people be protected. The sailors cast lots and one is chosen; but the next question is, Who is to execute him? Prayers are offered, and the Lord answers, casting "a mighty Fish into the boat." They starve again, cast lots again (excusing the one "that God hath acquitted"), and this time the Lord sends "a great Bird." After a final set of lots is cast, the third victim is saved when a sail appears. In another narrative in the collection, a comparable story is told: when a ship is stuck in ice, lots are cast but none of the crew wishes to be the executioner; providentially the loser dies as he prays, and taking this as a "good *Omen*" they eat him.[30] Sacrifice is made possible without murder, a logic of substitution that persists in some providential narratives up to the nineteenth century.[31]

In the eighteenth century, however, lots become progressively secularized, and doubt as to divination by lot increases. Later commentaries and sermons on Jonah stress that lots are not recommended; they dwell on the humanity of the heathen sailors rather than the violence of their act, their reluctance to abandon Jonah, or to resort to lots. The runner-up for the Seatonian prize in 1825, Edward Smedley, writes in his *Jonah: A Poem*, "him unwillingly they threw / A willing victim to the gulph."[32] George Abbott, Archbishop of Canterbury, in his *Exposition upon the Prophet Jonah* (1845) stresses their refusal to single him out, and the fact that they probably cast lots many times to confirm the verdict.[33] In *Man by Nature and by Grace: or, Lessons from the Book of Jonah* (1850), W. K. Tweedie comments that the Hebrew word translated "they took up" (in "they took up Jonah, and cast him into the sea") means "to exalt with respect."[34] The limits of the redemptive and sacrificial principle that underlies these actions are thus carefully established: these sailors do not *wish* to kill Jonah; when they do throw him overboard, it is in the name of a higher power rather than individual survival. The scheme that makes Jonah a type of Christ (and his three days in the fish's belly a type of Christ's descent to hell, Matthew 12:39–40) reinforces the sense that this is a symbolic action.

René Girard has argued that this story of sacrifice and substitution underlies much Western mythmaking, at least until its logic is rendered explicit in Christianity. For Girard, Caiaphas's words are those of a political calculus, the "transcendent qualities" of the scapegoat "replaced by the justification of social utility"[35]—precisely that which was condemned on the *Mignonette*. And indeed, if one looks at the operation of lots in a range of shipwreck narratives, one comes to see that it conceals a harsh scapegoating in which the expendable are made to carry the burden. As Neil Hanson urbanely remarks, "certain features recur in almost every instance." Despite the ritual of drawing lots (that is, a supposedly random distribution of victims), an almost inevitable order interposes itself: black people are eaten first; then cabin boys and women; steerage passengers are eaten before crew; then unpopular seamen and ancillary crew (cooks, and so on); with ordinary seamen and officers last.[36] The ritual of lots, that is, conceals the operation of power as chance even as it reveals itself within the individuals whose bodies are consumed.

Perhaps the most notorious example of racialized cannibalism of the kind suggested by Hanson's list is the wreck of the *Peggy* in 1765–6, one of the sources of Poe's *The Narrative of Arthur Gordon Pym*. On board the drifting wreck, the first and (as it turned out) only person to be killed was the slave Whitshire. The comments of the captain and his owner David Harrison nicely demonstrates the logic of sacrifice disguised as chance:

> [T]hey had taken a chance for their lives, and the lot had fallen on a Negro, who was part of my cargo.—The little time taken to cast the lot, and their private manner of conducting the decision, gave me some strong suspicions that the poor Ethiopian was not altogether treated fairly;—but, on recollection, I almost wondered that they had given him even the appearance of an equal chance with themselves.[37]

At the end of Harrison's printed narrative is, nevertheless, a legalistic "Protest for their indemnity" on behalf of the owners, including an insistence that the death of Whitshire *is* general average sacrifice:

> I, the said Notary, at his request do hereby solemnly protest, that all damage, loss, detriment, and prejudice, that shall, or may have happened, for, or by reason or means of the total loss of his before-mentioned sloop Peggy and her cargo; or the killing of the before-mentioned Negro slave, or black man, is, and ought to be, borne by the merchants, freighters, and others interested therein; the same having accrued in manner herein before particularly set forth, and not by or through neglect, default, coincurrence, direction, or mismanagement of him, the appearer. . . . (54–5)

A similar example is provided by William Boys's account of the loss of the *Luxborough Galley*, destroyed by fire in 1727. She was a slaver for the South Sea Company carrying six hundred slaves; after off-loading in Jamaica, she joined the navy. "Two black boys" who were sent for rum spilled some and decided to see if the liquid burned, creating an explosion. One boat got off, with twenty-two on board. On day five it was stormy and it was proposed "to throw overboard the two black boys . . . in order to lighten the boat"—on the model of Jonah (9). The boys naturally opposed this; they cast lots (though the captain refused to sanction the act). In any event, before anyone was killed, one of the boys and another man died; they and the subsequent dead were eaten before six survivors landed in

Newfoundland. The case of the *Mary*, reported in the *Gentleman's Magazine* in 1737, is an equally routine scapegoating. The slaver foundered off the Canaries; her cargo of slaves, who had been manning the pumps, were left to sink.[38] Eight crew members escaped in a boat and after some weeks began to eat each other. "Our Hunger then being intolerable, we were forc'd to kill one of our Companions to eat, and it was agreed together to begin with one of the Portuguese."[39] Even in texts in which the pathos of shipwreck is the subject, eating black people is acceptable. In a popular narrative, at least partly factual, *The Surprising yet Real and true Voyages and Adventures of Monsieur Pierre Viaud, A French Sea-Captain* (1771), it is the black servant who is bludgeoned to death by the hero and the female survivor for food—after the narrator has thought of the maritime custom of casting lots.[40] The 1774 American edition of this text binds it with Falconer's *The Shipwreck* under the heading "To the Sentimentalist in America," and indeed the narrative has many appeals to sentiment. But while Viaud calls himself a "barbarian" for killing his servant, the necessity (and legality) of doing so is never an issue.

Elsewhere, a rather different but closely related version of scapegoating operates, in which the person chosen by lot escapes because of the supposed willing intervention of another, usually a dispensable outsider. The popular maritime ballad known in English as "The Ship in Distress" (and under many different titles in versions in other European languages) is described by Brian Simpson:

> In most versions, the intended victim escapes at the last minute, or his escape is assumed, but the details differ. In some the lot falls on the captain; the cabin boy offers himself as a substitute, climbs the mast for a last look around, sees the Towers of Babylon and the captain's daughter, and marries her. In others the boy is offered the daughter and money as reward for acting as a substitute but asks for the ship instead. . . . A Scandinavian version has the king of Babylon in command; lots are drawn, and the unfortunate seaman who draws the fatal lot cannot decently be eaten, since he is closely related to the other sailors; one who is not related offers to die in his place and is sacrificed.[41]

This ballad has, it seems to me, a late recension in the "Titanic Toast," the oral recitation that circulated in African American communities soon after the *Titanic* went down in 1912. Its many versions describe Shine, a black stoker on this ship with no black crew. When the ship strikes the iceberg, he starts swimming, ignoring the pleas of the captain—who offers him his daughter and money—and passengers; he outswims the sharks and when the news breaks is drunk in a bar in New York. As Steve Beil and others have shown, this ballad relates to a widespread sense that the *Titanic* was the ship of Anglo-Saxon supremacy, as well as to reports that Jack Johnson, the black heavyweight, had been refused passage.[42] One might also link it to the decline, since the 1850s, in black participation in the merchant marine. But seeing it as "signifying" on "The Ship in Distress" also enables us to read it as a refusal of substitution and sacrifice: this black underling is not going to offer his place to *anyone*.

In the cases described above, the lack of comment on the collective decisions made is, perhaps, simply what one would expect: a version of the rapaciousness of slavery that in Equiano's *Interesting Narrative* is figured as a vision of white cannibalism. What is covered up is a sacrificial logic in which risk is not shared equally; it is redistributed toward the bodies of the socially and commercially dispensable—bodies that disappear. Where the presence of the victimized body can be reinserted into this story is in relation to a topos that I would christen "fresh meat." An example is provided by the wreck of the *Nottingham Galley* in 1710, which left a group of sailors on Boon Island off New England.[43] When a rescuer arrives on the rock, "as they were passing on towards the tent, the man casting his eye on the remains of the flesh, exposed to the frost on the summit of the rock, expressed his satisfaction at their not being destitute of provisions; and the master acquiesced in the justice of his sentiments, without unravelling the mystery." This wreck combined, interestingly enough, cannibalism and suggestions of insurance fraud. The master, John Deane, stressed that he was persuaded to divide the corpse of the carpenter only after entreaties from the crew and after "Abundance of mature Thought and Consultation"; he portrays himself as the hero of the hour, presiding over an unruly crew and spotting rescuers.[44] Three of the crew members, including the mate and boatswain, published an opposing account stressing the master's cowardliness and negligence, and claiming that the ship was overinsured and could therefore be wrecked at a profit; that in fact Deane had attempted to lose the ship earlier.[45] They also, implicitly, link the alleged fraud to meat hunger: in their account, he initiates the flesh eating, telling them it is no sin, and it is reported that "he barbarously told the Children in his Lodging, that he would have made a Frigassy of them if he had 'em in Boon Island" (18, 24). The narrative written by Deane and his brother Jasper (the main owner of the ship) has a rebuttal, probably added after the type was set up, claiming that the ship was not overinsured and that no one would deliberately wreck a ship on a remote spot, "where 'twas more than Ten Thousand to one, but every Man had perish'd" (22).

In a later example, the *Narrative of the Shipwreck and Suffering of Miss Ann Saunders* (1827), the frisson of cannibalism is tinged with what can only be described as a healthy pleasure in feminine fortitude. As the title page states, Saunders

> was a passenger on board the ship *Francis Mary*, which foundered at sea on the 5th Feb. 1826, on her passage from New Brunswick to Liverpool. Miss Saun-

ders was one of the six survivors who were driven to the awful extremity of subsisting 22 days on the dead bodies of such of the unfortunate crew as fell victims to starvation—one of whom was a young man to whom she was soon to be joined in marriage.[46]

The cannibalism began on day seventeen; Saunders—like Jonah's crew—resists for a day, but then takes not only to the eating of the dead but also to their preparation. In what seems like a bizarre parody of the "one flesh" of marriage, she pleads her claim to "the greater portion of his [her fiancé's] precious blood, as it oozed, half congealed, from the wound inflicted upon his lifeless body!!" Later, as the only person left on her feet, the "office" of cutting up the flesh falls to her. Her friend Mrs. Kendall also shows more pluck than most, eating the brains of a seaman and "declaring . . . that it was the most delicious thing she had ever tasted!" Rescue comes in the form of HMS *Blonde*. Here again is "fresh meat":

> When relieved, but a small part of the body of the last person deceased re-
> mained, and this I had cut as usual into slices and spread on the quarter deck;
> which being noticed by the Lieutenant of the Blonde . . . and before we had
> time to state to him what extremities we had been driven, he observed "you
> have got, I perceive, fresh meat!" but his horror can be better conceived than
> described when he was told that what he saw, were the remains of the dead
> body of one of our unfortunate companions. . . .[47]

The lieutenant may have been shocked; his captain might not have been: he was Lord Byron, inheritor of the title of the poet who had written of maritime cannibalism so graphically in *Don Juan*.

The visibility of the flesh of the dead has a counterpoint in stress on the actuality of violent sacrifice in the *Zong* case, most memorably depicted in Turner's famous painting *Slavers Throwing Overboard the Dead and Dying*, said to have its origins in the case and in the many descriptions of sharks savaging bodies in abolitionist poetry. In both the cannibal feast and the dead body of the slave, what is involved is a materialization of social meta-phor; and perhaps also a vision of that which resists exchange—the abject body that cannot be adequately symbolized within society's vision of what bodies are for.

We can draw some tentative conclusions from the linkage of sacrifice in insurance, lot drawing, and cannibalism that I have attempted to sketch. Sacrifice at sea is the original model for all risk in insurance; it corresponds to the sacrificial premium we all make so that others (or ourselves) are compensated in the event of disaster; so that, as well, a system of contrac-tual kinship may be maintained. Susan Mizruchi characterizes life insur-ance as "an act of sacrifical protection," at once a symbolic warding off of evil and a way of conceiving community and welfare within a humanitarian calculus.[48] This seems right; the stated legal principle underlying insurance is, after all, "the insurer's standing exactly in the place of the assured," a form of legally enforceable sympathetic identification. But in the case of life insurance the question of compensation is more troubled: others may be compensated, but that demands a victim whose losses are total, except to the extent that insurance reflects familial and social connectedness (we die happy knowing at least that others around us are secure). One name for the negative component of this victimage is slavery: the fate of the actual slave, who owes nothing to his owners; whose insurance involves no reciprocity; but perhaps also, in lesser degree, slavery as a metaphor for the subordination of person to another person, job, or social role; the sacrifice made by what Hegel calls the unhappy consciousness, the element of the self that denies social valuation, a value not defined by self-identity.

Another form of sacrifice at sea, the drawing of lots before the person is killed and ingested, provides a dark model here—a model in which the supposedly random operation of fate is mimicked by the lot, but which is in fact susceptible to human manipulation and scapegoating. And while scapegoats may be portrayed as willing, as in "The Ship in Distress" and indeed in many shipwreck narratives, this is always a point at issue, and the story often seems to conceal a violent subordination. When human beings secularize the distribution of risk and compensation, insurance becomes a reflection of social reality rather than a transcendent principle. In the case of the *Zong*, both of the definitions referred to above—commercial sacrifice; the sacrifice of bodies—were at work, as the lawyers involved seemed to know. The problem of distributing burdens is always predicated on the question of who is inside and who outside the circle of the assured (as Mizruchi makes clear when she points out that the Nazis forbade insurance on Jews). This is the case for slaves, but as we have seen, simply to ask the question, "Is a slave insurable, and under what circumstances?" is also to engage in a potential identification—which means that the famous slave insurance cases form part of a progressive history. In a culture of compensation, all losses must ultimately be covered, or leave a traumatic remnant—which is why the issue of reparation is still with us.

Notes

1. See Todd L. Savitt, "Slave Life Insurance in Virginia and North Carolina," *Journal of Southern History* 43 (1977), 583–600; Robert S. Starobin, *Industrial Slavery in the Old South* (New York: Oxford University Press, 1970).

2. Vivian A. Rotman Zelizer, *Morals and Markets: The Development of Life Insurance in the United States* (New York: Columbia University Press, 1979).

3. This question is asked, but not clearly answered, by Michael Sean Quinn, "Examining Slave Insurance in a World 150 Years Removed," *Insurance Journal*, July 24, 2000.

4.   On the evolution of these terms, see Victor Dover, *A Handbook to Marine Insurance* (London: Witherby, 8th rev. ed., 1987).

5.   Geoffrey Clark, *Betting on Lives: The Culture of Life Insurance in England, 1695–1775* (Manchester: Manchester University Press, 1999), 19.

6.   Clark, *Betting on Lives*, 22; Zelizer, *Morals and Markets*, 68–72.

7.   *The Marine Insurance Code of France, 1681*, trans. Douglas Barlow (Willodale, Ontario: author, 1989), 22–3. Barlow notes that Article 9 was largely copied from the *Guidon de la Mer*, a collection of precedents dating from the 1500s.

8.   John Wesket, *A Complete Digest of the Theory, Laws and Practice of Insurance* (London: Frys, Couchman and Collier, 1781), 72.

9.   Zelizer, *Morals and Markets*, 71.

10.   To some extent this history is also written into the history of the term *person*, which originally referred to a mask or persona, someone who acts a part, but later also referred to the body of a person (as opposed to the soul), and then to "the actual self or being of a man or woman" (*OED* 5), often used reflexively ("his own person"). The person is thus part of a history in which the self emerges as personal property; it achieves identity with it-self.

11.   See *Tatham vs. Hodgson* (1796), Charles Durnford and Edward Hyde East, *Term Reports in the Court of King's Bench* (London: J. Butterworth, 4th ed., 1794–1802), VI 656, in which slaves starved to death after a voyage was extended from six to nine weeks to more than six months. The judges ruled that it would undermine the recent act if the claim was allowed, since it meant that "every person going on this [or any] voyage should find his interest combined with his duty" (Lord Kenyon, 658); "natural death" thus must include starvation. Judge Lawrence stressed that "I do not know that it was ever decided that a loss arising from a mistake of the captain was a loss within the perils of the sea," citing the *Zong* case (659)—implying that a Captain is to blame even in such an extreme case. See also Laurence R. Baily, *Perils of the Sea, and their Effects on Policies of Insurance* (London: Effingham Wilson, 1860), 197–8.

12.   Herbert Klein, *The Middle Passage: Comparative Studies in the Atlantic Slave Trade* (Princeton, NJ: Princeton University Press, 1978), 153.

13.   Wesket, *A Complete Digest*, 525, 11.

14.   *Jones vs. Schmoll*, Guildhall Tr. Vac. 1785, Durnford and East, *Term Reports*, I 130n; James Allan Park, *A System of the Law of Marine Insurances* (London: T. Whieldon, 2nd ed., 1790), 56.

15.   See Howard Jones, "The Peculiar Institution and National Honor: The Case of the Creole Slave Revolt," *Civil War History* 21 (1975), 28–50; Maggie Montesinos Sale, *The Slumbering Volcano: American Slave Ship Revolts and the Production of Rebellious Masculinity* (Durham, NC: Duke University Press, 1997), chs. 3 and 5; also John Cullen Gruesser, "Taking Liberties: Pauline Hopkins's Recasting of the Creole Rebellion," John Cullen Gruesser (ed.), *The Unruly Voice: Rediscovering Pauline Elizabeth Hopkins* (Urbana: University of Illinois Press, 1996), 98–118. Douglass's "The Heroic Slave" has received extensive commentary.

16.   See Robert D. Meade, *Judah P. Benjamin: Confederate Statesman* (New York: Oxford University Press, 1943), 40–2.

17.   *Supreme Court: Edward Lockett vs. Merchants' Insurance Company*. Brief of Slidell, Benjamin and Conrad, for Defendants (New Orleans: n.p., 1842), 26–7. Ironically, Benjamin was himself later a slave owner and defender of the institution.

18.   Boulay Paty, cited *Lockett vs. Merchants' Insurance Company*, 33.

19.   *Thomas McCargo vs. Merchants' Insurance Company* (New Orleans: n.p., 1842).

20.   The appeal hearing took place on May 22, 1783; there is no record of a second case, and it is usually presumed the owners withdrew their case. See Park, *A System of the Law of Marine Insurances*, 62; Sylvester Douglas, *Reports of Cases Argued and Determined in the Court of King's Bench*, vol. 3 by Henry Roscoe (London: S. Sweet and Stevens and Sons, 1831), 233–5; and Robert Weisbord, "The Case of the Slave-Ship *Zong*, 1783," *History Today* 19 (1969), 561–7. Statutes subsequently passing included 30 G. 3, c. 33, *f.* 8 and 34 G. 3, c. 80, *f.* 10 prohibiting any losses due to throwing overboard, ill treatment, or natural death.

21.   The account here draws on the bound set of manuscript records of the case Granville Sharp had made from shorthand transcripts, "In the King's Bench, Wednesday May 21 1783" and other documents, National Maritime Museum, London, Rec/19. These are the "vouchers" that Sharp attached to his protest to the Admiralty: see Prince Hoare, *Memoirs of Granville*

Sharp, esq. (London: Henry Colburn, 1820), 242–4, appendix 8. Abbreviated forms have been spelled out.

22. Wilhelm Benecke [of Lloyds], *A Treatise on the Principles of Indemnity in Marine Insurance, Bottomry and Respondentia* (London: Baldwin, Cradock and Joy, 1824), 168.

23. Voucher 1, Plea to the Court of Exchequer, Hilary Term 23 Geo. 3, in Sharp Records, 132.

24. See *Captain [J. N.] Inglefield's Narrative, Concerning the Loss of His Majesty's Ship the Centaur, of Seventy-Four Guns . . . a new edition* (London: J. Murray, 1783).

25. Hoare, *Memoirs of Granville Sharp*, appendix 8, n.p.

26. Peter Fryer, *Staying Power: The History of Black People in Britain* (London: Pluto, 1984), 125; Edmund Heward, *Lord Mansfield* (Chichester: Barry Rose, 1979), 146.

27. A. W. Brian Simpson, *Cannibalism and the Common Law* [1984] (London: Hambledon Press, 1994), 251–2.

28. The case of the *William Brown (U.S. vs. Holmes)*, described in Simpson, *Cannibalism*, 162.

29. Simpson, *Cannibalism*, 249.

30. *Mr James Janeway's Legacy to his Friends, Containing Twenty Seven Famous Instances of God's Providences in and about Sea Dangers and Deliverances, with the Names of Several that were Eye-Witnesses to many of them. Wereto is Added a Sermon on the same Subject* (London: Dorman Newman, 1674), 3–6, 15.

31. See, for instance, *Melancholy Shipwreck, and Remarkable Instance of the Interposition of Divine Providence* (1834), related by Mrs. Mathews, a missionary's wife bound for India from Portsmouth. After sixteen days in an open boat, lots are proposed. She then gets them to defer a day and prays. They prepare lots, she gets another hour for prayer, and a sail appears.

32. Edward Smedley, *Jonah: A Poem* (London: John Murray, 1815), 6. The winning poem, by James W. Bellamy, manages not to mention the lots and Jonah's ejection. Neither is the issue raised in Jacob Durché's 1781 Humane Society sermon, on Jonah 2:5–6, which simply offers a moralization of straying.

33. George Abbott, D.D., *An Exposition upon the Prophet Jonah*, 2 vols. (London: Hamilton, Adams, 1845), vol. 1, 90; compare Thomas Harding, *Expository Lectures on the Book of Jonah* (London: A. Heylin, 1856), 45.

34. Rev. W. K. Tweedie, *Man by Nature and by Grace: or, Lessons from the Book of Jonah* (Edinburgh: Johnstone & Hunter, 1850), 72–3.

35. René Girard, *The Scapegoat* (London: Athlone Press, 1986), 113.

36. Neil Hanson, *The Custom of the Sea* (London: Doubleday, 1997), 138.

37. David Harrison, *The Melancholy Narrative of the Distressful Voyage and Miraculous Deliverance of Captain David Harrison of the Sloop Peggy* (London: James Harrison, 1766), 23. The case is discussed in Peter Thompson, "No Chance in Nature: Cannibalism as a Solution to Maritime Famine c. 1750–1800," Tim Armstrong (ed.), *American Bodies: Cultural Histories of the Physique* (New York: New York University Press, 1996), 32–44.

38. *Gentleman's Magazine* 89 (July 1737), 449–50.

39. Other examples include the *Francis Spaight* (1835), where the sailors bled and ate their way through four crew, beginning with a probably rigged ballot among the cabin boys; the *Exuine* and *Cospatrick*; and the *Sallie M. Stedman* off Cape Hateras in 1878, where a black sailor went mad and was killed and eaten. For others, see Simpson, *Cannibalism*, 128–33, 139; Hanson, *The Custom of the Sea*.

40. On the text's status, see the introduction to *Shipwreck and Adventures of Monsieur Pierre Viaud*, trans. and ed. Robin F. A. Fabel (Pensecola: West Florida University Press, 1990).

41. Simpson, *Cannibalism*, 141.

42. Steve Beil, *Down with the Old Canoe: A Cultural History of the Titanic Disaster* (New York: W. W. Norton, 1996).

43. *A Narrative of the Shipwreck of the Nottingham Galley, &c, publish'd in 1711. Revised and reprinted with additions in 1726* (London: n.p., n.d.), 20. On the case generally, see R. H. Warner, "Captain John Deane and the Wreck of the Nottingham Galley: A Study of History and Bibliography," *New England Quarterly* 68 (1995), 106–17.

44. *A Narrative of the Sufferings, Preservation and Deliverance of Capt. John Dean and Company* (London: R. Tookey, n.d. [1711]).

45. *A True Account of the Voyage of the Nottingham-Galley of London, John Dean Commander, from the River Thames to New-England* (London: S. Popping, n.d. [1711]). A pirated version of Deane's account, condensing it and converting the first person to third, appeared: *A Sad*

and Deplorable, but True Account of the Dreadful Hardships, and Sufferings of Capt. John Dean, and his Company, on Board the Nottingham Galley (London: J. Dutton, 1711).

46. *Narrative of the Shipwreck and Suffering of Miss Ann Saunders* (Providence, RI: Z. S. Crossman, 1827). Various editions of this narrative appeared, as well as accounts in the press. One could compare this marital communion to that in the wreck of the *George*, 1822: "Her wretched husband was compel'd / Her precious blood to taste" (quoted in Simpson, *Cannibalism and the Common Law*, 117).

47. *Shipwreck and Suffering*, 19–20. A letter from Lieutenant (later Rear Admiral) R. F. Gambier, describing the rescue, is in the National Maritime Museum, MS 73/073.

48. Susan L. Mizruchi, *The Science of Sacrifice: American Literature and Modern Social Theory* (Princeton, NJ: Princeton University Press, 1998), 256, 303–7.

CHAPTER 10

Cast Away

The Uttermost Parts of the Earth

PETER HULME

Je pense aux matelots oubliés dans une île.
Charles Baudelaire, "Le Cygne" (1857)

The phrase *sea change* can work in a number of ways. The sea, and its associated meanings, itself changed over the course of the period covered by this book, which has well and truly historicized the oceans. The sea also changes transitively, in at least two senses: the literal transformations brought about by salt water, from drowning to preservation; and the transformations experienced by those who cross the sea. The supposedly dramatic effects of this latter meaning have led to the phrase *sea change* indicating a *profound* transformation, one that is, by implication, not easily reversed. By the starting date of 1600, one might assume that Europeans were beginning to associate those profound transformations with the new experience of circumnavigating the world: Magellan and Drake had completed probably two of the longest voyages ever in terms of both distance traveled and time away from home. Circumnavigation led to more danger at sea than Europeans had previously experienced: more shipwrecks, more mutinies, more castaways. But there are, of course, no safe seas. Literally, as well as metaphorically, the narrowest straits are often the most perilous: so, in 1611, for example, the voyage from Naples to Tunis was a short journey in sea miles, but involved both a difficult maritime passage and a huge shift in terms of culture, religion, and ideology, certainly sufficient for sea changes to take place.

Indeed, the first appearance of the phrase *sea change* in English seems to be in Ariel's song from *The Tempest*, shortly after that return voyage from Tunis has ended in shipwreck. "Full fathom five thy father lies," sings Ariel:

> Of his bones are coral made;
> Those are pearls that were his eyes;
> Nothing of him that doth fade,
> But doth suffer a sea-change
> Into something rich and strange.
> Sea-nymphs hourly ring his knell.
> (1.2.397–402)[1]

This is profound transformation indeed—bones into coral, eyes into pearls, the human remains of a castaway become rich and strange; but, as so often in *The Tempest*, things are not what they seem. Ariel directs this song at Ferdinand as part of Prospero's scheme to lower the morale of the royal prince and make him properly susceptible to Miranda's kindness as well as to her beauty. In fact, as Ariel well knows, since he engineered the whole shipwreck, Ferdinand's father, Alonso, is alive and well on another part of the island: the song is, in one sense, a pack of lies. In another sense, though, the song tells a deeper truth. Alonso, in common with all the other characters in the play, has suffered a sea change: the return journey from Tunis to Naples has begun a process of transformation that will be overoptimistically summed up at the end of the play by Gonzalo as everyone finding themselves "when no man was his own" (5.1.213).

Nothing dramatizes the sea change better than being cast away, preferably on the kind of island, real or mythological, where metamorphoses are likely to take place. The trope of the castaway is very closely linked to the trope of the island, whose own significances are many and varied: a metaphor for retreat, for pleasure and desire, for redemption, for new beginnings, for control: for all kinds of sea change. Aside from the spirits of the island, almost all the characters in *The Tempest* are castaways: "we were all sea-swallowed, though some cast again," says Antonio (2.1.249), taking advantage of the theatrical pun on *cast*. Prospero and Miranda, and—separately—Sycorax have been cast away from their maritime communities by political enemies who, for whatever reason, did not want to simply kill them. All the other characters, with the exception of Caliban, who was born on the island, have been shipwrecked and cast away through Prospero's magic. Two of the play's further ironies are that Prospero has shared the castaway fate of Sycorax, the woman he likes to construe as his opposite, and that these two characters—cast away by nonmagical means—are both magicians whose magic was unable to prevent them being cast away.

According to Prospero, Sycorax was left on the island by sailors, her death sentence in Algiers commuted because of her pregnancy (1.2.264–8). Prospero and Miranda were cast adrift, again according to Prospero, in "a rotten carcase of a butt, not rigg'd, / Nor tackle, sail nor mast" (1.2.146–7)—a traditional form of punishment, it seems, for certain categories of crime, and particularly favored, one might speculate, by authorities unwilling to risk backlash from public execution and uncertain about the legitimacy, either secular or religious, of their actions.[2] To cast away in such a *navis unus pellius*, a ship of one skin, as it was traditionally called, was an attempt to leave the authorities' consciences clean: the sea—or at least God through his instrument the sea—would protect the innocent and condemn the guilty. Prospero's survival is, therefore, for Prospero, a mark of his innocence, although he is unwilling to apply the same yardstick to Sycorax, who also survived her ordeal, and he, in any case, survived in part because of Gonzalo's care package, which was not included in the original castaway scheme hatched by Prospero's enemy, Alonso.

The geography of *The Tempest* famously manages to combine that narrow world of the Mediterranean with a sense of the oceans beyond, conjured largely through the play's names: *Caliban* and *the Bermudas* invoke the Caribbean and the North Atlantic, while *Setebos*—Sycorax's god, according to Caliban—evokes a world as distant from London as it was possible to get in 1611, a world of giant Patagonian savages and cannibals, violent storms, and fraught relationships between Europeans and natives; all of which, like the name *Setebos* itself, could have come to Shakespeare through the accounts of either Magellan's transit through Patagonia, or Francis Drake's, or both: *Setebos* was a name both voyages recorded as a Patagonian god.[3] Both these voyages also provide, not irrelevantly for *The Tempest*, stories of leaders under pressure responding to threats of treason with decisive action: Magellan and Drake both executed potential traitors at exactly the same spot on the Patagonian coast; Drake dealing with his friend Doughty as Prospero in Milan had failed to deal with his brother Antonio. The executions also have a strong ritual and theatrical element to them, as if the imminence of the deadly passage around the Horn demanded a tightening of order, a spectacle to concentrate the minds of the crew.[4]

The name *Setebos* acts as a trace in Shakespeare's play of an imaginative geography of the world that began to take shape with Magellan's voyage but did not reach its full form until the very end of our period, in the late nineteenth century. For my purposes here, that imaginative geography had two elements that, although logically contradictory, were comfortably combined in colonial discourse. One element was, quite simply, the shape of the world, long *known* as round, but demonstrated by Magellan—in the truly founding gesture of globalization—to be interconnected through navigable seas.[5] The second element was the language in which geographical—and implicitly other kinds of relationships—were mapped onto the new globes that began to inscribe the findings of the circumnavigators: a defiantly planar language of center and periphery that has religious and classical origins but that was firmly secularized during the colonial period.[6] The key term here, as my title indicates, is *uttermost,* a word still frequently used today in connection with Patagonia to suggest its distance from the centers of civilization—wherever they may currently be found.[7]

The formation of this imaginative geography took a second significant step in the late eighteenth century, when the Bass Strait became the equivalent of Magellan's at the other side of the Pacific, both therefore acting as gateways to that new New World, both stretches of dangerous sea that would test the resolve of those desiring to pass through them to the Pacific beyond, and both peopled by the most depraved and savage of the indigenous populations that Europeans would describe—the Tasmanians now joining the Patagonians in that group.[8] In his essay commissioned by the French Institut National as a guide to the philosophers and scientists on Nicolas Baudin's expedition to Tasmania right at the beginning of the nineteenth century, the French scientist Joseph-Marie Degérando wrote this: "The philosophical traveller, sailing to the ends of the earth, is, in fact, travelling in time: he is exploring the past; every step he makes is the passage of an age. Those unknown islands that he reaches are for him the cradle of human society."[9] The idea that savages belonged to an earlier stage of human development had become an Enlightenment commonplace. What Degérando adds is the sense that the physical distance traveled could be correlated with the extent of the return into the human past. Since Patagonia and Tasmania were the "uttermost" parts of the earth, the farthest south that a European could travel before the welcome turn northward to the tropical world of the Pacific itself, their populations inevitably became cast as the "lowest" or "earliest" forms of human life. It was in Patagonia that Darwin, on board the *Beagle* in 1832, saw humanity in what he calls its "lowest and most savage state";[10] and soon afterward Nott and Gliddon's encyclopedic work, *Indigenous Races of the Earth,* introduced the Tasmanians by writing: "we have reached the lowest."[11] These peoples were often said—using words from *The Tempest*—to occupy "the dark backward and abyss of time" (1.2.50).[12]

This fundamental idea has been through many different versions. Most of them are evolutionary in the sense that Patagonians and Tasmanians are seen as "lowest" because they are either the first peoples to develop and therefore the most primitive, or the last to develop and therefore the least developed. (Racial theories are very adaptable.) But there was also a bio-geographical variant on the idea, which can perhaps be glimpsed in George Forster's early comment (on one of Cook's voyages) that the Patagonian Yámana people might be "the miserable out-casts of some neighbouring tribe," since nobody, he thought, would have *chosen* to live in what he saw as the hostile climate of Patagonia.[13] So the discourse for which *uttermost* is a key term has the population of "the uttermost part of the earth" as cast-aways, outcast by their more powerful neighbors.

Similar kinds of suggestions are found, at least implicitly, in the work of Darwin and Wallace, but these elements of biogeographical theory were most clearly expounded in the first twenty years of the twentieth century by writers such as W. D. Matthew, the Canadian paleontologist, William Johnson Sollas, the British geologist and anthropologist, and Griffith Taylor, the Australian geographer. Here, more explicitly, the Tasmanians and Patagonians were seen as coming last in the human race, temporal castaways in the sea of modernity, with that phrase *uttermost parts of the earth* reappearing as a sign of expul-sion, the result of a form of judicial casting away: what happened to Prospero and Sycorax but on a larger scale. In 1911 Sollas wrote that hunter-gatherers like the Patagonian and Tasmanian natives "have one by one been expelled and driven to the uttermost parts of the earth. . . . Justice belongs to the strong, and has been meted out to each race according to its strength; each has received as much justice as it deserved."[14] By 1911, the justice meted out by the strong had just about completed its genocidal course in these uttermost parts of the Earth. The patterns were remarkably similar in the two places. On closer inspection it had turned out that both Tasmania and Patagonia had cli-mates perfectly acceptable to northern Europeans and particularly hospitable to sheep. Sheep needed fences and shepherds. Fences disrupted indigenous hunting, so the natives killed the sheep and the shepherds killed the natives.[15]

The contradictions within that imaginative geography can be spelled out. Classical geography had established the existence of torrid, temperate, and frigid zones (or *klimata*) in the Northern Hemisphere, each usually given about thirty degrees of latitude, and with the inhabited lands *(oekemene)* clustered in the northern temperate zone. The belief in a designed world suggested the symmetrical existence of such zones and lands in the south, even if the lands were uninhabited. European voyages of discovery eventu-ally disproved the existence of any Terra Australis, but the symmetry of the globe was confirmed by the existence of the same three zones on the other side of the equator.[16] However, scientific thought—located ideologically if not physically in Europe—often refused that symmetry: at least one version of racial theory based its true original color in only the *northern* temperate zone.[17] And it was the widespread assumption that the globe had been peopled from north of the equator, from the Caucasus, that allowed the con-firmation of Tasmania and Patagonia as "uttermost," with all the implications of that term, while ignoring that all of Tasmania and most of Patagonia are less far south than Salisbury Plain is north; that both lie firmly within one of the globe's two temperate zones.

Being cast away is an ever-present danger of sea travel. In its simplest form, it just means being lost overboard, as is the castaway of Cowper's poem of that name or Pip in the chapter of *Moby-Dick* also called "The Castaway."[18] Shipwreck often leads to casting away, frequently en masse, as in *The Tempest*—it was not unusual for hundreds of sailors to be cast away together, though they might also be marooned by design, whether their own or someone else's. But the literary and cultural castaway as trope has tended to be isolated and on a deserted island, a figure as useful for various kinds of theorists as it is relatively rare in maritime history.[19]

In 1600, most of the world's islands of any size were actually inhabited, so most castaways encountered native populations. The castaway trope, if it used real toponyms, was likely to feature one of the three uninhabited islands of St. Helena, Mauritius, and Juan Fernández, all staging posts for imperial trade routes and therefore likely places for sailors to jump ship, be left behind by mistake, or be marooned by their captains.[20] For *Robinson Crusoe*, Defoe drew on elements of accounts of actual castaways on these islands, but then placed Crusoe's supposedly deserted island in the middle of one of the most densely populated parts of indigenous America, close to Trinidad and in the mouth of the Orinoco. Arguably the great cross-cultural narratives of *real* colonial encounter have been written by castaways who have had to come to terms, terms not of their own making, with the indigenous societies in which they have lived—Cabeza de Vaca on the Gulf Coast, John Byron in Patagonia.[21] The trope of the castaway either denies this encounter altogether or, as in *Robinson Crusoe*, recasts it as a traditional master-slave relationship, with Friday quickly becoming the good and helpful servant. Both Byron and Cabeza de Vaca suggested that degradation as a slave was part of the experience of European survival in castaway circumstances, so *Robinson Crusoe* exactly reverses the interpersonal dynamics of castaway and native.

One theory much enamored of the figure of the castaway was classical economics, for much the same reason as philosophical allegorists liked it: it seemed to offer the basic building blocks—a human being, an environment—without any of the complications that muddy the waters in actual historical contexts. The model would seem to come from chemistry: reduce to the elemental, place in an experimental situation, and watch developments. Marx was scathing about this procedure, pointing out that, despite the political economists' use of Robinson Crusoe stories, the basic state of humankind is actually social; but his remarks did not stop Robinson Crusoe subsequently becoming even more of a favorite example to neoclassical economics, so demonstrating that theory's deep, even pathological, commitment to an economic model divorced from historical real-ity.[22] As Marx implied, that commitment is ideoloical in the sense that it tells us about those theories' ideas of how markets should operate, rather than anything about how they actually do or ever have operated.[23]

If the ideological—and in this context deeply unrealistic—figure of Robinson Crusoe is central to capitalism's self-image: solitary, quietly heroic, re-creating civilization from scratch, the whole man recast from the broken mold that is modernity, his voluntary labor force committed to his wealth and well-being, then arguably we can look in the camera obscura of Marx's writings to see, standing on their feet, the real castaways of primi-tive accumulation: those cast out of their parishes by the rural enclosures (famously seen by Thomas More as a case of sheep eating people[24]), ending up as the "masterless men" of Shakespeare's day, and later that urban rag-gle-taggle of the Parisian streets that Marx came close to celebrating in "The Eighteenth Brumaire."[25] But the problem in this context with such a picture is that the narrowness of its frame of reference risks collapsing Defoe's genuinely Atlantic vision back into a story of internal European development. If the castaway trope is as "global" in its geography as *Robin-son Crusoe* suggests, then the "reality" behind it needs to match that scale. Marx's camera obscura needs to become a cosmorama.

Baudelaire's great poem, "Le Cygne" [The Swan], was published in 1857, not long after Marx's "Eighteenth Brumaire," and it reads like an elegy to the dispossessed, written out of an intimate knowledge of the life of that Parisian lumpenproletariat described by Marx. Baudelaire's analysis may have been shorter than Marx's, but his range was in some ways even wider.[26] As this essay's epigraph recalls, Baudelaire's poem remembered the sailors aban-doned on an island, more early victims of maritime capitalism; but his ar-chetypal castaway, based in part on a kitchen maid Baudelaire had known during his stay on the island of Mauritius, and in part on his mistress and muse, Jeanne Duval, is a thin and tubercular Negress searching with haggard eye in the Parisian fog for a glimpse of the palm trees she remembers from her island off the African coast—a wonderful reversal of the usual castaway trope and a rare moment of French anti-exoticism:

> Je pense à la négresse, amaigrie et phtisique,
> Piétinant dans la boue, et cherchant, l'oeil hagard,
> Les cocotiers absents de la superbe Afrique
> Derrière la muraille immense du brouillard . . .

> [I think of a Negress, thin and tubercular,
> Treading in the mire, searching with haggard eye
> For palm trees she recalls from splendid Africa,
> Somewhere behind a giant barrier of fog.][27]

Baudelaire's African in Paris brings another dimension to the castaway figure, which arguably has even more resonance at the beginning of the twenty-first century than it did in 1857, and which I will follow into the final part of the essay, but only after a still more global set of images is evoked to match the breadth of the colonial imaginary.

Although the trope of the castaway is usually limited to individuals or small groups, and almost exclusively European or North American, the colonial period saw many indigenous groups quite literally cast away, the most dramatic case possibly being the Black Caribs from St. Vincent, who in 1797 were rounded up, dumped on a small offshore island without a water supply, and those that survived then taken many hundreds of miles to the island of Roatan, off the Central American coast, where they were cast away and left to their own devices; Roatan having been chosen solely in an attempt to embarrass Spain, with whom Britain was then at war.[28] In a larger sense, the whole reservation system in North America could be seen as operating on the principle of creating enclosed islands within the larger sea of national sovereignty and casting away Indian groups onto those islands. In other cases, indigenous groups have survived only by casting themselves away, creating islands for themselves, usually on land that no one else wanted, at least at the time.

The great period of popularity of the fictional castaway stories—*Swiss Family Robinson, The Coral Island, Masterman Ready*, and many others—is marked toward beginning and end by the two genocides in Tasmania and Patagonia.[29] In both cases, the remnant indigenous populations themselves ended up cast away on an island—Flinders, off Tasmania, Dawson's in Tierra del Fuego—where they were herded into missions for their own supposed good, spreading physical disease and incubating psychological malaise. In both cases, the displaced natives could actually see their former lands from the islands on which they were imprisoned. Nostalgia, in what we might now consider its original sense of homesickness, permeates nineteenth-century colonial language, and Tasmania and Patagonia are both still full of lovingly re-created British architecture and gardens. But the term has a harder, medical edge in this period. The doctor treating the Tasmanians on Flinders Island is quoted as saying: "They pine away, not from any positive disease, but from a disease they call 'home sickness.'"[30] Around the turn of the century, Lucas Bridges visited Dawson Island where captured Selk'nam Indians were working in a sawmill, effectively prisoners. Bridges talked to a man he knew: "He seemed to have nothing whatever to complain of with regard to his treatment," writes Bridges, "but was terribly sad at his captivity. Looking with yearning towards the distant mountains of his native land, he said: 'Shouwe t-maten ya.' ('Longing is killing me.')"[31] He died shortly afterward. Bruce Chatwin, an astute reader of Thomas Bridges's famous Patagonian dictionary, concludes that the layers of metaphorical associations that made up what he calls their "mental soil" shackled the Indians to their homeland "with ties that could not be broken." When they were broken, by force, the Indians died.[32] This was nostalgia. These were castaways, removed from their lands so that Europeans could metaphorically lose themselves there.

All ideological work leaves discursive traces. Our language is full of them, even if the *Oxford English Dictionary* did its best to ignore or deny them. Crusoe's shipwreck maroons him on his island. *Maroon* may originally have been a Native Caribbean word meaning "wild" or "savage," adopted by the Spanish as *cimarrón,* used to describe Indians and animals, and later Africans, who had escaped confinement.[33] Borrowed by the French to describe a buccaneering practice, it ends upside down as an English term for confinement—precisely the opposite of its indigenous meaning. But then turning freedom into confinement was a process essential to imperial ends.

Globalization may in some sense be a singular process that can reasonably be dated to 1522 when the remnants of Magellan's expedition limped back into European waters, but its internal circuitry is always in flux. The planar dimension of the colonial imaginary that had *uttermost* as a key term was triangular: an apex—the scientific center of Europe—and two base points, Patagonia and Tasmania, with their associated straits. Metaphorically and often literally, that apex was itself a further set of straits, the Straits of Gibraltar, through which the great voyage of Columbus sailed to inaugurate the modern era and where Gonzalo wishes the story of *The Tempest* to be written with gold (5.1.205–8). Dante's Ulysses had, at least for later commentators, symbolized his rejection of ancient learning by sailing out through those straits into the Atlantic; and in 1620, shortly after *The Tempest* was written, and on the centenary of Magellan's departure, when Francis Bacon wanted to symbolize the establishment of a new science that had broken with its classical precedents, he used the image of a ship sailing through the Pillars of Hercules, leaving the Old World for a new world of knowledge.[34] In the colonial period, the circuits led outward, bringing back knowledge and trade and treasure from elsewhere. Outward, too, in the same year as Columbus passed through those straits, there began the flow of people, the expulsions of Muslims and Jews from Spain that helped establish the white and Christian Europe that would be the ultimate beneficiary of such global trade.

In 1973, a disturbing and would-be prophetic novel by the French writer Jean Raspail was published, called *The Camp of the Saints,* which reverses this circuitry, describing a passage *in.*[35] A pilgrimage of a million starving Indians storm on board ships in Calcutta harbor and sail around Africa, through the Straits of Gibraltar, and into the Mediterranean. French army units, ordered to fire on the invading masses, desert in droves, and the novel ends with the establishment of a new world order dominated by the forces of the previously dispossessed. In the preface to the novel's second edition,

Raspail explains that it was only "prudence" that had led him to displace the threat to Europe onto faraway India, from where it *actually* lies—on the shores of the Mediterranean, ready to follow what he calls the "mighty vanguard already here . . . in the bosom of a people that once was French."[36]

Raspail's novel is a fascist cry of despair at the white race's supposed failure of will, or of "soul" as he calls it. Its four English editions in the last fifteen years have been embraced by white supremacist organizations as a warning to the white race that it must be prepared to defend itself against the threatening tide of the dispossessed who will soon attempt to overthrow its long and deserved hegemony, unless that race rediscovers what Raspail unblinkingly calls "the inflexible courage to be rich."[37]

During the age of the sea, almost all actual castaways were involuntary victims of accident or malice and tried their utmost to return home. However, there has always been an undercurrent of voluntary castaways escaping the restrictions of home for the imagined freedoms of some South Sea island, or even involuntary castaways discovering to their surprise that they rather enjoy being cast away. Much, of course, has always depended on the nature of the life you're being cast away *from*. Crusoe, the fictional archetype, embodies the ambiguity: he wants to be "rescued," but is never happy at home. In the twenty-first century, the castaway trope is almost completely voluntary, whether it involves the luxury of one of the thousands of tropical hotels now called Castaways or the increasing numbers of people volunteering to be part of some televised piece of social engineering. The image of island fruitfulness has now been so comprehensively hijacked by international tourism that the "hard" alternative of an island that supposedly poses serious questions about survival has reemerged.[38]

Elsewhere, however, the sea still has its victims, and late capitalism still produces its castaways. To an extent rarely equaled since Shakespeare invented the phrase, those in search of a sea change to their lives are setting themselves on dangerous courses across water—Cubans and Haitians toward Florida, Southeast Asians toward Australia, Africans and other Asians toward Europe. Through one of the deepest ironies of modernity, these castaways often evade capture precisely because their technology is so outdated—they travel on vessels too small and unsophisticated to be spotted by their pursuers. But of course, consequently, many of the boats fail to reach their destination.

So in recent years the narrative premise of Raspail's novel has increasingly begun to look prophetic. In February 1993, a small rusting freighter called the *Golden Venture* carried refugees from China to Kenya and then Kenya to Rockaway, in the Queens district of New York City, where the boat ran aground, drowning several of the refugees. Then, early in 2001, even more pointedly, the *East Sea*, a freighter flying a Cambodian flag, was beached by its crew near Nice with a cargo of nearly one thousand Iraqi and Turkish Kurds packed into the hold in conditions very close to those described by Raspail for his Indian ship. Needless to say, these castaways did not take over the government of the world.

The Straits of Gibraltar are not in this sense the border between Morocco and Spain, or even Africa and Europe: they are the frontier between the First World and the Third, the Camp of the Saints and the tents of the wretched. Ceuta and Melilla, the two remaining outposts of Europe on North African soil, and perceived as susceptible entry points, have now been completely surrounded by armed fences and surveillance cameras, turning them into small fortresses, mimicking the larger European fortress, and forcing would-be entrants to brave a crossing of the straits. In the last few years, several *thousand* people have drowned trying to cross the Straits of Gibraltar in the rough-hewn wooden boats the Spanish call *pateras*, the modern equivalent of the *navis unus pellius*, the "boat of one skin."[39]

The beach resonates within the Western imagination as a symbol of paradise, and it has been made to resonate for postcolonial studies as a symbol of cultural encounter.[40] But nothing prepares one for the indifference to death that its pleasures now induce (figure 10.1).

> Those are pearls that were his eyes;
> Nothing of him that doth fade,
> But doth suffer a sea-change . . .
> Sea-nymphs hourly ring his knell.

Fig. 10.1 The beach at Zahara de los Atunes, Spain.

Notes

1. All *Tempest* quotations taken from William Shakespeare, *The Tempest*, ed. Stephen Orgel (Oxford: World's Classics, 1994).

2. J. R. Reinhard, "Setting Adrift in Medieval Law and Literature," *Publication of the Modern Language Association* 56 (1941), 33–68: 35. Prospero thinks that Alonso did not dare kill him and Miranda, "so dear the love my people bore me" (1.2.141). Compare "In addition to his shaping description of Miranda's passionate response, Prospero provides an explanatory historical gloss for the *pictura*. The ungovernable ship just lost is revealed to be a reparative echo of the long lost 'rotten carcase of a butt, not rigged, / Nor tackle, sail, nor mast' (I.ii.46–7) in which Prospero and Miranda were set adrift by the treachery of his usurping brother. Explaining the spectacle to Miranda, Prospero aims to explain her to herself. The butt is another version of the *topos* of the ship of state, one known to scholars as the rudderless boat: it appears as a juridical trial or punishment described in legal codes, chronicles, and saint's lives, and as a central, organizing image in the romance adventures of Chaucer's and Gower's Constance and her sources and analogues so beloved by English readers from the thirteenth century to Shakespeare's time. The scene that we, with Miranda, are instructed to imagine (it is not staged), casts Prospero in a role held by saints, exiled criminals, and innocent virgins. We must consider which best diagnoses him." Elizabeth Fowler, "The Ship Adrift," Peter Hulme and William H. Sherman (eds.), *"The Tempest" and Its Travels* (London: Reaktion, 2000), 37–40: 39; and V. A. Kolve, "The Man of Law's Tale: The Rudderless Ship and the Sea," *Chaucer and the Imagery of Narrative: The First Five Canterbury Tales* (London: Edward Arnold, 1984), 297–358.

3. *The Tempest* is often supposed to draw on the shipwreck of the *Sea-Venture* on the Bermudas, where the new governor of Virginia was cast away with the entire crew of the ship—the castaway incident with which Peter Linebaugh and Marcus Rediker begin their book *The Many-Headed Hydra: The Hidden History of the Revolutionary Atlantic* (London: Verso, 2000), which provides the larger canvas for the castaway scenes sketched here.

   Shakespeare's knowledge of Pigafetta's account probably came via the translation in Richard Eden's *The History of Trauayle in the West and East Indies* (London: Richarde Iugge, 1577). See Antonio Pigafetta, *The First Voyage around the World (1519–1522): An Account of Magellan's Expedition*, ed. Thedore J. Cachey Jr. (New York: Marsilio Publishers, 1995).

4. After Doughty had been condemned to die, "our generall proposed vnto him this choice: *Whether he would take, to be executed in this Iland? or to be sett a land on the maine? or returne into England, there to answer his deed before the Lords of her maiesties Councell?*" [Francis Fletcher], *The World Encompassed By Sir Francis Drake* [1628], facs. ed. (Amsterdam: Theatrum Orbis Terrarum, 1969), 31. Assured as he was of an eternal inheritance in a better life, "*he feared, if he should be set a land among Infidels, how he should be able to maintaine this assurance, feeling in his owne frailtie, how mighty the contagion is of lewd custome.*" Opting to lose his head, "he left vnto our fleete, a lamentable example of a goodly gentleman, who in seeking aduancement vnfit for him, cast away himselfe" (33). Fletcher's wording is interesting, given that Doughty chose death precisely in order *not* to be cast away, a fate he clearly saw as worse than death.

5. "Modernity arose out of the world ocean, first made appropriately spatial in Magellan's westward journey across the Pacific." Christopher L. Connery, "The Oceanic Feeling and the Regional Imaginary," Rob Wilson and Wimal Dissanayake (eds.), *Global / Local: Cultural Production and the Transnational Imaginary* (Durham, NC: Duke University Press, 1996), 204–31: 209. And compare Jerry Brotton, *Trading Territories: Mapping the Early Modern World* (London: Reaktion, 1997).

6. And that survives today: how often is somewhere described as "remote" with no felt need to explain the point from which it may be remote, and no sense that that point is as "remote" from the somewhere as vice versa?

7. Colin McEwan, Luis A. Borrero, and Alfredo Prieto (eds.), *Patagonia: Natural History, Prehistory and Ethnography at the Uttermost End of the Earth* (London: British Museum Press, 1997). Milton's lines convey the paradox: "To the uttermost convex / Of this great round" (*Paradise Lost*, 7.266); as if a "round" could have an outermost point.

8. See Clive Gamble, "Archaeology, History and the Uttermost Ends of the Earth—Tasmania, Tierra del Fuego and the Cape," *Antiquity* 66 (1992), 712–20: 714.

9.   Joseph-Marie Degérando, *The Observation of Savage Peoples*, trans. F. T. C. Moore (Berkeley: University of California Press, 1969), 63; the French original is reprinted in Jean Copans and Jean Jamin, *Aux origines de l'anthropologie française: les mémoires de la Société des Observateurs de l'Homme en l'an VIII* [1799–1805] (Paris: Le Sycomore, 1978), 127–70. Compare Miranda J. Hughes, "Philosophical Travellers at the Ends of the Earth: Baudin, Péron and the Tasmanians," R. W. Home (ed.), *Australian Science in the Making* (Cambridge: Cambridge University Press, 1988), 23–44; and Rhys Jones, "Philosophical Time Travellers," *Antiquity* 66 (1992), 744–57.

10. Charles Darwin, *Journal of Researches into the Natural History and Geology of the Countries Visited during the Voyage round the World of H.M.S. "Beagle"* . . . [1845] (London: John Murray, 1905), 483. It was to Patagonia that the missionary on the *Beagle* was headed to fulfill the biblical command to bear Christian witness "unto the uttermost part of the earth," a task later undertaken by Thomas Bridges, whose son, Lucas, called his extraordinary family history *Uttermost Part of the Earth* (London: Hodder & Stoughton, 1951).

11. Josiah C. Nott and George R. Gliddon, *Indigenous Races of the Earth; or, New Chapters of Ethnological Enquiry* (Philadelphia: J. B. Lippincott, 1857), 637.

12. See Francis Spufford, *I May Be Some Time: Ice and the English Imagination* (London: Faber and Faber, 1996), 213.

13. George Forster, *A Voyage Round the World* (London: R. White, 1777), vol. 2, 505; quoted in Ernesto Piana et al., "Chronicles of 'Ona-Ashaga': Archaeology in the Beagle Channel (Tierra del Fuego–Argentina)," *Antiquity* 66 (1992), 771–83: 773.

14. W. J. Sollas, *Ancient Hunters and Their Modern Representatives* (London: Macmillan, 1911), 382–3. Compare Gamble, "Archaeology, History and the Uttermost Ends of the Earth"; Peter J. Bowler, "From 'Savage' to 'Primitive': Victorian Evolutionism and the Interpretation of Marginalized Peoples," *Antiquity* 66 (1992), 721–9; Nancy J. Christie, "Environment and Race: Geography's Search for a Darwinian Synthesis," Roy MacLeod and Philip E. Rehbock (eds.), *Darwin's Laboratory: Evolutionary Theory and Natural History in the Pacific* (Honolulu: University of Hawaii Press, 1994), 426–73; Henrika Kuklik, "Islands in the Pacific: Darwinian Biogeography and British Anthropology," *American Ethnologist* 21, no. 3 (1996), 611–38; Tim Murray, "Tasmania and the Constitution of 'the Dawn of Humanity,'" *Antiquity* 66 (1992), 730–43; and on the general intellectual background, Greta Jones, *Social Darwinism and English Thought: The Interaction between Biological and Social Theory* (Brighton: Harvester Press, 1980); Peter J. Bowler, *Theories of Human Evolution: A Century of Debate, 1844–1944* (Oxford: Basil Blackwell, 1987); Gillian Beer, *Open Fields: Science in Cultural Encounter* (Oxford: Clarendon Press, 1996); Clive Gamble, *Timewalkers: The Prehistory of Global Colonization* (Cambridge, MA: Harvard University Press, 1994); Adam Kuper, *The Invention of Primitive Society: Transformations of an Illusion* (London: Routledge, 1988); Fiona J. Stafford, *The Last of the Race: The Growth of a Myth from Milton to Darwin* (Oxford: Clarendon Press, 1994); and Milford Wolpoff and Rachel Caspari, *Race and Human Evolution: A Fatal Attraction* (Boulder, CO: Westview Press, 1997).

15. On the genocide of the indigenous Tasmanians and Patagonians, see Brian Plomley, *Friendly Mission: The Tasmanian Journals and Papers of George Augustus Robinson 1829–1834* (Hobart: Tasmanian Historical Research Association, 1966); and *Weep in Silence: A History of the Flinders Island Aboriginal Settlement* (Hobart: Blubber Head Press, 1987); Lyndall Ryan, *The Aboriginal Tasmanians* [1981] (St. Leonards, New South Wales: Allen & Unwin, 1996); Mateo Martinic Beros, "Panorama de la colonización en Tierra del Fuego entre 1881 y 1900," *Anales del Instituto de la Patagonia* 4, nos. 1–3 (1973), 5–69; "El genocidio Selk'nam: nuevos antecedentes," *Anales del Instituto de la Patagonia* 19 (1989–90), 23–8; and Anne Chapman, *El Fin de un Mundo: Los Selk'nam de Tierra del Fuego* (Buenos Aires: Vazquez Mazzini, 1989). For general background, see Mark Cocker, *Rivers of Blood, Rivers of Gold: Europe's Conflict with Tribal Peoples* (London: Jonathan Cape, 1998).

16. See David N. Livingstone, "The Moral Discourse of Climate: Historical Considerations on Race, Place and Virtue," *Journal of Historical Geography* 17, no. 4 (1991), 423–34; and, more generally, Clarence J. Glacken, *Traces on the Rhodian Shore: Nature and Culture in Western Thought from Ancient Times to the End of the Eighteenth Century* (Berkeley: University of California Press, 1976); and Denis Cosgrove, *Apollo's Eye: A Cartographic Genealogy of the Earth in the Western Imagination* (Baltimore: Johns Hopkins University Press, 2001).

17. Comte de Buffon, *Histoire naturelle, génerale et particulière*, 44 vols. (Paris: Imprimerie Royale, puis Plassan, 1744–1804), vol. 3, 528; quoted in Glacken, *Traces on the Rhodian Shore*, 591.

18. William Cowper, "The Castaway" [1799], *The Poetical Works of William Cowper*, ed. H. S. Milford (London: Oxford University Press, 1934), 431–2; and Herman Melville, *Moby-Dick; or, The Whale* [1851], ed. Harold Beaver (Harmondsworth: Penguin, 1986).
19. See Edward E. Leslie, *Desperate Journeys, Abandoned Souls: True Stories of Castaways and Other Survivors* (Boston: Mariner Books, 1988). Of general relevance here is Hans Blumenberg, *Shipwreck with Spectator: Paradigm of a Metaphor for Existence* [1979], trans. Steven Rendall (Cambridge, MA: MIT Press, 1997).
20. See Richard H. Grove, *Green Imperialism: Colonial Expansion, Tropical Island Edens and the Origins of Environmentalism, 1600–1860* (Cambridge: Cambridge University Press, 1996), 42–7, on St. Helena, Mauritius, and related aspects of island discourse.
21. See Rolena Adorno and Patrick Charles Pautz (eds.), *Álvar Núñez Cabeza de Vaca: His Account, His Life and the Expedition of Pánfilo de Narváez*, 3 vols. (Lincoln: University of Nebraska Press, 1999); and John Byron, *The Narrative of the Honourable John Byron . . .* (London: S. Baker et al., 1768).
22. See Karl Marx, *Capital: A Critique of Political Economy, Vol. 1*, trans. Ben Fowkes (Harmondsworth: Penguin, 1976), 169; Ian Watt, "*Robinson Crusoe* as a Myth," *Essays in Criticism* 1, no. 2 (1951), 96–119; Michael White, "The Production of an Economic *Robinson Crusoe*," *Southern Review* 16, no. 2 (1982), 115–42; and compare Gillian Hewitson, "Deconstructing Robinson Crusoe: A Feminist Interrogation of 'Rational Economic Man,'" *Australian Feminist Studies* 20 (1994), 131–49: 147n1. Adam Smith imaginatively re-created the development of human society through its four principal modes of subsistence by imagining a dozen people settling an uninhabited island. See Ronald L. Meek, *Social Science and the Ignoble Savage* (Cambridge: Cambridge University Press, 1976), 117.
23. "[T]he instrumentally rational, self-interested and radically separate individual who, it is alleged, can be found throughout history and across cultures, alone on an island, or in a society which is conceptualised as the sum of 'isolated' individuals." Hewitson, "Deconstructing Robinson Crusoe," 134. In one version, the singular drawback of Crusoe's isolation when it comes to modeling trade is overcome by having him make contracts with himself. Hal Varian, *Intermediate Microeconomics* (New York: W. W. Norton, 2nd ed., 1990), chapter 28, quoted in Hewitson, "Deconstructing Robinson Crusoe," 143. This is a model that might be said to have an attenuated notion of the social world.
24. See Thomas More, *Utopia* [1516], trans. Paul Turner (Harmondsworth: Penguin, 1965).
25. See Richard Halpern, *The Poetics of Primitive Accumulation: English Renaissance Culture and the Genealogy of Capital* (Ithaca, NY: Cornell University Press, 1991); and A. L. Beier, *Masterless Men: The Vagrancy Problem in England, 1560–1640* (London: Methuen, 1985). Juan Luis Vives used the phrase *cast out* to refer to the poor of the period. *On Assistance to the Poor*, trans. Sister Alice Tobriner, *A Sixteenth-Century Urban Report* (Chicago: University of Chicago Press, 1971), vol. 2, 36, quoted in Halpern, *The Poetics of Primitive Accumulation*, 74. Karl Marx, "The Eighteenth Brumaire of Louis Bonaparte," *Surveys from Exile*, ed. David Fernbach (Harmondsworth: Penguin, 1973), 143–249: 197.
26. Baudelaire was himself a kind of castaway in that he jumped ship at L'Ile de Bourbon on what was supposed to be a voyage to India. "Le Cygne" recasts "A une Malabaraise" (written 1841 after this trip). Compare Françoise Lionnet, "Reframing Baudelaire: Literary History, Biography, Postcolonial Theory, and Vernacular Languages," *Diacritics* 28, no. 3 (1998), 63–85.
27. Quoted from Charles Baudelaire, *The Flowers of Evil*, trans. James McGowan (Oxford: Oxford University Press, 1993), 176–7.
28. See Nancie L. Gonzalez, *Sojourners of the Caribbean: Ethnogenesis and Ethnohistory of the Garifuna* (Urbana: University of Illinois Press, 1988).
29. Desert island stories were particularly popular between 1788 and 1910, the high period of the second British Empire: Kevin Carpenter lists five hundred for England alone. Quoted in Louis James, "Unwrapping Crusoe: Retrospective and Prospective Views," Lieve Spaas and Brian Stimpson (eds.), *Robinson Crusoe: Myths and Metamorphoses* (Basingstoke: Macmillan, 1996), 1–9: 2.
30. James Bonwick, *The Last of the Tasmanians; or, The Black War of Van Diemen's Land* (London: Sampson Low, Son, & Marston, 1870), 390, who makes the connection with Ranz des Vaches and the Swiss.
31. Bridges, *Uttermost Part of the Earth*, 267.

32. Bruce Chatwin, *In Patagonia* (London: Picador, 1979), 130, reading Thomas Bridges, *Yá-mana-English: A Dictionary of the Speech of Tierra del Fuego*, ed. Ferdinand Hestermann and Martin Gusinde [1933] (Buenos Aires: Zagier y Urruty, 1987). As Chatwin wrote in a letter to his wife: "the colonisers did a very thorough job, and this gives the whole land its haunted quality." Nicholas Shakespeare, *Bruce Chatwin* (London: Harvill Press, 1999), 297; and compare Manfred Pfister, "Bruce Chatwin and the Postmodernization of the Travelogue," *Literature, Interpretation, Theory* 7, nos. 3–4 (1996), 253–67: 254. On the haunted landscape of Tasmania, see Henry Reynolds, *Fate of a Free People* (Ringwood, Victoria: Penguin, 1995), 1.

33. See José Juan Arrom, "Cimarrón: Apuntes sobre sus primeras documentaciones y su probable origen," José Juan Arrom and Manuel A. García Arévalo, *Cimarrón* (Santo Domingo: Fundación García-Arévalo, 1986), 13–30.

34. "I put out on the deep and open sea / With one boat only, and the company / Small as it was, which had not deserted me." Dante Alighieri, *The Divine Comedy*, trans. C. H. Sissons (Manchester: Manchester University Press, 1980), 113; and Francis Bacon, *Instauratio Magna* (London: Joannem Billium, 1620), frontispiece.

35. "The camp of the saints" is a biblical reference, from the Book of Revelation (20:9), in which Satan is released from his one-thousand-year imprisonment and unleashes the forces of Gog and Magog, which "compassed the camp of the saints about," until the fire from heaven came down to devour them.

36. Jean Raspail, *The Camp of the Saints* [1973], trans. Norman Shapiro (Petoskey, MI: Social Contract Press, 1995), xv. Raspail also wrote about the indigenous Fuegians: *Who Will Remember the People?* [1986], trans. Jeremy Leggatt (San Francisco: Mercury House, 1988), and the indigenous Caribs: *Bleu caraïbe et citrons verts: mes derniers voyages aux Antilles* (Paris: Éditions Robert Laffont, 1980). Compare Peter Hulme, *Remnants of Conquest: The Island Caribs and Their Visitors, 1877–1998* (Oxford: Oxford University Press, 2000), 277–83.

37. Raspail, *The Camp of the Saints*, xvi. For a balanced assessment, see Connolly and Kennedy, http://www.theatlantic.com/atlantic/election/connection/immigrat/kennf.htm (August 10, 2001).

38. See the various *Survivor* TV programs.

39. Jeremy Harding, *The Uninvited: Refugees at the Rich Man's Gate* (London: Profile Books and London Review of Books, 2000), 103. Compare Sarah Collinson, *Shore to Shore: The Politics of Migration in Euro-Maghreb Relations* (London: Royal Institute of International Affairs, 1996); and Phil Marfleet, "Europe's Civilising Mission," Phil Cohen (ed.), *New Ethnicities, Old Racisms?* (London: Zed Books, 1999), 18–36.

40. See Lena Lenček and Gideon Bosker, *The Beach: The History of Paradise on Earth* (London: Secker and Warburg, 1998); and Greg Dening, *Islands and Beaches: Discourse on a Silent Land: Marquesas 1774–1880* (Honolulu: University Press of Hawaii, 1980).

Select Bibliography

Albion, Robert Greenhalgh. *Five Centuries of Famous Ships: From the Santa Maria to the Glomar Explorer* (New York et al.: McGraw-Hill, 1978).

Andrews, Kenneth R. *The Elizabethan Seaman* (London: National Maritime Museum, 1982).

Armitage, David. "The Empire of the Seas," *The Ideological Origins of the British Empire* (Cambridge: Cambridge University Press, 2000), 100–24.

Astro, Richard (ed.). *Literature and the Sea* (Corvallis: Oregon State University Press, 1976).

Auden, W. H. *The Enchafèd Flood, or The Romantic Iconography of the Sea* (London: Faber and Faber, 1951).

Babcock, F. Lawrence. *Spanning the Atlantic* (New York: Knopf, 1931).

Bachelard, Gaston. *Water and Dreams: An Essay on the Imagination of Matter* [French original 1942], trans. Edith Farrell (Dallas: The Dallas Institute of Humanities and Culture Publications, 1983).

Barnes, Robert. *Sea Hunters of Indonesia: Fishers and Weavers of Lamalera* (New York: Oxford University Press, 1996).

Bass, George F. (ed.). *History of Seafaring* (London: Thames and Hudson, 1972).

Behrman, Cynthia Fansler. *Victorian Myths of the Sea* (Athens: Ohio University Press, 1977).

Beil, Steve. *Down with the Old Canoe: A Cultural History of the Titanic Disaster* (New York: W. W. Norton, 1996).

Bender, Bert. *Sea-Brothers: The Tradition of American Sea Fiction from Moby Dick to the Present* (Philadelphia: University of Pennsylvania Press, 1988).

Blumenberg, Hans. *Shipwreck with Spectator: Paradigm of a Metaphor for Existence* [German original 1979], trans. Steven Rendall (Cambridge, MA, and London: MIT Press, 1996).

Bolster, Jeffrey. *Black Jacks: African American Seamen in the Age of Sail* (Cambridge, MA: Harvard University Press, 1997).

Bowen, Frank C. *A Century of Atlantic Travel, 1830–1930* (London: Sampson Low, Marston and Co., 1932[?]).

Boxer, C. R. *The Dutch Seaborne Empire* (New York: Penguin, 1990).

Braudel, Fernand. *The Mediterranean and the Mediterranean World in the Age of Philipp II*, trans. Siân Reynolds, 2 vols. (London: Fontana, 1975).

Brooks, George. *The Kru Mariner* (Newark: University of Delaware Press, 1972).

Brown, E. D. *The International Law of the Sea*, 2 vols. (Aldershot, Hants, and Brookfield, VT: Dartmouth, 1994).

Burg, B. R. *Sodomy and the Pirate Tradition* (New York: New York University Press, 1995).

Burton, Valerie. "Counting Seafarers: The Published Records of the Registrar of Merchant Seamen, 1849–1913," *Mariner's Mirror* 71 (1985), 305–20.

———. "The Making of a Nineteenth-Century Profession: Shipmasters and the British Shipping Industry," *Journal of the Canadian Historical Association* 1 (1990), 97–118.

———. "Household and Labour Market Interactions in the Late Nineteenth Century British Shipping Industry: Breadwinning and Seafaring Families," T. W. Guiannane and P. Johnson (eds.). *The Microeconomic Analysis of the Household and the Labour Market, 1880–1939* (Seville: Universidad de Sevilla, 1998), 99–109.

———. " 'Whoring, Drinking Sailors': Reflections on Masculinity from the Labour History of Nineteenth-Century British Shipping," Margaret Walsh (ed.), *Working Out Gender* (Aldershot et al.: Ashgate, 1999), 84–101.

Carlson, Patricia Ann (ed.). *Literature and Lore of the Sea* (Amsterdam: Rodopi, 1986).

Carretta, Vincent. "Olaudah Equiano or Gustavus Vassa? New Light on an Eighteenth-Century Question of Identity," *Slavery and Abolition* 20, no. 3 (1999), 96–105.

Carson, Rachel. *The Sea around Us* [1951] (New York: Mentor, 1989).

Chaudhuri, K. N. *Trade and Civilisation in the Indian Ocean* (New York: Cambridge University Press, 1985).

Chappell, David. *Double Ghosts: Oceanian Voyagers on Euroamerican Ships* (Armonk, NY: M. E. Sharpe, 1997).

Cockcroft, Robert. *The Voyages of Life: Ship Imagery in Art, Literature and Life* (Nottingham: Nottingham University Art Gallery, 1982).

Cohen, Daniel A. (ed.). *The Female Marine and Related Works: Narratives of Cross-Dressing and Urban Vice in America's Early Republic* (Amherst: University of Massachusetts Press, 1997).

Cohn, Michael, and Michael Platzer. *Black Men of the Sea* (New York: Dodd, Mead, 1978).

Collinson, Sarah. *Shore to Shore: The Politics of Migration in Euro-Maghreb Relations* (London: Royal Institute of International Affairs, 1996).

Connery, Christopher L. "The Oceanic Feeling and the Regional Imaginary," Rob Wilson and Wimal Dissanayake (eds.), *Global/Local: Cultural Production and the Transnational Imaginary* (Durham: Duke University Press, 1996), 284–311.

Coote, John (ed.), *The Faber Book of the Sea* (London: Faber, 1989).

——— (ed.). *The Faber Book of Tales of the Sea* (London: Faber, 1991).

Corbin, Alain. *The Lure of the Sea: The Discovery of the Seaside in the Western World, 1750–1840* [French original 1988], trans. Jocelyn Phelps (Cambridge: Polity Press, 1994).

Corris, Peter. *Port, Passage and Plantation* (Melbourne: University of Melbourne Press, 1973).

Cosgrove, Denis. *Apollo's Eye: A Cartographic Genealogy of the Earth in the Western Imagination* (Baltimore: Johns Hopkins University Press, 2001).

Creighton, Margaret, and Lisa Norling (eds.). *Iron Men, Wooden Women: Gender and Seafaring in the Atlantic World, 1700–1920* (Baltimore: Johns Hopkins University Press, 1996).

Deng, Gang. *Chinese Maritime Activities and Socioeconomic Development, c. 2100 B.C.–1900 A.D.* (Westport, CT: Greenwood, 1997).

Dening, Greg. *Islands and Beaches: Discourse on a Silent Land: Marquesas 1774–1880* (Chicago: Dorsey Press, 1980).

———. *Mr Bligh's Bad Language: Passion, Power and Theatre on the Bounty* (Cambridge: Cambridge University Press, 1992).

———. *The Death of William Gooch: History's Anthropology* (Honolulu: University of Hawaii Press, 1995).

Diedrich, Maria, et al. (eds.). *Black Imagination and the Middle Passage* (Oxford: Oxford University Press, 1999).

Dover, Robert. *A Handbook to Marine Insurance*, 8th rev. ed. (London: Whiterby, 1987).

Edmond, Rod. *Representing the South Pacific: Colonial Discourse from Cook to Gauguin* (Cambridge: Cambridge University Press, 1997).

Edwards, Philip. *The Story of the Voyage: Sea-Narratives in 18th Century England* (Cambridge: Cambridge University Press, 1994).

———. *Sea-Marks: The Metaphorical Voyage, Spenser to Milton* (Liverpool: Liverpool University Press, 1997).

Elias, Norbert. "Studies on the Genesis of the Naval Profession," *British Journal of Sociology* 1 (1950).

Falconer, Alexander Frederick. *Shakespeare and the Sea* (London: Constable, 1964).

Finney, Ben R. *Hokule 'a: The Way to Tahiti* (New York: Dodd, Mead, 1979).

———. *Voyage of Rediscovery: A Cultural Odyssey through Polynesia* (Berkeley: University of California Press, 1994).

Foster, John Wilson. *The Titanic Complex* (Vancouver: Belcouver Press, 1997).

———— (ed.). *Titanic* (Harmondsworth: Penguin, 1999).

Fricke, Peter H. (ed.). *Seafarer and Community: Towards a Social Understanding of Seafaring* (London: Croom Helm, 1973).

Fry, Henry. *The History of the North Atlantic Steam Navigation—with Some Account of Early Ships and Shipowners* [1896] (London: Cornmarket Press, 1969).

Fulford, Tim, and Peter J. Kitson (eds.). *Romanticism and Colonialism: Writing and Empire, 1780–1830* (Cambridge: Cambridge University Press, 1998).

Gilroy, Paul. *The Black Atlantic: Modernity and Double Consciousness* (Cambridge, MA: Harvard University Press, 1993).

Gordon, Paul, and Danny Reilly. "Guest Workers of the Sea: Racism in British Shipping," *Race & Class* 28, no. 2 (autumn 1986), 73–82.

Grant de Pauw, Linda. *Seafaring Women* (Boston: Houghton Mifflin, 1982).

Hamilton-Paterson, James. *Seven Tenths: The Sea and Its Thresholds* (London: Hutchinson, 1992).

Hanson, Neil. *The Custom of the Sea* (London: Doubleday, 1997).

Harding, Jeremy. *The Uninvited: Refugees at the Rich Man's Gate* (London: Profile Books and the London Review of Books, 2000).

Hattendorf, John (ed.). *Maritime History*, 2 vols. (Malabar, FL: Krieger, 1996).

Hau'ofa, Epeli, et al. (eds.). *A New Oceania: Rediscovering Our Sea of Islands* (Suva: School of Social and Economic Development, University of the South Pacific, 1993).

Hau'ofa, Epeli. "The Ocean in Us," *The Contemporary Pacific* 10 (1998), 391–410.

Hay, Douglas, et al. *Albion's Fatal Tree: Crime and Society in Eighteenth-Century England* (New York: Pantheon, 1975), 167–88.

Henningsen, Henning. *Crossing the Equator: Sailor's Baptisms and Other Initiation Rites* (Copenhagen: Munksgaard, 1961).

Howell, Colin, and Richard Twomey (eds.). *Jack Tar in History: Essays in the History of Maritime Life and Labour* (Fredricton, New Brunswick: Acadiensis Press, 1991).

Hulme, Peter. *Colonial Encounters: Europe and the Native Caribbean, 1492–1797* (London: Methuen, 1986).

————. *Remnants of Conquest: The Island Caribs and Their Visitors, 1877–1998* (Oxford: Oxford University Press, 2000).

Hulme, Peter, and William H. Sherman (eds.). *"The Tempest" and Its Travels* (London: Reaktion, 2000).

Hyde, Francis. *Cunard and the North Atlantic, 1840–1973: A History of Shipping and Financial Management* (London: Macmillan, 1975).

Irwin, Geoffrey. *The Prehistoric Exploration and Colonisation of the Pacific* (Cambridge: Cambridge University Press, 1992).

Klausmann, Ulrike, et al. (eds.). *Women Pirates and the Politics of the Jolly Roger* (Montreal and London: Black Rose, 1997).

Klein, Bernhard (ed.). *Fictions of the Sea: Critical Perspectives on the Ocean in British Literature and Culture* (Aldershot et al.: Ashgate, 2002).

Klein, Bernhard, and Gesa Mackenthun (eds.). *Das Meer als kulturelle Kontaktzone: Räume, Reisende, Repräsentationen* (Konstanz: Universitätsverlag Konstanz, 2003).

Klein, Herbert. *The Middle Passage: Comparative Studies in the Atlantic Slave Trade* (Princeton, NJ: Princeton University Press, 1978).

Kramer, Jürgen. "The Sea Is Culture," Bernhard Klein and Jürgen Kramer (eds.). *Common Ground? Crossovers between Cultural Studies and Postcolonial Studies* (Trier: Wissenschaftlicher Verlag, 2001), 101–12.

Kunzig, Robert. *The Restless Sea: Exploring the World Beneath the Waves* (New York: W. W. Norton, 1999).

Kyselka, Will. *An Ocean in Mind* (Honolulu: University of Hawaii Press, 1987).

Lemisch, Jesse. "Jack Tar in the Streets: Merchant Seamen in the Politics of Revolutionary America," *William and Mary Quarterly* 25, no. 3 (1968), 371–407.

Lenček, Lena, and Gideon Bosker. *The Beach: The History of Paradise on Earth* (London: Secker and Warburg, 1998).

Leslie, Edward E. *Desperate Journeys, Abandoned Souls: True Stories of Castaways and Other Survivors* (Boston: Mariner Books, 1988).

Lincoln, Margarette. "Shipwreck Narratives of the Eighteenth and Early Nineteenth Century," *British Journal for Eighteenth-Century Studies* 20 (1997), 155–72.

Lincoln, Margarette (ed.). *Science and Exploration in the Pacific: European Voyages to the Southern Oceans in the Eighteenth Century* (Suffolk and Rochester, NY: Boydell and Brewer, 1998).

Linebaugh, Peter. "All the Atlantic Mountains Shook," *Labour/Le Travailleur* 10 (1982), 87–121.

Linebaugh, Peter, and Marcus Rediker. *The Many-Headed Hydra: Sailors, Slaves, Commoners, and the Hidden History of the Revolutionary Atlantic* (Boston: Beacon Press, 2000).

Lloyd, Christopher. *The British Seaman, 1200–1860: A Social Survey* (London: Collins, 1968).

Louis, W. Roger (gen. ed.). *The Oxford History of the British Empire*, 5 vols. (Oxford: Oxford University Press, 1998).

Lydenberg, Harry Miller. *Crossing the Line* (New York: New York Public Library, 1957).

Marsh, Arthur, and Victoria Ryan. *The Seamen: A History of the National Union of Seamen* (Oxford: Malthouse Press, 1989).

Mason, Michael, et al. *The British Seafarer* (London: Hutchinson/BBC/The National Maritime Museum, 1980).

McEwan, Colin, Luis A. Borrero, and Alfredo Prieto (eds.). *Patagonia: Natural History, Prehistory and Ethnography at the Uttermost End of the Earth* (London: British Museum Press, 1997).

McPherson, Kenneth. *The Indian Ocean: A History of People and the Sea* (Delhi: Oxford University Press, 1993).

Michelet, Jules. *The Sea* [1861], trans. W. H. D. Adams (London: n.p., 1875).

Milne, Gordon. *Ports of Call: A Study of the American Nautical Novel* (Lanham and London: University Press of America, 1986).

Moore, Clive. *Kanaka: A History of the Melanesian Mackay* (Port Moresby: University of Papua New Guinea, 1985).

Morison, Samuel Eliot. *The Maritime History of Massachusetts* (Boston: Houghton Mifflin, 1921).

Norling, Lisa. *Captain Ahab Had a Wife: New England Women and the Whalefishery, 1720–1870* (Chapel Hill: University of North Carolina Press, 2000).

Panikkar, K. M. *India and the Indian Ocean: An Essay on the Influence of Sea Power in Indian History* (London: Allen and Unwin, 1951).

Parry, J. H. *The Discovery of the Sea: An Illustrated History of Men, Ships and the Sea in the Fifteenth and Sixteenth Centuries* (New York: Dial Press; London: Weidenfeld and Nicolson, 1974).

Peck, John. *Maritime Fiction: Sailors and the Sea in British and American Novels, 1719–1917* (Basingstoke: Palgrave, 2001).

Perez-Mallaina, Pablo. *Spain's Men of the Sea* (Baltimore: Johns Hopkins University Press, 1998).

Petroff, Peter, and John Ferguson. *Sailing Endeavour* (Sydney: Maritime Heritage Press, 1994).

Pettinger, Alasdair (ed.). *Always Elsewhere: Travels of the Black Atlantic* (London: Cassell, 1998).

Philbrick, Thomas. *James Fenimore Cooper and the Development of American Sea Fiction* (Cambridge, MA: Harvard University Press, 1961).

Phillips, Caryl. *The Atlantic Sound* (New York: Knopf, 2000).

Prager, Ellen J. *The Oceans* (New York: McGraw Hill, 2000).

Raban, Jonathan (ed.). *The Oxford Book of the Sea* (Oxford: Oxford University Press, 1991).

Rankin, Hugh F. *The Golden Age of Piracy* (Williamsburg, VA: Colonial Williamsburg; New York: Holt, Rinehart and Winston, 1969).

Rediker, Marcus. *Between the Devil and the Deep Blue Sea: Merchant Seamen, Pirates, and the Anglo-American Maritime World, 1700–1750* (Cambridge: Cambridge University Press, 1987).

Reid, Anthony. *Southeast Asia in the Age of Commerce 1450–1680. Vol. 2: Expansion and Crisis* (New Haven, CT: Yale University Press, 1993).

Reid, Anthony (ed.). *Southeast Asia in the Early Modern Era: Trade Power and Belief* (Ithaca, NY: Cornell University Press, 1993).

Rennie, Neil. *Far Fetched Facts: The Literature of Travel and the Idea of the South Seas* (Oxford: Oxford University Press, 1995).

Rice, E. E. (ed.) *The Sea and History* (Stround: Sutton Publishing, 1996).

Ritchie, Robert. *Captain Kidd and the War against the Pirates* (Cambridge, MA: Harvard University Press, 1986).

Ross, Ernest Carson. *The Development of the English Sea Novel from Defoe to Conrad* (Ann Arbor: Edwards Bros., 1925).

Sager, Eric W. *Seafaring Labour: The Merchant Marine of Atlantic Canada, 1820–1914* (Kingston: McGill Queen's University Press, 1989).

Sandin, Benedict. *The Sea Dayaks of Borneo Before White Rajah Rule* (London: Macmillan, 1967).

Scammell, G. V. *Ships, Oceans, and Empire: Studies in European Maritime and Colonial History, 1400–1750,* Variorum Collected Studies Series (Aldershot et al.: Ashgate, 1995).

Schmitt, Carl. *Land and Sea* [German original 1944], trans. Simona Draghici (Washington, DC: Plutarch Press, 1997).

Scott, Julius Sherrard III. "The Common Wind: Circuits of Afro-American Communication in the Era of the Haitian Revolution", Ph.D. dissertation, Duke University, 1986.

Skallerup, Harry R. *Books Afloat and Ashore: A History of Books, Libraries, and Reading among Seamen during the Age of Sail* (Hamden, CT: Archon, 1974).

Smetherton, Bobbie B., and Robert M. Smetherton. *Territorial Seas and Inter-American Relations* (New York: Praeger, 1974).

Smith, Roger C. *Vanguard of Empire: Ships of Exploration in the Age of Columbus* (New York and Oxford: Oxford University Press, 1993).

Smith, Vanessa. *Literary Culture and the Pacific: Nineteenth-Century Textual Encounters* (Cambridge: Cambridge University Press, 1998).

Spate, O. H. K. *The Spanish Lake* (Canberra: Australian National University Press, 1979).

Spratt, H. Philip. *Transatlantic Paddle Steamers* (Glasgow: Brown, Son and Ferguson, 1961).

Springer, Haskell (ed.). *America and the Sea* (Athens: University of Georgia Press, 1995).

Spufford, Francis. *I May Be Some Time: Ice and the English Imagination* (London: Faber and Faber, 1996).

Stark, Suzanne. *Female Tars: Women Aboard Ship in the Age of Sail* (London: Pimlico, 1998).

Tanner, Tony (ed.). *The Oxford Book of Sea Stories* (Oxford: Oxford University Press, 1994).

Treneer, Anne. *The Sea in English Literature: From Beowulf to Donne* (Liverpool: University Press of Liverpool; London: Hodder and Stoughton, 1926).

Wallerstein, Immanuel. *The Modern World System: Capitalist Agriculture and the Origins of the European World Economy in the Sixteenth Century* (New York: Academic Press, 1974).

Ward, R. Gerard (ed.). *American Activities in the Central Pacific* (Ridgewood, NJ: Gregg Press, 1966).

Warner, Oliver. *English Maritime Writing: Hakluyt to Cook* (London: Longmans, 1958).

Warren, James Francis. *The Sulu Zone, the World Capitalist Economy and the Historical Imagination* (Amsterdam: VU Press, 1998).

Waters, David W. *The Art of Navigation in England in Elizabethan and Early Stuart Times,* 3 vols. (Greenwich: National Maritime Museum, sec. ed. 1978).

Watson, Harold Francis. *The Sailor in English Fiction and Drama, 1550–1800* (New York: Columbia University Press, 1931).

Weibust, Knut. *Deep Sea Sailors: A Study in Maritime Ethnology* (Stockholm: Nordiska Museet, 1969).

Wolf, Eric. *Europe and the People Without History* (Berkeley: University of California Press, 1982).

Wood, Marcus. *Blind Memory: Visual Representations of Slavery in England and America, 1780–1865* (Manchester: Manchester University Press, 2000).

Contributors

Tim Armstrong is reader in modern English and American literature at Royal Holloway, University of London. His recent publications include *Modernism, Technology and the Body: A Cultural Study* (1998), and *Haunted Hardy: Poetry, History, Memory* (2000). He is currently working on a cultural history of modernism, and on a longer-term project concerning narratives of disaster and risk, of which his essay in this collection forms a part.

David A. Chappell is associate professor of Pacific islands history at the University of Hawaii. He is the author of *Double Ghosts: Oceanian Voyagers on Euroamerican Ships* (1997). He was book review editor for the *Journal of World History* from 1997 to 2002, and has published ten articles in various journals of Pacific, world, African, and maritime history.

Greg Dening writes what he would call "double-visioned" eighteenth-century histories of Oceania—historical ethnographies and ethnographic histories of both sides of Pacific island beaches. *Islands and Beaches* (1981), *Mr Bligh's Bad Language* (1992), *The Death of William Gooch* (1996), *Performances* (1996), and *Readings/Writings* (1998) would be samples of his work. He is currently adjunct professor at the Centre for Cross-Cultural Research, Australian National University. He "adjuncts" by conducting postgraduate workshops on the creative imagination in the presentation of knowledge.

Peter Hulme is professor in literature at the University of Essex. His most recent books are *Remnants of Conquest: The Island Caribs and their Visitors,*

1877–1998 (2000) and two co-edited projects: *"The Tempest" and Its Travels* (2000) and the *Cambridge Companion to Travel Writing* (2002).

Bernhard Klein is lecturer in literature at the University of Essex. He is the author of *Maps and the Writing of Space in Early Modern England and Ireland* (2001) and a forthcoming study on the uses of history in contemporary Irish literature. He has edited several collections of essays, including *Fictions of the Sea: Critical Perspectives on the Ocean in British Literature and Culture* (2002).

Gesa Mackenthun teaches American studies at the University of Rostock, Germany. Her research in the fields of colonial discourse in the early modern period, postcolonial theory, and the impact of the Atlantic slave trade on antebellum American literature has culminated in two books, *Metaphors of Dispossession: American Beginnings and the Translation of Empire, 1492–1637* (1997) and *Fictions of the Black Atlantic in American Foundational Literature* (forthcoming from Routledge in 2004).

Alasdair Pettinger is an independent scholar based in Glasgow, Scotland. He is the editor of *Always Elsewhere* (1998), an anthology of travel writings of the Black Atlantic, and has published articles on travel writing and African American cultural history. He is currently working on a study of Frederick Douglass, Scotland, and the South.

Marcus Rediker is professor of history at the University of Pittsburgh. He is author (or coauthor) of *Between the Devil and the Deep Blue Sea: Merchant Seamen, Pirates, and the Anglo-American Maritime World, 1700–1750* (1987), which won the Organization of American Historians' Merle Curti Social History Award and the American Studies Association's John Hope Franklin Prize; the American Social History Project's *Who Built America? Working People and the Nation's Economy, Politics, Culture, and Society, Vol. 1* (1989); and (with Peter Linebaugh) *The Many-Headed Hydra: Sailors, Slaves, Commoners, and the Hidden History of the Revolutionary Atlantic* (2000), which won the International Labor History Book Prize. His new book, *Villains of All Nations: Atlantic Pirates in the Golden Age*, will be published by Beacon in the U.S., Verso in the U.K., in spring 2004.

Vanessa Smith is an ARC Queen Elizabeth II fellow in the School of English, Art History, Film and Media at the University of Sydney. She is the author of *Literary Culture and the Pacific: Nineteenth-Century Textual*

Encounters (1998) and co-editor of *Exploration and Exchange: A South Seas Anthology 1680–1900* (2000), as well as *Islands in History and Representation* (2003).

James Francis Warren is professor of Southeast Asian modern history at Murdoch University, Australia. He is currently a visiting professor at the Asia Research Institute, National University of Singapore. He is a fellow of the Australian Academy of Humanities and the author of seven books, including *Iranun and Balangingi: Globalization, Maritime Raiding and the Birth of Ethnicity* (2002).

Index

Abbott, George, 177; *Exposition upon the Prophet Jonah*, 177
Acadia (ship), 159
Aitken, James, 116
Algerine Captive, The (Tyler), 135
America, a Prophecy (Blake), 111, 112–6, 119, 129, Fig. 6.1
Amistad (ship), 142
Ancient Voyagers in the Pacific (Sharp), 26
Annales historians, 69
Annis, John, 134
Antony and Cleopatra (Shakespeare), 95, 97–9, 105, 136
Aotourou, 45–8, 49–50, 53n32
Apotheosis of Captain Cook (painting), 19; Fig. 1.3
Archivo de Indias, 69
Attucks, Crispus, 118
Auden, W. H., 13–14

Bachelard, Gaston, 14
Bacon, Francis, 195
Bailey, James Earl, 83
Bailyn, Bernard, 25
Baird, Reverend Dr. Robert, 158
Baker, Sir George, 176
Bakhtin, Mikhail, 148n51
Balangingi, 55, 56, 57–8, 62, 63, 64, 65, 68–9, 70–1
Banks, Sir Joseph, 48, 82
Barclay, Alexander, 94

Baré, Jeanne, 40, 42, 43–5, 51, 52n18, 53n32
Barlow, Douglas, 169, 183n7
Barlow, Joel, 134
Barnes, Robert, 66
Barnum, Phineas T., 158–9
Barthes, Roland, 13, 17
Baudelaire, Charles, 187, 193–4, 200n26; "Le Cygne," 187, 193–4, 200n26
Baudin, Nicolas, 190
beach, 13, 197
beachcomber, 16, 53n30, 81
Beagle (ship), 190, 199n10
Beaufort, Francis, 24
Behn, Aphra, 95, 100, 101, 127; *Oronooko*, 95, 100–101, 102, 127
Beil, Steve, 179
Bellamy, James W., 184n32
Beloved (Morrison), 144
Benito Cereno (Melville), 136, 142–3, 144, 145, 148n46, 148n51
Benjamin, Judah P., 172
Between the Devil and the Deep Blue Sea (Rediker), 3
Bhabha, Homi, 83
Bikini, bikini, 18
Black Atlantic, 2, 5, 6, 136, 142, 143, 144, 146
Black Atlantic, The (Gilroy), 5, 85
Blake, William, 111, 112, 116, 117, 119, 120, 122, 125, 129, Figs. 6.1, 6.2, 6.3; *America, a Prophecy*, 111, 112–6, 119, 129, Fig. 6.1

Bligh, William, 43, 44
Blonde, HMS (ship), 181
Bob, Jo (of Rarotonga), 84
border, concept of, 58–9
Borges, Jorge Luis, 148n46
bottomry agreement, 168
Boudeuse (ship), 45
Bougainville, Louis de, 38, 39–40, 42, 43, 45, 46–8, 50, 52n18, 53n32
Bounty (ship), 5, 43, 133, 145
Boy, William, 178
Brant, Sebastian, 93–4, 145; *Das Narrenschiff*, 93–4, 145
Bridges, Lucas, 194, 199n10
Bridges, Thomas, 194, 199n10
Brown, Clarissa and Josephine, 153
Brown, William Wells, 149–51, 163, 172
Burke, Edmund, 117
Burney, Fanny, 49
Burrop, Charles M., 152
Butler, Judith, 41
Byron, John, 192

Cabeza de Vaca, Alvar Núñez, 192
Calhoun, John, 146n4
Callum, Sir John, 48
Cambria (ship), 158, 160
Camp of the Saints, The (Raspail), 195–6
cannibalism, maritime, 167, 175–82
canoes, 18, 19, 28–33
Carpenter, Kevin, 200n29
Carretta, Vincent, 104, 108n57
Carson, Rachel, 23; *The Sea around Us*, 23
Carteret, Philip, 52n11
Celebes Seas, *see* Sulu and Celebes Seas
Centaur (ship), 174
Channing, William Ellery, 157
Chappell, David, 48
Chatwin, Bruce, 194–5, 201n32
Child, Lydia Maria, 172
Civilising Process, The (Elias), 24
Clark, Geoffrey, 168, 169
Clarkson, Thomas, 117
Coetzee, J. M., 103
Cohen, Daniel, 41
Colbert, 168; *Ordonnance de la Marine*, 168–70
Coleridge, Samuel Taylor, 117
Collingwood, Luke, 173, 174; *see also Zong*
Columbus, Christopher, 91, 92, 93, 94, 106n10, 131, 195

Common Sense (Paine), 115
compass, 17, 30, 31
Condamine, Charles Marie de la, 50, 51
contact zone, 2, 162
Cook, James, 16, 18, 19–23, 25, 47–8, 81–2, 132, 191, Figs. 1.3, 1.4; journal of (on the *Endeavour*), 21
Cooper, James Fenimore, 140, 145
Coral Island, The (Ballantyne), 194
Cortés, Hernán, 132
Cospatrick (ship), 184n39
Cowper, William, 192
Craft, William and Ellen, 153
Creighton, Margaret, 4; *Iron Men, Wooden Women*, 4
Creole (ship), 171
Cromwell, Oliver, 121
Crow, Jim, *see* Jim Crow
Cugoano, Ottobah, 117
Cunard Line, 151, 154, 157–8, 162
Cunard, Edward, 153, 154
Cunard, Nancy, 153
Cunard, Samuel, 152, 154
Custom of the Sea, 176
"Cygne, Le," (Baudelaire), 187, 193–4, 200n26

D'Aguiar, Fred, 6
Dale, Thomas, 124
Dana, Richard Henry, 83
Danckaerts, Jaspar, 123
Dante Alighieri, 195
Darwin, Charles, 20, 190, 191
Davenport, Mr., 173–4
Deane, John, 180
Declaration of Independence, 112
Defoe, Daniel, 95, 101, 192; *Robinson Crusoe*, 95, 101–3, 192–3, 196
Degérando, Joseph-Maria, 190
Dekker, Rudolf, 41
Delano, Amasa, 78, 79
Delany, Martin, 136, 148n39
Deng, Gang, 76
Dening, Greg, 5, 86, 145; *Mr Bligh's Bad Language*, 5
Derrida, Jacques, 17
Despard, Edward Marcus, 119, 124
Dillon, Peter, 81
Docker, Hilton, 79
Don Juan (Byron), 181
Doughty, 189, 198n4
Douglas, Bronwyn, 47

Douglass, Frederick, 136, 148n39, 151–3, 154, 157, 158, 159, 160–2, 165n63, 172; "The Heroic Slave," 172; *My Bondage and My Freedom*, 151; *Narrative of the Life of Frederick Douglass*, 160
Drake, Francis, 17, 187, 189
DuBois, W. E. B., 156
Durché, Jacob, 184n32
Duval, Jeanne, 193
Dwight, Timothy, 134

East India Company, 79–80
East Is a Big Bird (Gladwin), 16, 27
East Sea (ship), 196
Edwards, Bryan, 127
"Eighteenth Brumaire, The" (Marx), 193
Einstein, Albert, 14
Elias, Norbert, 24–5; *The Civilising Process*, 24
Emmanuel Appadocca (Philip), 136, 139–41, 142, 148n39
Endeavour (ship), 18, 19, 20–1, 28, Figs. 1.1, 1.8
Equiano, Olaudah, 95, 99, 103–5, 108n57, 117, 119, 122, 134, 180; *The Interesting Narrative*, 95, 103–5, 180
Eratosthenes, 22
Etoile (ship), 46, 53n32
Europa (ship), 153
Europe and the People without History (Wolf), 69
Exposition upon the Prophet Jonah (Abbott), 177
Exuine (ship), 184n39

Falconer, William, 179; *The Shipwreck*, 179
Fanon, Frantz, 26
Fesche, Charles-Félix-Pierre, 45
Finney, Ben, 18, 27, 28; *Hokule'a: The Way to Tahiti*, 27
Forster, George, 191
Forster, Johann Reinhold, 24, 39, 40
Fort Venus, 22–3, Figs. 1.5, 1.6
Foucault, Michel, 2, 17, 93, 143, 148n46; *Madness and Civilization*, 2
Francis Spaight (ship), 184n39
Freneau, Philip, 134
Freud, Sigmund, 13
Fugitive Slave Law, 140, 162

Gage, Thomas, 117
Gainza, Francisco, 64

Gama, Vasco da, 76, 82
Garber, Marjorie, 37, 41
Garnet, Henry Highland, 152–3, 165n67
Garrick, David, 49
Gatty, Harold, 26; *Raft Book*, 26
Geertz, Clifford, 17
general average (in marine insurance), 168, 171, 173, 174, 178
George III, King, 19, 20, 119
Gérando, Joseph-Maria de, *see* Degérando, Joseph-Maria
ghat-serang, 79
Gillies, John, 97, 108n40
Gilroy, Paul, 5; *The Black Atlantic*, 5, 85
Ginsberg, Elaine K., 44; *Passing and the Fictions of Identity*, 44
Girard, René, 177
Gladwin, Thomas, 16, 27; *East Is a Big Bird*, 16, 27
Gliddon, George R., 190; *Indigenous Races of the Earth*, 190
Golden Venture (ship), 196
Grampus (ship), 138
Gregson vs. Gilbert, 172; *see also Zong*
Gronniosaw, James Albert Ukawsaw, 117
Grotius, Hugo, 107n26
Guha, Ranajit, 78
Guidon de la Mer, 183

Hakluyt, Richard, 99; *Principal Navigations*, 99
Halcon, Don Jose Maria, 65
Hall, John, 83
Hanson, Neil, 177–8
Hardy, Thomas, 119
Harrison, David, 178
Hawkins, Sir John, 120
Heersink, Christiaan, 66
Heim, Jacques, 18
"Heroic Slave, The," (Douglass), 172
Heyerdahl, Thor, 26
Heywood, Mr., 173
Hokule'a (canoe), 18, 19, 28–33, Figs. 1.2, 1.9, 1.10, 1.18
Hokule'a: The Way to Tahiti (Finney), 27
Homer, 133; *The Odyssey*, 133
homesickness, 194
Hongi Hika, 82
Hopkins, Pauline, 172
Hughes, Langston, 153
Hutchinson, John, 160, 161

Indigenous Races of the Earth (Nott and Gliddon), 190
Inglefield, J. N., 174
insurance, of slaves, 167–82; life, 167–82
Interesting Narrative, The (Equiano), 95, 103–5, 180
Iranun, 55, 56, 57–8, 62, 63, 64, 65, 66, 67, 68–9, 70–1
Iron Men, Wooden Women (Creighton and Norling), 4
Irwin, Geoffrey, 16
islands, islanders, 15–16, 27, 188

Jefferson, Thomas, 112
Jim Crow, 83, 154–5
John (ship), 83
Johnson, Jack, 179
Jonah, biblical story of, 176, 177
Jonah: A Poem (Smedley), 177
Jones vs. Scholl, 171
journal of Captain Cook (on the *Endeavour*), 21
Judkins, Captain, 154, 158–9, 160, 162

Kadu of Woleai, 83
Kanaka, Sam, 83
kanakas, 77, 83–4
Karcher, Carolyn, 142
Klein, Bernhard, 13, 136
Kotzebue, Otto von, 83
Kru, 76, 77, 85–6, 87

Las Casas, Bartolomé de, 106n2
lascars, 76–7, 79–81, 83, 84, 87, 89n69
Leach, E. R., 60
Ledyard, John, 136
Lévi-Strauss, Claude, 14
Lewis, David, 27, 29; *We, the Navigators*, 27
Lewis, Martin, 6
Life of Marcus Antonius (Plutarch), 97
Lockyer, Robert, 124
Long, Edward, 127
Loutherbourg, Philippe Jacques de, 20, Fig. 1.3; *Apotheosis of Captain Cook*, 19; Fig. 1.3
Luxborough Galley (ship), 178
Lyotard, Jean-François, 28

MacIver, Charles, 152, 158
Mackenthun, Gesa, 13
Madness and Civilization (Foucault), 2
Magellan, Ferdinand, 187, 189, 190, 195

Mai, *see* Omai
Making of the English Working Class, The (Thompson), 116
Man by Nature and by Grace: or, Lessons from the Book of Jonah (Tweedie), 177
Manila-men, 75, 77–9, 83, 84, 87
Mansfield, Lord, *see* Murray, William
Many-Headed Hydra, The (Rediker and Linebaugh), 111, 120
Mardi (Melville), 131–3, 134, 146n4
mare clausum, 107n26
mare liberum, 107n26
maritime archaeology, 7
maroon, 195
Marx, Karl, 121, 192–3; "The Eighteenth Brumaire," 193
Mary (ship), 179
Masterman Ready (Marryat), 194
Matthew, W. D., 191
McMahon, Elizabeth, 51n1
McPherson, Kenneth, 76
Melville, Herman, 75–6, 77, 79, 81, 84, 131, 133, 136, 142, 144, 146, 163; *Benito Cereno*, 136, 142–3, 144, 145, 148n46, 148n51; *Mardi*, 131–3, 134, 146n4; *Moby-Dick*, 75, 84, 136, 142, 143–4, 192; *Redburn*, 163; *Typee*, 84
Merchant of Venice, The (Shakespeare), 97, 172
Michelet, Jules, 14
Middle Passage, 85, 101, 105, 121, 122, 138, 146, 170
Mignonette (ship), 176, 177
Mill, John Stuart, 136
Mizruchi, Susan, 181, 182
Moby-Dick (Melville), 75, 84, 136, 142, 143–4, 192
Montaigne, Michel de, 118
More, Thomas, 93, 118, 193
Morrison, Toni, 144; *Beloved*, 144
Morton, Samuel G., 136
Mr Bligh's Bad Language (Dening), 5
Mr James Janeway's Legacy to His Friends, 176–7
Murray, William, Lord Mansfield, 170, 171, 175
My Bondage and My Freedom (Douglass), 151

Nahelia (canoe), 28
Nainoa, 29–32, Figs. 1.12, 1.17

Narrative of Arthur Gordon Pym, The (Poe),
   136, 137–9, 142, 178
Narrative of the Life of Frederick Douglass
   (Douglass), 160
*Narrative of the Shipwreck and Suffering of
   Miss Ann Saunders,* 180
Narrenschiff, Das (Brant), 93–4, 145
Nautilus (ship), 24, 140
navis unus pellius, 189, 197
Nayler, James, 123
Nelson, Dana, 139
Nemo, Captain, 24, 140
Neptune, 125, 127, 129, Fig.6.2
Niña (ship), 106n6
Norling, Lisa, 4; *Iron Men, Wooden Women,* 4
nostalgia, 194–5
Nott, Josiah C., 136, 190; *Indigenous Races of
   the Earth,* 190
Nottingham Galley (ship), 180
Núñez de Balboa, Vasco, 17

Odyssey, The (Homer), 133
Omai (pantomime), 19, 20
Omai, 16, 47–50
Opukahaia, Henry, 84
Ordonnance de la Marine (Colbert),
   168–70
Oronooko (Behn), 95, 100–101, 102, 127
Oxford English Dictionary, 195

Paine, Tom, 115, 116, 118–9; *Common
   Sense,* 115
Park, James, 170; *A System of the Law of
   Marine Insurances,* 170
Park, Mungo, 136
Parker, Richard, 176
Parry, J. H., 24, 91–2
Passing and the Fictions of Identity
   (Ginsberg), 44
patera, 197
Pauw, Linda Grant de, 52n6
Peggy (ship), 178
Pequod (ship), 75, 143–4, 145, 146
Pericles (Shakespeare), 96
Perils of the Sea, 168, 170, 173
Pérouse, La (ship), 81
Philip, Maxwell, 136, 139, 141; *Emmanuel
   Appadocca,* 136, 139–41, 142, 148n39
Philippine National Archive, 69
Phipps, John, 134
Piailug, Mau, 28, 32
Picasso, Pablo, 14

Pigot, Mr., 174
Pinta (ship), 106n6
piracy, pirates, 56, 60, 63, 65, 66, 67, 68, 70
Plutarch, 97; *Life of Marcus Antonius,* 97
Poe, Edgar Allan, 136, 137, 178; *The
   Narrative of Arthur Gordon Pym,* 136,
   137–9, 142, 178
Pol, Lotte van de, 41
Presgrave, Edward, 65
Priber, Christian Gottlieb, 118
Principal Navigations (Hakluyt), 99
Proteus, 133–4
Public Records Office, 69
Pukui, Mary Pukena, 28
Putnam, Caroline, 153, 166n67

racial segregation, 154–7, 160
Raft Book (Gatty), 26
Raspail, Jean, 195–6, 197; *The Camp of the
   Saints,* 195–6
Reard, Louis, 18
Redburn (Melville), 163
Rediker, Marcus, 3; *Between the Devil and
   the Deep Blue Sea,* 3; *The Many-Headed
   Hydra,* 111, 120
Redmond, Charles Lenox, 155
Rennie, Neil, 51
Resolution (ship), 18
Rice, Thomas D., 155
Ricoeur, Paul, 17
Rijksarchief, 69
Rimspeak, 18
Robinson Crusoe (Defoe), 95, 101–3, 192–3,
   196
Robinson, Amy, 44, 45
Rousseau, Jean Jacques, 82, 118
Rowson, Susanna, 135, 147n14; *Slaves in
   Algiers,* 147n14

sacrifice (at sea), 173, 181
Sallie M. Stedman (ship), 184n39
Salter, Joseph, 80
San Dominick (ship), 145
Santa María (ship), 93, 95, 106n6
Schmitt, Carl, 95–6
Schur, Alex, 3, 5, 25, 93
Scott, James, 74n26, 78
Sea around Us, The (Carson), 23
sea change, concept of, 187–8
sea fiction, 6
"Sea Is History, The" (Walcott), 1–2
sea loan, 168

sea, "discovery of," 6, 24, 68, 92; as "great connector," 60; historicization of, 14–16; language of, 15–16; as *vacuum domicilium*, 68
Sea-Venture (ship), 198n3
Selden, John, 107n26
Selk'nam Indians, 194
Shakespeare, William, 95, 96–9, 118, 136, 188, 189, 196, 198n3; *Antony and Cleopatra*, 95, 97–9, 105, 136; *The Merchant of Venice*, 97, 172; *Pericles*, 96; *The Tempest*, 96, 104, 188–9, 192, 195, 198n3; *Twelfth Night*, 97
Sharp, Andrew, 26, 32; *Ancient Voyagers in the Pacific*, 26
Sharp, Granville, 117, 173, 174–5, 176, 183n21
Shine, 179
"Ship in Distress, The," 179–80, 182
Ship of Fools, The (Brant), *see Narrenschiff*
ships, and gender, 4; as social spaces, 4, 5, 25, 145–6, 158, 160; steamships, transatlantic, 149–63; historical and fictional ships/canoes by name: *Acadia*, 159; *Amistad*, 142; *Beagle*, 190, 199n10; *HMS Blonde*, 181; *Boudeuse*, 45; *Bounty*, 5, 43, 133, 145; *Cambria*, 158, 160; *Centaur*, 174; *Cospatrick*, 184n39; *Creole*, 171; *East Sea*, 196; *Endeavour*, 18, 19, 20–1, 28, Figs. 1.1, 1.8; *Etoile*, 46, 53n32; *Europa*, 153; *Exuine*, 184n39; *Francis Spaight*, 184n39; *Golden Venture*, 196; *Grampus*, 138; *Hokule'a*, 18, 19, 28–33, Figs. 1.2, 1.9, 1.10, 1.18; *John*, 83; *Luxborough Galley*, 178; *Mary*, 179; *Mignonette*, 176, 177; *Nahelia*, 28; *Nautilus*, 24, 140; *Niña*, 106n6; *Nottingham Galley*, 180; *Peggy*, 178; *Pequod*, 75, 143–4, 145, 146; *Pérouse, La*, 81; *Pinta*, 106n6; *Resolution*, 18; *Sallie M. Stedman*, 184n39; *San Dominick*, 145; *Santa María*, 93, 95, 106n6; *Sea-Venture*, 198n3; *Titanic*, 179; *Zong*, 6, 167, 172–5, 182
shipwreck, 175–6
Shipwreck, The (Falconer), 179
Simpson, Brian, 176, 179
Slavers Throwing Overboard the Dead and Dying (Turner), 181
Slavery Era Insurance Policies Bill, 167
slavery, slaves, slave raiding, slave trade, 55, 61, 62, 63, 65–7, 68, 69, 70–1, 72, 85, 133, 134, 138, 142, 149, 167–82, 192
Slaves in Algiers (Rowson), 147n14

Smedley, Edward, 177; *Jonah: A Poem*, 177
Smith, Adam, 200n22
Society for the Protection of Asiatic Sailors, 79–80
Sollas, William Johnson, 191
Southey, Robert, 117
Sparrman, Andreas, 18
Spence, Thomas, 118, 119
Stark, Suzanne, 41
Stedman, John Gabriel, 125, 127
Stranger's Home, 79
Sulu and Celebes Seas, 58, 60, 65, Fig. 3.1
Sulu Zone 1768–1898, The (Warren), 69
Sulu Zone, 55–74
Sulu-Mindanao, *see* Sulu Zone
Sundquist, Eric, 142, 148n51
Surprising yet Real and true Voyages and Adventures of Monsieur Pierre Viaud, A French Sea-Captain, The, 179
Swiss Family Robinson (Wyss), 194
System of the Law of Marine Insurances, A (Park), 170

Tabili, Laura, 79
Tacky, 124
Tama, 84
Taosug, 59, 61, 63, 65, 70, 71, 72
Taylor, Griffith, 191
Te Pehi, 82
Tempest, The (Shakespeare), 96, 104, 188–9, 192, 195, 198n3
Thompson, Edward, 116; *The Making of the English Working Class*, 116
time, "regional," concept of, 60–1
Titanic (ship), 179
"Titanic Toast," 179
Torres, Luís de, 92
Tuitui, 84
Tupaia, 81–2, 87
Tupou, King of Tonga, 82
Turner, Joseph Mallord William, 181; *Slavers Throwing Overboard the Dead and Dying*, 181
Turner, Nat, 137
Turner, Victor, 5
20,000 Leagues Under the Sea (Verne), 24
Tweedie, W. K., 177; *Man by Nature and by Grace: or, Lessons from the Book of Jonah*, 177
Twelfth Night (Shakespeare), 97
Tyler, Royall, 135; *The Algerine Captive*, 135
Typee (Melville), 84

Vancouver, George, 18
Venus, Fort, *see* Fort Venus
Venus, Transit of, 21–3, Fig. 1.7
Verne, Jules, 24; *20,000 Leagues Under the Sea*, 24
Visram, Rozina, 79, 81
Voyage of Rediscovery (Finney), 27
Voyage to the South Seas, A (Bligh), 43

Walcott, Derek, 1–2, 3, 6; "The Sea Is History," 1–2
Wallace, Alfred, 191
Warburton, George, 160–2, 165n63
Ward, Samuel Ringgold, 153, 154, 162
Washington, George, 123
Watkins, James, 153
waves, 15–16

We, the Navigators (Lewis), 27
Webber, John, 20, Fig. 1.4
Wedderburn, Robert, 122
Wesket, John, 169, 171
Wheatly, Phyllis, 117
Wigen, Kären, 6
Wittgenstein, Ludwig, 17
Wolf, Eric, 3, 69, 86; *Europe and the People without History*, 69
Wordsworth, William, 117
world-system theory, 69

Yámana, 191

zone, concept of, 58–9
Zong (ship), 6, 167, 172–5, 182